FATAL ATTRACTION

WHEN LOVE TURNS TO MURDER

Edited by Mike James

True Crime Library – No. 2
A Forum Press Book
by the Paperback Division of
Forum Design,
P.O. Box 158, London SE20 7QA.

An Imprint of True Crime Library
© 1992 by Mike James
Reprinted 1994 **1995**
All rights reserved

Typeset by T.S. Typesetting,
1 Park Avenue, West Wickham, Kent BR4 9JU.
Printed and bound in Great Britain by
HarperCollins Manufacturing, Glasgow.

ISBN No: 1 874358 01 X

For Jeanette

In the True Crime Library series:

CONTENTS

EDITOR'S NOTE

The crime passionel has long been the foundation for the murder mystery. Agatha Christie's Miss Marple encountered it repeatedly in English country houses. Dashiell Hammett's hard-bitten Sam Spade was forever unmasking the femme fatale. While Raymond Chandler's more erudite Philip Marlowe, walking the mean streets of the city, knew them too.

In the pages that follow, you will read about the true-life crimes of passion; and discover that the line between fact and fiction is paper thin. The lethal ladies may not always be beautiful and the men propping up the eternal triangle may not always resemble matinee idols. But the passions that drive them down that dark road to death and disaster seldom vary.

A softly whispered "I love you" can melt the hardest heart. They can also prove to be the most dangerous words in the English language. For love and hate are opposite sides of the same coin; and passion runs eternally along the borderline of madness.

In this collection of stories, you will find a mix of love, jealousy and hate, lust, longing and loneliness. . . mild, gentle little mistresses who picked up a gun and a knife and became something else. . . marauding husbands who couldn't resist the forbidden fruit. . . vengeful wives prepared to destroy and be destroyed. As the man said: "Heaven has no rage, like love to hatred turned. Nor hell a fury, like a woman scorned."

But don't imagine for a single moment that this is simply the story of another world and that we can watch it from the sidelines. It's our world too, yours and mine. And if we allow our own passions to become unbridled, we too could travel down that dark and dangerous road.

Mike James

1

SHE HAD TO KILL

David Duncan

There are people who, although giving every appearance of being normal, are like kegs of dynamite. They wear ordinary faces, lead commonplace, inconspicuous lives. There is no way you can know them for what they truly are, for human nature is not to be melted in the crucible and tested in the laboratory. Yet, in the secret recesses of their emotions, a powder train has been laid – built up slowly, grain by grain, of stored-up hate, goading vengefulness, or consuming jealousy. Then the spark falls and there erupts a shattering explosion of berserk human violence.

Just such an explosion took place in Somerville, Massachusetts, on August 24th, 1953.

The local branch of the state's Unemployment Security Division opened as always at 9 o'clock. There were the usual Monday morning noises in the sun-splashed office, the buzzing of telephones, the hum of many voices, high heels clicking on the hardwood floor, girls clacking on typewriters. Mildred McDonald too was at her desk, but her machine was strangely silent. She sat staring, almost trance-like, at a small calendar tucked into the open drawer of her desk.

"Have a tough week-end, honey?"

Mildred's swivel chair rasped sharply as she turned to

face a pretty blonde. "Oh, it's you, Gert." Mildred smiled. It was a weak smile that belied the clammy paleness under her rouge and the odd glitter of her eyes.

"Sure it's me," Gertrude Marshall said good-naturedly. "Who else? How about a light, honey?" She put a cigarette between her lips and reached for Mildred's shoulder bag lying on the desk. Mildred grabbed it first and clutched it to the breast of her neat, brown checkered blouse.

The blonde stared at her in surprise. "My, aren't we jumpy today. All I wanted was a match, Millie."

"I'm awfully sorry." Mildred fumbled in the bag and brought out a packet of matches. With nervous fingers she scraped a match into flame and held it to the tip of the cigarette as Gert leaned over towards her. The blonde's eyes wandered to the calendar in the drawer. It was folded to the April page, and Sunday, the 26th, was circled in heavy red crayon.

"Listen, Millie," Gert urged softly, "why don't you forget the guy? A girl with your looks –"

"Why can't people mind their own business?" Mildred banged the drawer shut. She bit her lower lip to steady its tell-tale quiver.

"Honey, I was only trying to help," the blonde said gently. "What's a pal for?"

Mildred pressed her friend's hand. "I know, Gert. I shouldn't have said what I did. It's just that I don't like to talk about it."

"You should talk about it and get it out of your system. So the lug brushed you off and got married on the 26th.

"Why make a memorial day out of it? There are plenty of other fish in the sea. Go out on a toot, play the field, loosen up. The best way of forgetting one guy is to find yourself another."

This was good advice, and no one realized it better than Mildred herself. *Forget Joe!* She kept repeating the words as she slid paper into the typewriter roller and tapped out the date. *Forget Joe!* Simple enough to say. For months, long terrible months filled with a sharp, biting anguish, she had been trying to do just that. The trouble was that Joe would not be forgotten. Somehow she could not think of anything without Joe popping into the picture. Joe taking her to the movies. Joe squiring her to parties. Joe covering her with sand at the beach. He had monopolised her thoughts for almost three years – gay, happy years in which they had spent innumerable hours together.

Mildred jerked the sheet from the typewriter and tore it fiercely into tiny scraps. She looked furtively around, her eyes misted. A thin pinched line of white silhouetted the curving fullness of her trembling lips. No one must know that she had typed Joe's name, over and over again, across the glazed blankness of the paper.

At half-past ten she went over to the desk of William R. Ward. Mr. Ward was manager of the branch office. He pushed back the file he was working on and nodded genially.

"Morning, Mildred," he said. "How's it going today?"

"I don't feel very well, Mr. Ward."

"Why, I'm sorry to hear that, Mildred," Ward said, his voice solicitous. His inquiring gaze studied the pretty secretary, noting the ruffled brown curls and the distraught face. The pupils of her eyes had dwindled to black pinpoints in hazel irises as cloudy and opaque as frosted glass.

"You don't look good, for a fact," the manager admitted.

"Will it be all right if I take the day off?" she asked.

"Of course," Ward said. "You go on home and take care of yourself. And don't worry about anything."

At her desk, Mildred took out her lipstick and touched up the rough spots her worrying teeth had gnawed. The perfect oval of the smooth, youthful face in the mirror stared back at her with almost glacial calmness. She put the lipstick back into the shoulder bag but did not close the lid. Her eyes were fixed on the grey metal object inside, a large object which left scant room for her compact and other accessories. Its long snout shone dully, pointed like a ghostly, warning finger.

Strange about the gun. Mildred could not recall just when the thought of it had first stolen into her mind, then burgeoned like an insidious seed, slowly sending out tenacious roots to clamp around her tortured brain. At first it had been like a game of make-believe such as children play. She had imagined herself with a pistol, frightening Joe, making him squirm and plead. She would see herself, cool and completely self-possessed, pointing the menacing gun at him and –

At this point the picture would invariably blur. She could never quite visualize what was to happen next, nor just how the cold menace of the firearm would alter things. There was Joe's wife, not to be dissolved into thin air by the mere mesmeric wave of a gun. Pauline was a reality no magic could make disappear.

Mildred went downstairs and out into the hot sunlight of the street. She walked uptown, a vivid graceful figure in brown. The bag, dangling from her left shoulder, was heavy with its sinister burden. She kept it firmly against her side under the pressure of a white, rounded arm almost bare in the short-sleeved, brown-checkered blouse. Her summery skirt was brown, too; swirling with every stride of her long straight legs. Strollers glanced appreciatively at the seductive figure of the girl, but she was not aware of their interested glances. There was purpose in her every step, but it was the purpose of a sleepwalker.

She was still thinking of the long-barrelled pistol so bulky in her bag. Methodically she reviewed the past months, trying to isolate the precise moment when the dream-game had crystallized into urgent need. Just before she went on holiday Mildred decided. She nodded vigorously. Yes, it must have been then. Only that could explain why she had chosen Springfield, 100 miles away, to spend those lonely two weeks.

No one knew her in Springfield. Presumably, she had gone there to try to arrange a transfer to the state office there. No one had asked embarrassing questions on that fateful day of July 17th when she presented herself demurely at the police station. She was in need of a gun, "for protection", she informed the sergeant. She was a girl alone in a strange city.

There had been no reason to suspect her request, and the application was granted as a matter of routine. She had plonked down 50 cents and received the permit. With a permit she could buy the gun.

It was a two-mile walk to the DiRocco family home where Joe had brought his bride to live. Mildred quickened her step when she passed Oliver Street. Angry colour stained the white of her throat. It was here that she had first flashed the gun at Joe, right here on the corner. He hadn't been much impressed. To make matters worse he had treated her like a cranky child. Hardly more than a week ago, that had been, but it seemed like an eternity. First, she had tried calling at the house. Joe isn't home, they had told her . . . Joe's at the beach . . . Joe went to the movies with Pauline . . . Finally she had caught up with him on Oliver Street. Joe was alone, a paper bag of groceries in his arm, three neatly folded newspapers tucked into his pocket. The infuriatingly perfect picture of the happy young groom hurrying home to the loving little wife.

There had been shocked surprise in his dark eyes when she confronted him. But it was the glimmer of pity in them that had really burned her up.

Snapping open the bag, she had showed him the gun. "Joe, I'm going to shoot you." She had tried to make her voice icy and menacing, but somehow he had detected her indecision. He had known right off that she didn't mean it. The things he said to calm her had seared into her mind like acid in a steel plate. At last he'd sent her home like a spanked child. She flushed at the painful memory.

Overhead, the midday sun burned like a red-hot cauldron. Mildred's forehead was clammy with perspiration when she turned off Broadway into Minnesota Avenue. For an instant she felt giddy in the August heat, but the rat-tat-tat of her heels never faltered on the simmering pavement. Somewhere a church clock chimed 12 times as she reached number 29, the large brown frame house that she knew so well.

She climbed the porch steps and rang the bell. The door opened and a childish pert face peered at her in surprise. It was Mary DiRocco, Joe's 14-year-old sister. There was ice in Mildred's eyes as she looked at the elfin figure. Mary was a DiRocco and all the DiRoccos were her enemies.

"Joe isn't home," Mary said quickly. It was the old refrain that Mildred had such good cause to recognize. She pushed her foot across the threshold before Mary could slam the door.

"I want to speak to your mother," Mildred said tonelessly.

"Ma's not home either," Mary declared. "She's in Boston. She went shopping."

Mildred searched the child's face. Mary seemed to be telling the truth. "I'll wait," Mildred decided. "There are several things I think she ought to know."

"About Joe?"

"Yes, about Joe."

"Ma may not be back for quite some time," Mary said hopefully.

"I'm perfectly willing to wait." Mildred pushed past the hesitant child. Reluctantly, Mary led the way into the kitchen.

"Pa should be home any minute," Mary offered.

Mildred shrugged. Why argue with a child? She lit a cigarette, filled her lungs with its soothing fragrance. She had nervously stubbed out five half-smoked cigarettes by the time Angelo DiRocco let himself in the front door.

"Hello, Mildred," he said slowly. "You waiting for Joe?

He's at the office."

"I know, Mr. DiRocco. I wanted to speak to Mrs. DiRocco."

"I see." DiRocco sat down at the table "All I want is a sandwich, Mary. I'm not very hungry."

He gulped his food hurriedly. The tense-faced girl sat smoking, silent. Her fingers caressed the smooth leather of the brown shoulder bag.

"Listen, Mildred," Angelo DiRocco said at last. "Why don't you give this up? It's no good for you and no good for Joe."

"Give what up, Mr. DiRocco?"

Angelo sighed. "You know what I mean, Mildred. This mooning over Joe. He's my boy, and a fine boy, yet I tell you he's not worth it. No man is. When two young people find they're not right for each other, it is best they part like friends. You're so pretty, Mildred, and so young – you are twenty-five?"

"Yes, Mr. DiRocco."

"You'll find somebody else. A girl like you can have the best."

Mildred's eyes flicked over him dreamily. It was as if an icicle had brushed his face. He sighed again. "Why don't you run on home? What you're doing can only make you more unhappy."

"If you don't mind, Mr. DiRocco, I'll smoke another cigarette," Mildred said. "Maybe by then Mrs. DiRocco will be home."

Angelo shrugged. He left the house to go back to work. Mary and Mildred were alone.

"Why don't you let Joe alone?" Mary asked. "He's so happy with Pauline."

"What do you know about it?" Mildred snapped scornfully.

"I know that he's crazy about her," Mary retorted. She jumped from the chair. "You'd better go now. If you don't, I'm going to call my aunt."

Mildred groped in her bag. "Sit down, Mary."

The little girl turned, her eyes growing enormous at the sight of the revolver in Mildred's hand. She shrank back into her chair, terrified.

The telephone rang. Mildred said huskily, "You can answer it, Mary, but be careful what you say."

Mary went to the hall with shaking legs. There was a quaver in her voice when she spoke into the mouthpiece. Mrs. Frances Agostino, a cousin, was on the line. Mary spoke to her briefly, not daring to give the alarm. Her wide eyes were fixed fearfully on the pistol.

Later, Mildred motioned the child into the bedroom and ordered her to lie down. Mary obeyed, the cloudy hazel eyes with contracted pupils piercing her like dagger points.

"Won't you please go?" Mary begged.

Mildred shook her head dully. An annoying pulse fluttered in the hollow of her throat. She stared at the gun in her hand almost unbelievingly, seeming to view it through a veil of cobwebs. There was a rushing noise in her head, and the pistol acted weirdly, taking oddly distorted, fantastic shapes. It distended and swelled with evil power. Had she ever intended using the gun – really using it? Up to now she had insisted upon looking at it as a prop in a make-believe play. Even the box of shells she had regarded as harmless toys. The box was in her purse, minus the nine bullets she had only that morning put into the cylinder. She passed her hand tiredly over her face as if to brush away the bothersome mist.

There was a sound outside the house. Mary, who had been watching Mildred in fascinated horror, made a move as if to get off the bed. Flame erupted in Mildred's brain and flame burst from the muzzle of the pistol.

Mary moaned and clutched her stomach. Red covered her hand and dripped onto the counterpane.

The room was filled with repeated gun shots, so fused that the din was one continuous roar. A finger kept plucking at the trigger, again and again and again. Almost with surprise Mildred noted that the finger was her own.

Mary lay sprawled on the bed like a broken doll, motionless in a pool of crimson.

Mildred opened her shoulder bag. It was as if she were watching some stranger, a twin who brought out a knife with a glinting blade, who walked slowly to the bed and did terrible things to Mary's soft, slim throat. Still dazed, she gripped the dead girl under the armpits and dragged her towards the kitchen.

It was about half past one when Mildred opened the front door and stepped out onto the porch. She almost collided with Bob DiRocco, Joe's younger brother.

"Well, Mildred," he began, "what are you doing here?"

"I wanted to speak to your mother," Mildred said coolly.

Bob frowned. "She isn't home. Didn't Mary tell you?"

"Yes, she did."

Mildred passed by him and walked down the street towards Broadway. Bob looked after her, puzzled. He had never seen Mildred like this – rapt, remote, her eyes harried as if they would blot out an ugly picture.

He went inside the house. "Mary!" he called out.

There was no answer. He looked for her in the kitchen, and it was there that he first smelled the thick, acrid fumes of smoke from the basement. He paused at the head of the cellar stairs and looked down at a smouldering heap of papers, magazines, rags – and something else. In the half-light Bob had difficulty recognizing the fire for what it was. Then a sudden shocking awareness sent him flying down the stairs like a person demented. Sobbing wildly, he beat out the flames with his hands and dragged his sister's corpse from its improvised pyre.

He ran across the street to the Thomas Heggerty home. Mrs. Heggerty promptly telephoned the authorities. Soon a fire department rescue squad, a doctor and the Somerville police were gathered at the scene. While Captain LeRoy Pierce talked to Bob DiRocco, Dr. Andrew Guthrie examined the body and Sergeant Joseph Dole looked over the house.

In the cellar Dole found an almost empty can of motor oil. The papers and magazines, ignited by the killer, were drenched with this fluid. There was little blood on the floor and the detective looked elsewhere in the house for the actual scene of the murder. He found it in Mary's bedroom on the first floor. The counterpane was drenched with blood and the detective dug two slugs out of the mattress and another pair from the wall.

"Twenty-twos," he told Captain Pierce.

The captain nodded. "Then it must have been one of those target pistols with the long barrel. They hold nine rounds. Doc Guthrie says the girl has five slugs in her."

The medical man had more than that to tell the officers. "In addition to being shot," he said, "an attempt was made to cut her throat – but not with a very sharp weapon. There are four slash wounds on the neck, all of them superficial."

One bullet had shattered Mary's left wrist and another her jaw. A third had pierced her abdomen and a fourth was lodged in her head, just behind the left ear. But it was the fifth which had produced instant death. This had entered her back, severing the aorta, the main artery to the heart.

Lieutenant of Detectives James Conniff and Edward Kelly of the state police joined the investigators late that afternoon. By that time there was little doubt about the identity of the killer who had shot and attempted to burn Mary DiRocco. The police also learned that they had just missed her. A bartender in a tavern on Broadway, two blocks from the DiRocco home, reported that a girl of Mildred McDonald's description had entered soon after the murder. She'd ordered a beer and stayed at the tavern till 2.20. The police arrived at 2.30.

Although Mildred was known to have drunk alcohol only once before in her life, there was no doubt of the identification. The alarm went out.

Mildred was not to be found at her home. Captain Pierce spread the alert throughout New England by teletype and radio. All bus and railroad stations were alerted. The teletype order described Mildred as "very pretty, five feet four, one hundred and fifteen pounds. She has large hazel eyes with long lashes, short and curly brown hair." It wound up ominously, "She may be armed and should be considered dangerous."

Only one aspect of the gruesome crime still puzzled the cops. If Mildred McDonald had a grievance against Joseph DiRocco, her boyfriend for more than two years, she had conceivably plotted vengeance against him. But why had she killed Mary, a child who had never done her any harm?

The bizarre case inevitably made sensational headlines. Two prominent Somerville families were involved. Mrs. Angelo DiRocco's brother was Gabriele F. Piemonte, former president of the Boston City Council. Mildred's father, Alfred J. McDonald, taught printing in Northeastern Junior High School and was a part-time instructor at Boston University. Mildred's stunned family was at a loss to explain the tragedy. There seemed no reason for the violent turn her broken romance had taken. She was a pretty girl, vivacious and popular. She could have had her pick of eligible beaus.

By Tuesday morning the cops had picked up her trail. She had been seen riding a bus to Sullivan Square in Boston. At Park Square in that city a girl of her description had purchased a bus ticket to New York City. Word was flashed there.

The streets in the heart of Manhattan's entertainment district were crowded at 8 p.m. Patrolman George Grace, one of New York's finest, was slated to take up traffic duty at the intersection of 43rd Street and Eighth Avenue. Ordinarily he was assigned to downtown duty, but on Tuesday night he had been detailed to handle the Times Square crowds. While waiting to take up his post, he spent a few minutes on the corner, skimming over the evening papers. The tabloids that night were plastered with full-page cover shots of Mildred McDonald.

Grace, 34, and a cop for eight years, had many aptitudes, one of which was an eagle eye for detail. This he ascribed to his training during World War II when he started in service as a private in the infantry and emerged as a commissioned officer in the air force.

Now, on the other side of 43rd Street, a girl was passing by, a pretty girl with curly brown hair, a white blouse, and a bright red skirt. A shoulder bag hung at her side. She seemed to be walking aimlessly, a dazed, confused expression on her pale face. It was the face that jolted Patrolman Grace.

Grace hurried across the street and tapped the girl politely on the arm. "Pardon me, Miss," he said. "Would you mind telling me your name?"

The girl didn't seem at all surprised.

"Mary Anderson," she said dully.

Where are you from?"

"Springfield, Massachusetts. I came here two days ago."

It was clear to Patrolman Grace that the girl was in a state of shock and hardly aware of what was happening.

"Name the big streets running off the main drag in Springfield," Grace ordered.

The girl stumbled over her words, hesitated, lost.

"May I take a look inside your pocketbook?" Grace asked.

Wordlessly, she took the strap from her shoulder and handed over the bag. In an instant Grace knew that his hunch had paid off. In the bag were identity cards with the name Mildred McDonald.

At the 54th Street Police Station, the girl made no further effort to deny that she was the fugitive wanted in Somerville. To Detective Francis Ryan she confided that she was living at the YWCA on Hudson Street. Ryan didn't press the dazed girl with any further questions at the time, but sent two plainclothesmen to search her room at the hostel.

There, in an imitation alligator skin handbag, police

found the murder gun. There was also a box of .22 calibre bullets, nine empty shells wrapped in a handkerchief, and a bloodstained brown skirt. The police also found a paring knife, wiped clean, and the pistol permit.

The girl made a pathetic figure as she sat in the police squad room, surrounded by scarred furniture and the sombre grilles on the sealed windows. This time Detective Ryan went straight to the point.

"Mildred, did you kill Mary DiRocco?"

"No – no, I didn't," the girl whispered.

"But you did go to her house? You did talk to her? You were seen."

"I went there. But I didn't kill Mary."

"But this is your gun?" Ryan held out the long-barrelled target pistol.

The girl drew back, her hand to her mouth. She stared at the revolver with terror. "Yes – yes," she stammered, "but I only bought it to scare Joe. I wouldn't hurt Mary. Everyone knows I wouldn't do a thing like that."

For nine hours the prisoner persisted in her claim of innocence. When Lieutenant Detective David B. Murphy, of the Massachusetts State Police, and Somerville Detective Robert T. Brady reached New York from Somerville early Wednesday morning, they took up the questioning. Hours later, Mildred McDonald made a complete confession which she signed.

In her statement, the girl claimed she had no intention to commit violence when she set out for the DiRocco home on Monday morning.

"I was humiliated," she explained. "I went with the fellow for two years. I thought we were going to be married. Then he brushed me off. That's what I had against Joe. And that's what I was going to tell his mother."

While waiting, she engaged in conversation with Mary, who kept praising Joe's wife, Pauline.

"I took the inference that I was being belittled about Joe's marriage to Pauline," she said. When Mary finally ordered her from the house and threatened to telephone for help, Mildred had snatched her gun out and ordered Mary not to touch the phone. She permitted Mary to lie down in the bedroom. Later, when the phone rang, she permitted Mary to answer. The caller was Mary's cousin. Mildred became panicky during this conversation, somehow getting the idea that she was being tricked.

Later, when a noise seemed to come from the front door, Mary started to move from the bed. "I went stark mad," Mildred said. "Everything reeled around me. I was just plain crazy." That was when Mildred started shooting. The prisoner claimed to have only a dim recollection of slashing the child's throat. After setting the body afire, she tried to extinguish the flames by dousing the body with water, she said.

Mildred McDonald waived extradition. Police plans to fly her back to Somerville were stymied when the airline with whom passage was booked, balked. "Civil Aeronautics Bureau regulations prohibit airlines from carrying a person who may endanger his own or another passenger's health," the airline stated. One classification for such a person, the line added, was a prisoner in custody of a legal guard. On Thursday, August 27th, Mildred was returned to Somerville by train. A warrant had already been issued, charging her with murder. She was promptly arraigned in District Court, where she pleaded not guilty and was moved to a cell in the Somerville station house, directly across the street from the offices of the Unemployment Security Division where she had worked for eight years.

On September 9th a grand jury of 17 men and 5 women returned an indictment charging Mildred McDonald with the murder of Mary DiRocco.

Two months later on November 13th, 1953 Mildred McDonald pleaded guilty to second-degree murder and was sentenced to life imprisonment.

2

A BED FULL OF BLOOD

Brian T.B. Hart

At about 9 o'clock on the morning of Monday, December 28th, 1863, a group of small children gathered at the front door of a house in York Street, St. Helens. One of them knocked, and they stood waiting for admittance, impatient to be indoors out of the cold.

There was nothing unusual in this occurrence, for the house was also their school, run by 31-year-old Mary Woods. In those days education was neither free nor compulsory. The government only contributed a few thousand pounds towards the nation's schools and the resultant education system by any standards was a haphazard hit-and-miss affair.

Charitable institutions and the various churches ran some schools, but most of the children's education was provided by private teachers like Mary Woods. When the teacher was female as in this case the schools were popularly referred to as "Dame Schools."

On that Monday morning, the first day back after the Christmas holidays, the children knocked repeatedly, each time louder than the last. As the minutes ticked away and there was still no response they became increasingly alarmed. Eventually some of them went to the nearby house of Miss Woods' sister to tell her. She hurried back with the children, afraid that perhaps Miss

Woods was ill, for she was a cripple and often in poor health. Still there was no response from inside the house, but then two workmen came along, and at the sister's request they prepared to break down the front door. At that moment, however, it was discovered that the back door of the house was unlocked.

The workmen, whose names were Harrison and Monsdell, entered and, seeing that the ground floor was empty, went upstairs. On the wall of the landing opposite one of the bedrooms, they saw marks of blood. Monsdell peered round the bedroom door. In the bed, covered in blood, was a man with his throat slashed open, but miraculously still alive. The two workmen rushed from the house without exploring further, and raised the alarm.

Police Constable Turner soon arrived and found the stricken man still lying in the bed full of blood. At first the constable thought the victim was alone in the bed, but the injured man motioned for him to turn back the bedclothes. When he did he got a shock he would remember for the rest of his life. There sprawled out with her throat cut open and covered in thick, congealing blood was the body of Mary Woods. On the floor near her side of the bed lay a razor, open, and also covered with blood.

Dr. Blundell and his assistant Mr. Rigg were sent for, and Rigg stitched up the man's gaping wound.

The injured man, James Clitheroe, was moved to an adjoining room to be properly and cleanly attended to. As news of the horrid deed spread throughout the neighbourhood, crowds gathered outside the house to speculate on what was going on inside. Some of them even managed to get in, so Clitheroe had a constant stream of visitors for the rest of the day. Relatives, friends and curious onlookers passing in and out of the room.

Because his injuries prevented him from speaking, every now and then the bedbound patient would raise himself weakly on one elbow and attempt to mime, for the benefit of the curious, exactly what had happened.

On Saturday, January 2nd, 1864, at the inquest on Mary Woods, the verdict was that she had been wilfully murdered by James Clitheroe. What evidence they had to arrive at such a conclusion is not known, but the basis of it appears to be that he was the only one to survive.

The trial for his life began on March 22nd, 1864, at the Spring Assizes before Mr. Justice Wills.

It emerged that James Clitheroe was a 32-year-old married man with five children and had worked at the nearby Pocket Nook plate-glass works for 18 years. Some of Clitheroe's children were pupils at Mary Woods' school, and he often called at the schoolhouse. To supplement her income Mary sold beer supplied to her by a local brewery where her father and brother worked. Clitheroe began visiting Mary, ostensibly at first to buy beer. But soon it became well known in the district that James and Mary were having an affair. It was even rumoured that Clitheroe's wife knew of the intimate relationship and had come to terms with it.

On the Sunday evening prior to the schoolteacher's death, Clitheroe and his wife had tea with Mary Woods at her home at about 5 o'clock. They sat together until eight, when Clitheroe said he had a headache and would go for a walk in the fresh air. He told his wife she must go home shortly, and then left her with Miss Woods. He walked only as far as the Carter's Arms, a public house in nearby Duke Street, where he stayed for about an hour, during which time he drank three pints of beer.

Witnesses recalled that he seemed nervous and uneasy, standing up and sitting down repeatedly, and pacing the floor. Whilst he was there the conversation among the customers turned to a man called Townley, who had recently been found guilty of murder in Derbyshire. Clitheroe joined in, and as he left the pub said, "In the morning there will be a greater bother than ever was made about Townley."

After leaving the Carter's Arms it was presumed he

returned to Miss Woods' house in York Street and spent the night with her until next morning when she was found dead and he injured.

In court the prosecuting barrister, Mr. Higgins, read out a statement that Clitheroe had made to the police.

"We made it up to cut our throats, she being uneasy. She told me there was a razor in the drawer under the looking glass, I fetched the razor, got into bed, and first cut my throat. She said to me, 'Jim you've done it now, I'll die with you,' I pushed the razor to her, and she took it up, and cut her throat."

The prosecution contended that this statement in itself was enough to convict Clitheroe of murder. Mr. Higgins told the court, "When two persons make an agreement to destroy life and commit suicide, and one of them is successful in effecting that purpose, and kills himself or herself, and the other escapes, then it is murder in point of law, on the part of the one who so escapes."

In other words, it did not matter whose hand had held the razor that had cut Mary Woods' throat and ended her life. It may have been her own or it may have been Clitheroe's, but whichever was the case, Mr. Higgins contended, then if Clitheroe was party to a suicide pact then he was guilty of the murder of Mary Woods.

P.C. Turner then gave evidence of how he had entered the house, and what he had found there. He also read a further statement from Clitheroe given to the constable.

"We made it up to cut our throats about four or half past four in the morning. I found a razor in the drawer in the looking glass, I got out of bed and fetched the razor. I first cut my throat, and kissed her and gave the razor to her. She said 'You have done it now, I'll die with you.' The razor belonged to her father, and she used it for cutting corns.

About five o'clock in the morning, about half an hour after we had cut our throats, I got out of bed, put my hand against the wall, and looked at her, and saw she was dead, I said. 'Lord save me, she's dead and I'm living.' About eight o'clock in the morning I again got up, and went downstairs, and unlocked the back door, so that if anyone came they might get in. I then went back to bed again where you found me."

John Rigg, the doctor's assistant, described to the wide-eyed members of the jury the wound of the dead woman.

"Her throat was cut deeply, the wound being about five inches in length, right across the throat. It was one wound and had been inflicted from right to left. It was perfectly straight. It could have been done by her own hand, and from the appearance of the wound I am of the opinion that it had been so inflicted by herself."

The defence barrister, Mr. Torr, in his final speech asked the jury to consider the case as one of suicide, and not of murder. He spoke very eloquently for an hour and a quarter on the prisoner's behalf, but it was to no avail. The judge instructed the jury on the law in his closing speech, and the law was so explicit, and his instructions so clear on the subject, that the verdict was a mere formality. He told the jury:

"If two persons were to plot together that one of them should kill a third person, the two would be equally guilty in point of law, even supposing they were not both present. Applying those principles of law, which were also principles of everyday common sense, to the present case, it was clear that if the prisoner took the life of Mary Woods by cutting her throat, by his own act he was guilty of murder and if they agreed together to commit suicide in company, by cutting his or her own throat, even supposing the prisoner did not hold the razor, if it was in pursuance of agreement and counsel that had passed between them on the subject, he would be guilty of murder, and as answerable for the act as though he had himself done it, because it was the result of his counsel and agreement."

The jury retired for a mere 20 minutes before returning with a verdict of guilty. It only remained for the judge to don the black cap and pronounce sentence of death in the traditional manner.

In the following weeks two petitions were forwarded to the Home Secretary in an effort to save the condemned man. The first bore over a hundred signatures collected in the St. Helens area, and was forwarded by the Reverend Mocatta. The second was drawn up by Mr. Torr, the defending barrister, with signatures of four of the jury, and 13 barristers. The reply from the Home Office was short and to the point.

Whitehall, 12th April, 1864.

Rev. Sir,

I am directed by the Secretary, Sir George Grey to acknowledge the receipt of a memorial, lately presented by you on behalf of James Clitheroe, now under sentence of death for murder. I am to acquaint you, that after a full consideration of the circumstances, Sir George Grey regrets that he can see no sufficient ground to justify him in advising Her Majesty to interfere with the due course of law.

I am, Rev. Sir,

Your obedient servant,

H. Waddington

The execution was set for noon on Saturday, April 16th, 1864, at Kirkdale Gaol, Liverpool. On Friday the scaffold was built in a corner of the prison yard, and at five that afternoon, William Calcraft the executioner arrived, taking up his quarters at the gaol.

It was to be a public execution, and on the Saturday

morning, crowds arrived from many parts of the country by train, while others walked from St. Helens, and nearby villages to see Clitheroe executed. Bands of musicians entertained the assembled throng, and nearby public houses were packed to capacity. As the time approached, however, a hush fell upon the crowd. The condemned man and his executioner ascended the gallows steps. The noose was placed around the prisoner's neck. A few words were exchanged between the two, and then the noose was repositioned. Calcraft shook hands with the prisoner and then stepped aside. In a few seconds the trap-door on which Clitheroe stood dropped open with a fearful noise, and he was launched into eternity. As the drop took the full weight of the body the wound in his neck, which had only partially healed, burst wide open, with blood gushing out as he fell.

The next edition of the *St. Helens Newspaper* commented:

"How long are these horrible exhibitions to disgrace our land, and brutalise our population? Can it any longer be said that such scenes are a terror to evil doers or a prevention of the horrible crimes they are meant to punish?

"Is it not time that the legislature should take steps to amend the law with regard to executions and, if they are not prepared to abolish capital punishment, surely something might be done less offensive to public decency, and less stimulating to vice and immortality."

We still do not know the motive for the suicide pact between Mary Woods and James Clitheroe. The reports of the court proceedings hold no clues, neither does Clitheroe's last letter to his wife from the death cell. In the letter he still maintained his innocence, and still did not understand that it was not necessary for him to personally cut his lover's throat to be found guilty of murder.

In part his letter read:

"Dear wife I take the opportunity of solemnly declaring I am innocent of the murder of Mary Woods, if I were guilty I would confess. I am responsible in another case for her life, for I agreed to cut my own throat, and then handed the razor to her for which I am now truly sorrowful."

3

TRAIN RIDE TO ETERNITY
R.D. Kingslyn

The benches were jammed with people waiting for trains. Luggage stood about in clusters and porters darted through the crowd, taking suitcases from overburdened travellers. Down near the gates a policeman idly paced back and forth with measured steps, seemingly unaware of the press and bustle of the crowd.

He yawned, and as he did a girl on one bench jerked her newspaper down and peered quickly at the clock on the station wall. The face that had been hidden behind the paper was beautiful, brightened with wide, intelligent eyes and crowned by a halo of softly gleaming dark hair. But there was tension in the rigid set of her well-rounded form as a heavy-footed stranger stamped closer.

The officer shot a quick glance towards her and the paper moved up, covering her face. The fingers of one hand dug deeply, nervously, into a moist palm.

Twenty minutes before train time. Twenty minutes to decide whether to forget the man or to go through with it.

The thought pounded through Wanda Stopa's brain. Forget the man! She read the same line of one article six times, then darted another glance at the officer, who still strolled back and forth before the gates through which she must pass.

She had been a fool, no question about it. A fool to speak as frankly and vindictively as she had done last night. A fool to allow those pretenses and arty boastings to provoke her into a genuine boast, into a threat which was not vain but of volcanic reality. Suppose someone had not been as drunk as he appeared to be, and the policeman at the gates had been posted to intercept her?

Wanda stiffened, her face whitened. They were calling her train now, booming out the word "Chicago!" The big patrolman seemed to be singling her out with glaring eyes. And within her a hammer kept beating away, warning her to forget, to slink back to her flat in Greenwich Village and let the terrible thing in her heart die.

She watched the others go through the gate. She sat on the bench, her legs suddenly heavy, the newspaper cast aside in her intense concentration. Her eyes were on the hands of the clock.

In three minutes the train would leave . . .

Wanda leapt to her feet. She swayed a moment, as though faint, then swiftly gathered her handbag and over-night case and hurried towards the platform gate. The guard, beginning to swing it shut, stopped and stared at her.

The burly patrolman fixed her with a suspicious look. Wanda slipped through.

She rushed down the steps, into the first carriage, found a seat, felt the first rumblings as the train began to roll slowly. She fumbled within the purse, let her fingers curl around the cold, reassuring butt of her .38 calibre revolver.

Wanda had made the most momentous decision of her life. She had the weird sensation that she had boarded this train years ago, back in the "Little Poland" district of Chicago, and that now, as the rails clicked beneath her, she was merely rushing to the end of a long trip.

It had all began when her father, a sculptor, emigrated

from Warsaw and settled in the large Polish colony in Chicago. Wanda Stopa and her two older brothers, Henry and Walter, had grown up in Augusta Street. Young Wanda was bright, her school marks never falling below 90.

She was always thought to take after her grandfather, an authentic nobleman of Warsaw who had lost his inherited lands after he participated in a Polish uprising against the Czar.

She achieved a brilliant scholastic record and entered law school, where her progress was no less noteworthy. In her last year at the school, her parents resolved to return to the ancient homeland for a visit. All the Stopas were enthusiastic about the trip except Wanda, who stated frankly that she was not going with them.

Remaining behind, the girl lived quite properly at a residence club for employed young women and college girls. But she then, began to "go Bohemian", a fad of young people years ago.

Even so, Wanda displayed extraordinary force of character in this new phase of her life. She stayed out to all hours and still managed to get up early. Although she went into the studio set, there was no decline in the excellence of her studies. Her graduation with honours was inevitable.

It was soon after this that Wanda met a young man variously known as Zdzislaw Glasko, Vladimir Glaskov, or Theodore Glaskoff. He was also sometimes honoured with the title of "Count".

Glaskoff was certainly Russian, rather tall and with a marked military bearing. He claimed he had been a captain before the Revolution in 1917.

Wanda Stopa, brilliant student but groping sophisticate, was greatly attracted to him. And so, with a courtship that lasted but a week, the pair stole off to Crown Point, Indiana, and were married.

The Count, however, soon succeeded in making her miserable and exercised a strange and deplorable power over her. Glaskoff introduced Wanda to certain radical publications but far worse, he introduced his young wife to morphine.

Unhappiness in her marriage, a fast life-style, bitter disagreements with her family had not retarded Wanda's career as a lawyer. She had been appointed to serve on the staff of the United States attorney in Chicago following her highly publicised graduation and admission to the bar at the age of 21, the youngest in Illinois history. Soon she became a full-fledged assistant to the federal prosecutor, respected for her keen mind and unsparing application to any task or assignment.

Recognition in her case was sensational, almost too easy. For soon President Warren Harding's attorney general, Harry M. Dougherty, honoured Wanda Stopa with an appointment as a deputy assistant attorney general of the United States.

However, in the spring of 1922, Wanda, still disconsolate over her marriage, attended one more studio party, and there she met a romantically inclined poised and interesting man of middle age, a prosperous advertising executive – Yeremya Kenley Smith.

Their introduction at the party had barely developed when Kenley Smith began telling anyone who would listen that in Wanda he had found the brainiest girl he had ever met.

Smith had a studio on East Ohio street. He also had a wife. But Vieva Dawley Smith was at once represented to Wanda as a gifted musician and an understanding wife, most of the time absorbed in matters musical. She had no desire to interfere with Smith's own affairs and didn't even mind if they involved girls, young or not.

Moreover, said Smith, Vieva had a romantic attachment of her own. A composer was almost ready to sweep her off, whereupon Kenley Smith would be given a divorce and his freedom to marry again immediately.

So he and the brainy young lady lawyer began to be seen everywhere, together becoming inseparable companions; attending all the parties. And it was a literal fact that Mrs. Kenley Smith did not object to this or suspect anything other than that her husband was being a patron of the arts.

She met Wanda and extended to the girl hospitality and kindness.

Smith had told his wife all about Wanda's unfortunate marriage to Glaskoff, and she believed that her husband was generously helping Wanda to disengage herself from this wedlock, but when Smith's own divorce plans lagged, Wanda openly displayed her impatience.

Finding that Kenley could neither be cajoled nor threatened, Wanda decided to try the old dodge of jealousy. With dramatic abruptness she dropped out of Smith's life, disappeared. That is, she journeyed to Detroit – allowing Smith to believe that this manoeuvre might mean a reconciliation with "Count" Glaskoff. And it worked.

After three barren months without Wanda, Kenley Smith trekked to Detroit and brought her back.

She now considered him virtually her fiancé. But the captivated young attorney could sell none of this to a jury of Stopas, now returned to Augusta Street from their visit to Poland.

"No," said firm and old-fashioned Mama Stopa.

Again and again Wanda asked leave to bring Kenley around to meet her folks. But Mrs. Stopa refused. "A man, no matter how rich, who makes love to a nice girl when he already has a wife is no good – and will not be welcomed in this house," Mrs. Stopa said firmly.

Hating her family's attitude, Wanda continued to ignore reality and to lavish her adoration upon Kenley Smith. But not until December of 1923 did she give any demonstration of the extent of this infatuation. Barging in on the Smiths, Wanda forced a showdown. Blunt questions were asked – and bluntly answered.

"Do you want me to divorce you?" Vieva Smith inquired.

"Yes," said Kenley Smith.

"Then you do desire to marry Wanda?"

"No," Smith said at once, thus settling nothing.

However, he then advised Wanda to forget all about him, and then made certain that she wouldn't by offering to pay her an allowance of $150 a month "for a few months, to go to New York and make a new start".

There were so many people who loved and admired Wanda Stopa and would have been shocked to hear that she needed a new start. Wasn't the girl still an accomplished student of the law and a practising attorney?

No, she wasn't. The true answer was a sad one. For Wanda, frustrated, bewildered, unhappy and resentful, had ditched the promising career of her youth – that dazzling youth way back in the summer of 1921, a mere two years and six months before.

She went to New York for the new start, to Greenwich Village to become a writer.

In January of 1924, Wanda enrolled in a school to take courses in fiction writing and journalism.

She was already enrolled in the giddy round of studio parties, for she had brought along from Chicago all the membership cards: youth, good looks, pretty clothes, recklessness, a despondent and mysterious air, instinctive generosity and something to be generous with – money.

She not only paid her own bills promptly in the Village, but began helping out pinched and struggling friends and neighbours.

Her stories came back from the magazines, to which she had over-confidently submitted them. But, needing to supplement her allowance, she got a good job with a law firm, one of whose partners was Joseph Tumulty, who had been the noted private secretary of President Woodrow Wilson.

This could have been a real opportunity. And Wanda followed it up by securing a second job, helping to compile a legal textbook.

She was not yet a writer, but she was employed and busy with work she thoroughly understood. And around her was the gaiety of the Village. But still she couldn't forget Kenley Smith.

She wrote to him regularly and about this time composed as preposterous a letter as any girl in love ever sent to a man twice her age.

"I sincerely wish for your success and happiness more than anything and I feel that my attachment for you has become a sort of millstone around your neck; that you never intended it to reach the hectic state it has. That is my fault. I am exceptionally romantic and you are romantic to me.

"I know you love me but it is not a deep, integral part of yourself. You have not found yourself in love any more than you have in art; and I feel that my love for you is a real drawback to yourself in art.

"I have known you so intimately for two years without being of assistance, but instead a bad influence, then my withdrawal should have the opposite effect. Therefore, I am withdrawing, and I am doing it in no half-way fashion this time, my dear. Go on with your little love affairs, if you like, without thought of what it may be doing to me. Only consider me as a friend."

Then she set down a schedule of meals and sleep for Kenley Smith. He was to go to bed at eleven and rise with equal regularity at seven, eat at certain fixed hours and work hard.

"You will be surprised," she wrote, "how long the day will seem and how much you can accomplish."

And, finally, she got around to the naive proposition that she return unobtrusively to Chicago:

"Once a week I will go to your little house, put it in order, bring you your laundry, which I will have sent out, and on its return I will look over the clothes and mend them as may be necessary, replacing them in their proper drawers at some time not during your working hours.

"At no time during the week, except on Saturday, when I shall change your linen and clean house for you, will I intrude upon you. I promise, however, to hold myself in readiness to come to you whenever you may wish."

Presumably, this was expected to magnetise Smith to New York as once before she had drawn him to Detroit. But when her benefactor failed to respond, this item went ominously into her diary:

"Paid Nick $250 for the impregnated candy."

Wanda sent the candy by parcel post to Kenley Smith, retaining only one creamy chocolate, rich in cyanide, for herself. This she was to consume after receiving confirmation of the sudden demise of Kenley and perhaps Vieva Smith.

It was a dramatic idea, akin to keeping that last cartridge for yourself to avoid capture and torture by besieging savages.

Only Smith didn't partake of the candies. Nor did he treat Vieva Smith to one. He had listened to too many of Wanda Stopa's startling threats and suicide pact proposals. So he just threw Wanda's $250 chocolates into the dustbin.

Smith might have called in the police. Instead, he gave thought to avoiding a public scandal. He decided to take no action, even though Wanda proved utterly shameless about admitting her murder attempt.

"It is quite fitting," she wrote to him, "that I should send poisoned sweets to the man who has ruined my life with poisoned sweetness."

In a moment of fury she telephoned the Smiths' suburban cottage in Palos Park, saying that she would come on to Chicago to settle matters once and for all. She wrote to Smith reproachfully in a similar vein. But it all began to sound like a false alarm, and Smith dismissed it from his mind. However, what Kenley Smith didn't know was that Wanda soon committed herself to a showdown by boastful words spoken before many of her intimates.

On Tuesday night, April 22nd Wanda threw her biggest party, and before it broke up the unpredictable beauty had delighted many, and puzzled the more sober by giving away nearly everything she owned.

Clothing, books, objects of art, jewellery – saying she would not need gold trinkets where she was going.

In a kind of frenzy, Wanda had given away something else. Her bursting desire for retribution!

"I'm leaving for Chicago in the morning," she had announced.

"I've got some unfinished business to attend to. I have to kill a woman – and maybe a man, too."

One of the crowd burbled drunkenly. "Attaboy, Wanda old girl. If this woman has got in your lovely hair, you go right ahead and kill her."

There had been an uproarious burst of laughter from Wanda's guests, a swell of sound that had washed over her fury, and continued to return, to ring in her ears, as she tossed restlessly on her bed that night. Now, as Wanda Stopa hurtled along the steel rails towards Chicago, the laughter still mingled with the rail clicks and the pounding of the engine.

At seven o'clock on the morning of Thursday, April 24th, Wanda's lifelong trip began to near its end. She had arrived in Chicago. She no longer was visibly anxious or ill at ease. She had had all the hours of her journey in which to confirm her purpose and fortify her considerable self-assurance and aplomb. And yet she now cast a wary eye about her.

What troubled her still were those silly, bragging admissions of hers at the farewell party which she had elected to throw for her Greenwich Village pals. If any one of them had talked, detectives sent from Chicago headquarters might be waiting here – waiting for her.

She looked carefully yet unobtrusively about her.

She saw no one that she took to be a detective. It was too early in the morning for many people to be about and even the taxis were few. She located the far from elegant private taxi of an elderly man whose name was Ernest T. Wood.

Since the morning was raw, Wood had the window curtains in place on his cab. He seemed quite eager about picking up a fare.

His passenger announced her destination as Palos Park – the home of a Mr and Mrs. Y. Kenley Smith. Wood, as they bowled along, admitted that he had never been to the suburb before, but he said he could ask people and locate the Kenley Smiths' residence.

The obliging Ernest Wood stopped the first time to ask if he could look at a suburban resident's telephone book. That got him and his passenger the right house number on 89th Street in Palos Park. But Wood, still rather unsure of himself, halted a second time to ask.

This inquiry he addressed to 74-year-old Mrs. Emma Adams, who told him, "That's the house, right over there."

Her cabby singled out a cottage just down the street. The driver thanked her and rolled on in his curiously curtained vehicle. Mrs. Adams then set off for the corner post office when she met Henry Manning, coming from the shop as Mrs. Adams approached it. "I see you're going to have company at your house," she said. "They came in a car. The man asked me directions. That's how I know." Henry Manning, though only five years Mrs. Adams' junior, was still energetic and fairly agile. He was employed by Kenley Smith as gardener.

"I'll have to get right home," he told Mrs. Adams. And he began to hurry.

Manning knew that Mrs. Smith was alone in the cottage, ill in bed with influenza.

When the curtained taxi drew up in front of the Smith home, Wanda Stopa leapt out. She left her case in the car and carried her handbag in her right hand. The girl went almost at a run to the front door of the cottage. Still clutching her handbag rather grimly, she pressed the doorbell.

On this morning Vieva Dawley Smith was expecting the daughter of a neighbour to come over and sit with her. On hearing the bell, she got up out of bed and slipped into a wool dressing gown and answered the door.

"Why, Wanda – " she gasped.

Wanda Stopa pushed past Vieva Smith and demanded, "Where is Kenley? Why isn't he here?"

"Kenley went off to business some while ago," Vieva explained. "Was he supposed to be here? That is, did he expect you to come here?"

"Of course he did. Or he should have. I never go to his office – you should know that. And I wrote. You must have seen my letter. I said I was coming on out for a final showdown."

"Oh, that," said Vieva.

"Yes, that!" Wanda's voice was harsh and her large eyes were dark with fury.

Kenley's wife had heard so many threats from this girl before. She even turned her back on Wanda, to return to the bedroom. But she didn't get back into bed. She sat on the edge of it, wondering what she could say to appease this maddened young woman.

Wanda was prowling about outside the bedroom.

"There is no one here," said Vieva calmly. "And I wouldn't be in, either – except I have had this flu."

"There is always something the matter with you," Wanda said crossly. "Why don't you do the decent thing, set him free, divorce him?"

Vieva answered with patience. "I thought we had been all over that the last time. I wouldn't hold my husband if he wanted his freedom. He doesn't want a divorce. He has said that over and over. You heard him and accepted the arrangement and went away to New York. It was an extremely generous arrangement, if you ask me. You might as well resign yourself to the fact that Kenley doesn't love you now – assuming he ever thought he did. And even with a divorce, he would not marry you."

Wanda stood in the doorway of the bedroom. She hardly seemed to be listening. Her smouldering glance was confused and menacing. "How do you suppose I am going to take care of myself?" she demanded irritably.

"It is no affair of mine," said Vieva. "But you do have your profession. Whatever happened to the law, Wanda? Weren't you the youngest attorney ever admitted to the Illinois bar? Why, you were actually appointed a deputy assistant attorney general of the United States – you, hardly more than a girl."

"You don't have to tell me what I *was*," Wanda snapped. "If it gives you pleasure, Mrs. Smith, you might tell me what your husband has made of me. After what's happened I expect him to pay my bills. And if he refuses, I'll kill him – or blind him for life."

"Wanda!"

The girl also seemed to be deeply shocked by her latest threat. However, at that moment the gardener, Henry Manning, dashed breathlessly upon the scene. Wanda was no stranger to the hired hand. Henry had seen her at least once before and often heard her threats discussed.

"The missus is not well today," said Henry Manning. "You shouldn't have come here like this. She is not to be disturbed, miss."

"Oh, no?" In a split second Wanda resumed her arrogant and menacing attitude. "I've come quite a long way just to deal with her. And she is as well this minute as she'll ever be again in her life."

Henry Manning made a mistake, however heroic, by attempting to push the obsessed young woman out of Vieva Smith's bedroom. Wanda snapped open her handbag, and dipping into the bag, came up with a .38 revolver.

"Take your filthy hands off me, you – serf!" Wanda screamed.

Vieva then realised that this weapon made the old, futile threats new and real. She sprang up, clutching her robe about her, ran to a partly opened window, threw up the sash and jumped out. From the ground floor window it was only a short drop to the garden.

Wanda Stopa pulled the trigger twice.

Henry Manning released her with the first shot, pitched backwards and lay still. Wanda fired the revolver twice more, but now she was taking low and careful aim from the bedroom window through which Vieva Smith had fled.

Vieva, running for her life across the lawn towards a neighbour's house, heard the shots that struck Manning. Then she felt the third and fourth bullets whistle past her with breath-stopping nearness. Vieva ran faster than she had since her childhood. And she made it.

Luckily, her nearest neighbour was Mrs. George Hermanson, whose husband was chief of police of Palos Park. Mrs. Hermanson immediately telephoned her husband and passed the terrible news and a warning was given to Kenley Smith at his office in Chicago.

Peering cautiously from a window near the telephone, both women saw Wanda Stopa, incredibly unflustered, almost nonchalant, leave the home.

By the time Chief Hermanson, with two of his men, could get to his own home, the strange curtained taxi was out of sight and although Mrs. Hermanson had taken a good look at the car, it did not have a licence plate on the back.

There was no first aid which the police could bring to Henry Manning. The gardener was dead. Examination disclosed that he had died instantly from a single shot lodged near the heart.

Mrs. Kenley Smith talked freely to detectives who came out to Palos Park. She considered herself a lucky woman – two revolver bullets had nicked her fluttering robe, but missed her. It was Mrs. Smith who gave the authorities and the newspapers the story of Wanda's grudge.

Wanda's party friends the night before were interviewed and told of Wanda's weird actions, and of the threat to kill a woman in Chicago.

While police in New York were back-tracking on Wanda's motive for murder, Chicago detectives ran the murder car to earth. Old Ernest Wood was found and asked about his missing licence plate. He said that it had dropped off and had been lost. He had put in for a new one and had been authorised to drive about the city and try to earn his living while waiting for the replacement. This explanation turned out to be the truth.

Wood readily described every minute of his drive with Wanda. He said she hadn't even appeared excited when she beat her retreat from the Palos Park cottage. She had ordered him to drive straight to the Illinois Central depot, but at 20th and Michigan Avenue she had stopped him, paid him $12 then hurried away on foot. This had been a good mile from the railroad station.

If Wanda had taken the Illinois Central, she had probably gone to Detroit, a city with which she was particularly familiar. And soon in the Motor City two detective officers, Lieutenants Roach and Wilson, were out checking her possible arrival, trying to trace her to some former abode or, perhaps, the home of a friend.

Wilson checked all the hotels, beginning with the most obscure. He was hunting a fugitive, one whose story and photograph had been spread over America's front pages. When he came to ring up Detroit's best known hotel, the Statler, he learned that a recent arrival was a Mrs. Ted Glaskoff. He promptly headed for the Statler.

Wanda Stopa, meanwhile, had written her mother a brief letter. In the envelope she now placed her remaining worldly possessions: $150 in currency, a 1,000 mark Polish government bond, and a $200 insurance policy with the Polish Woman's Alliance, made out in favour of her mother. Having addressed the envelope, Wanda went down to the lobby to stamp and post her letter. Here a fellow-guest, Eugene Chloupek of Indianapolis, noticed the attractive girl, thought she reminded him of someone, then caught a glimpse of the name written on the envelope. Stopa! Chloupek unfolded his morning newspaper, looked again at the picture of the missing killer, Wanda Stopa. Wanda had disappeared into an elevator. But Chloupek rushed over to notify a desk clerk. Lieutenants Roach and Wilson were there, checking the registration of Mrs. Ted Glaskoff, New York City. Breathless, Chloupek told them his story, and the police hurried upstairs. "I am terribly ill – " a weak voice was heard gasping to a Statler switchboard operator from the room taken by young Mrs. Glaskoff.

Detectives, a hotel doctor and other hotel officials arrived outside Wanda's door. An assistant manager used his master key. Wanda Stopa was still alive when they broke in, but in less than a minute she fell over, dead. She had swallowed cyanide of potassium.

Roach and Wilson examined the woman's baggage and came across a few articles a diary and several evidently cherished story manuscripts. In her purse they found the .38 revolver, with four discharged cartridges. It was later proved by ballistics experts that this was the weapon that had been used to kill gardener Henry Manning.

Coroner Charles Earle arrived, inspected the body of the so-called countess, and issued a certificate permitting its removal. When the body had been carried to the waiting ambulance, Charles and Wilson made a quick search of the room, swung the door shut and clasped a padlock to it.

Wanda's train trip had ended.

4

EMILY'S LOVER HAD A TICKET TO THE GALLOWS

Jack Carter

It was on the floor in the bedroom of their comfortable suburban home in Pagoda Avenue, Richmond, Surrey, that Mrs. Jessie Mahon discovered by accident a neatly-folded cloakroom ticket for left luggage at Waterloo Station.

There was no question but that it had dropped from the waistcoat pocket of her husband, a 35-year-old sales manager – but for reasons best known to herself, Mrs. Mahon did not return it to her husband.

Patrick Mahon was five feet eleven inches tall, broad-shouldered, blue-eyed, handsome, dashing and debonair, and his faithful wife suspected him of having yet another affair with another woman.

He had been absent from home on several occasions, and, since Mrs. Mahon had had similar sort of trouble with him before, she decided that this time she might do something about it.

So she kept the cloakroom ticket. Shortly afterwards she met a very close friend with whom she discussed her fears concerning her husband.

"Why not," said the friend, "go and see a private detective and get him to find out what he is doing and who, if anyone, he is seeing?"

And so, on May 1st of that year – 1924 – Mrs. Mahon, unbeknown to her husband, called on Mr. John Beard, a private inquiry agent at Richmond, and told him that she suspected that her husband was leading a double life.

Patrick Mahon, she told the inquiry agent, had been absent from home on numerous occasions. She'd had trouble with him over a woman some years before, but that had blown over.

Now she suspected he was up to his old tricks.

Mr. Beard asked her whether she had done anything about it. Had she, for instance, searched the pockets of her husband's suits?

Mrs. Mahon replied that this was not possible because he always took his clothes with him into the bathroom. All she had found, she said, was a ticket for a bag at Waterloo Station.

It was evident by this time that Mrs. Mahon, if she did find evidence of her husband's infidelity, was contemplating divorce proceedings, and at Mr. Beard's request she handed him the cloakroom ticket.

The former Yard detective thought that the bag or case or whatever it was at Waterloo Station might provide some evidence to this effect and he arranged to go there and have it examined in the presence of the wife.

Fortunately for Mrs. Mahon at that time, Mr. Beard did not let her see the contents of the Gladstone bag which the attendant at Waterloo Station handed over in return for the ticket.

He took one look inside the bag and immediately shut it. He returned it to the attendant, and hurriedly telephoned Scotland Yard.

From that moment the Gladstone bag was under constant surveillance by two Scotland Yard detectives.

For what the inquiry agent had seen did not look like providing evidence of unfaithfulness or grounds for divorce.

It bore all the signs that somewhere, somehow, a dreadful murder had been committed.

Mr. Beard did not tell Mrs. Mahon what he had found and what, as a result, he suspected. He told her instead that a watch would be kept on her husband to see what he was up to.

And so the Yard men waited and watched, and Mrs. Mahon did as she was instructed. She did not mention the Gladstone bag to her husband.

By a strange coincidence it was on that same day – May 1st – that the unsuspecting Patrick Mahon arrived at Waterloo Station and claimed the Gladstone bag. And, as soon as he claimed it, the waiting detectives stepped forward and arrested him.

For inside that bag were two heavily bloodstained pieces of silk, torn and bloodstained garments, and a large clasp knife.

At Scotland Yard that day, Mahon was asked to explain the contents of the bag, and the story he eventually told, and the statement he signed on May 2nd, revealed one of the most ghastly and repulsive murders on record at Scotland Yard.

And there can be no doubt that it was the jealousy of the "other woman" – Miss Emily Beilby Kaye – which was one of the basic causes of it.

Mahon's statement was as follows:

"I first met Miss Kaye about ten months ago in London. I became on intimate terms with her about six or seven months ago. Intimacy took place on several occasions at various places.

"On April 12th, I met her at Eastbourne and we went to the Langley Bungalow. I stayed with her until Monday, April 17th. On the previous day we came up to London to see some friends and post some letters.

"We returned to Langley the same night. During that night – the 16th – we quarrelled over certain things, and in a violent temper she threw an axe at me.

"It was a coal axe. It hit me a glancing blow. Then I saw red and we fought and struggled. She was a very big girl. She appeared to be quite mad with anger and rage.

"During our struggle we overturned a chair and she struck her head on an iron coal scuttle, which appeared to stun her. This happened at midnight. I attempted to revive her, but found that she was dead. I put the body in the spare bedroom and covered it up with her fur coat.

"I came up to London on the morning of April 17th and returned to Langley at night, fairly late, taking with me a knife which I had bought in a shop in Victoria Street, and a small saw.

"When I got back to Langley I was still so upset and worried that I could not carry out my intentions to decapitate the body.

"I did so on Good Friday. I severed the legs from the hips, the head, and left the arms on. I then put the various parts in a trunk and locked it."

Mahon continued his grisly tale to the effect that he returned to London on Monday, the 21st, and to Langley once again on the following day.

"On that day," he went on, "I burned the head in the sitting-room grate. I next burned the feet and legs in the same grate, and returned to London that Tuesday night.

"On Friday, April 25th, I returned to Langley, I boiled some portions (of the body) in a large pot in the bungalow. I cut other portions up small, put them in a brown bag, and threw them out of the train while I was travelling between Waterloo and Richmond at about ten p.m. on Sunday, April 27th.

"As I could not dispose of all the portions I went on to Reading. Next morning I came to London and left the bag (the Gladstone bag) in the cloakroom at Waterloo Station on the Monday morning."

Mahon was detained while the Scotland Yard men inquired further into this horrible tale.

There were a lot of things they wanted to know. In particular why, if as Mahon said Miss Kaye died in an accidental fall, should he adopt such dreadful means to dispose of the body?

Why did he not report the accident? Why did he go to

such cunning and dreadful pains to conceal the actual cause of her death?

The Yard men soon found the bungalow which Mahon had rented for his week-end with Miss Kaye. It was an old Coastguard cottage known as The Officer's House, at Langley Bungalows, Westham, Pevensey Bay.

And they soon learned more about Miss Kaye, an intelligent woman of 38, and book-keeper to a firm in the City who lived alone at a hotel in Guildford Street, London.

She was known as a charming woman, athletic, fond of tennis and golf, and the possessor of the most beautiful hair.

Detectives who went to the bungalow made further grisly discoveries. There they found four portions of a woman's body in a trunk, and a quantity of garments covered in blood. A hat-box in which were pieces of boiled flesh; a saucepan containing reddish fluid and a tenon saw with flesh adhering to it. In the grate of the dining-room among the ashes there was what appeared to be a wedding ring.

In the scullery they found the broken shaft of an axe which fitted another part found in the coal-house.

In the sitting room where the quarrel took place there were large stains of blood on the boarding of the floor, on the carpet and on the felt.

And while detectives and their medical aides were examining these most gruesome discoveries, others were making inquiries in the area of the bungalow, and into the pasts of both Mahon and Miss Kaye.

During the course of these inquiries they received other reports of a woman having been seen at the bungalow *after,* according to Mahon, Miss Kaye had met her death. And the description given of this woman made it quite apparent that it was not Miss Kaye.

Even the case-hardened detectives did not think it possible that with the body of one woman in the bunga- low Mahon would invite another to stay with him there, but they pursued this line of inquiry with astonishing results.

They eventually found this woman who agreed that during that fateful Easter week-end she had met Mahon and, at his invitation, had stayed with him in the bungalow from Friday, April 18th until Easter Monday, April 21st.

All that time, of course, and unknown to her, Miss Kaye's body was in an adjoining room which Mahon had kept locked.

The inquiries became even more grim when medical experts gave it as their opinion that Miss Kaye could not have died in the way that Mahon had described. They said that the coal-scuttle, on which Mahon said she had fallen during the struggle, was far too flimsy to have caused injuries which resulted in her immediate death.

On May 6th, Patrick Mahon was charged with the wilful murder of Emily Beilby Kaye. On the following day, he appeared at Hailsham magistrates court, where, following the preliminary hearings, he was committed for trial at Lewes Assizes.

His trial opened on July 15th, 1924, before Mr. Justice Avory, Sir Henry Curtis-Bennett appeared for the prosecution, and Mr. J. D. Cassels, K.C., M.P., for the the defence. Mahon pleaded not guilty.

In the meantime, of course, the persistent Scotland Yard men had made inquiries about the knife and saw, which Mahon said he had bought in Victoria Street, London, on April 17th, and they had been told by the shopkeeper that he *had* sold these articles – not on the 17th, but on April 12th.

This information put an entirely different complexion on Mahon's story of an innocent accident and his shocking attempt to dispose of the body.

If Mahon had bought the saw and the knife on April 12th it was particularly significant, because that was the very day that he had arranged to meet Miss Kaye at Eastbourne for their week-end at the bungalow.

The police had also learned that Miss Kaye was pregnant at the time of her death, that she had given Mahon a good deal of the £600 she had saved, and that she was pressing him to leave his wife and go with her to South Africa.

Sir Henry Curtis-Bennett presented these damning facts to Mr. Justice Avory and the jury. The case for the prosecution, he said, was that Mahon had purchased the knife and the saw on April 12th, having in mind that day . . . murder.

On that day, he said, the position was that Miss Kaye's money had practically disappeared and she was pressing him to go away with her. On the following day, something had to happen and "Mahon had either to break with her, go abroad with her, or to see to it that she was not to go. So, according to the Crown, he took to this desolate beach the cook's knife and saw.

"Dr. Bernard Spilsbury [the famous Home Office pathologist] could find no marks on the body which would suggest the cause of death," Sir Henry stated.

"Must they not assume that signs of the cause of death were present on the head and neck? It might have been, as the Crown suggested, that when Miss Kaye was struck a fatal blow with the axe she fell near the cauldron, "but it was not the fall which caused her death, but the blow which caused her to fall."

Miss Kaye, said Sir Henry, had accumulated some £600. On February 16th she drew out four £100 pound Bank of England notes – three of which were cashed by Mahon, each one in a false name and giving a false address. Two were cashed before Miss Kaye's death, and the third after.

In the witness box, Mahon was calm. His attitude was easy and his voice cultured. He answered readily, and made no secret of the fact that his visit to the bungalow with Miss Kaye that week-end was something in the nature of a "love experiment".

It was, in effect, he said, to convince her that he did not love her sufficiently to go away with her, and he reiterated his version of her death by accident following a quarrel.

And it was during his description of that quarrel that he showed the one sign of emotion and the stress through which he was passing.

"She leapt," he said, "across the room clutching at my face . . ." – then suddenly Mahon swayed forward over the witness stand until his head hung level with the front rail. He burst into a fit of weeping so violent that his body shook.

But in less than a minute the sudden storm was over. He had regained control and he continued answering questions as before.

Sir Henry Curtis-Bennett continued to cross-examine him with penetrating force.

"Did you say that Miss Kaye's intention of going to Eastbourne with you was to convince you that you could be happy with her?

Mahon answered: "Yes."

"What was *your* intention?"

"To convince her that I did not love her sufficiently. I thought she would discover it."

"If that was so, why did you not say to her, 'This relationship must now stop?'"

"I did."

"You did? It is your case that this unmarried lady was seducing you – seducing you away from your wife?"

"It might be so put."

"Is it a fact?"

"Yes."

"How long did you think it was going to take to finish this 'love experiment' with Miss Kaye?"

"I meant to stay there only three or four days."

"And then?"

"I intended to make a clean breast of the whole thing to my wife."

"Then why go with Miss Kaye at all?"

"Because I had promised."

Mahon constantly denied that he had murdered Miss

Kaye, or that he knew she was pregnant. Under pressure, however, he admitted that she had told him she was "in trouble".

He maintained that her death was accidental, and the defence asked the jury to accept that Miss Kaye, knowing that Mahon was a married man, allowed her affection for him to increase and to go on increasing.

"Might they not consider," said Mr. Cassels in defence, "this as a case of a woman after another woman's husband?"

There was, in fact, evidence to the effect that Miss Kaye had fallen genuinely in love with the handsome Mahon, and there is no doubt that when she knew she was pregnant she insisted that he should finally break with his wife.

But Mahon, despite his behaviour towards his wife and his previous treatment of her, would not agree. And that, it is believed, was the cause of the fatal quarrel.

Miss Kaye demonstrated the fatal error of jealousy – jealousy that turned to hate when Mahon refused to continue his association with her.

Hence the quarrel. Hence death.

And no doubt the jury bore in mind these facts when considering their verdict: Why did Mahon buy the knife and the saw on April 12th? Why, if he had decided to end his affair with Miss Kaye, did he agree to go away with her? Why did he make such dreadful efforts to dispose of the body and thus prevent any identification of the cause of death? And why did he not confess to his wife *before* the week-end, rather than after as he said he intended to do?

It took the jury a mere forty-six minutes to make up their minds that Mahon was guilty of murder.

Asked if he had anything to say before sentence of death was passed on him, Mahon looked squarely at Mr. Justice Avory and said, "I feel too conscious of the bitterness and unfairness of the summing-up which you have uttered to say anything except that I am not guilty of the murder."

It was only after they had reached the verdict that the

jury were told of Mahon's past, and it caused something of a sensation – for this was not an innocent, debonair man by any means.

Mahon was now shown to be a convicted burglar, forger, thief and hypocrite.

It was revealed that in 1916 – eight years before – he entered a bank at Sunningdale, Berkshire, through a window and was disturbed by an eighteen-year-old girl who screamed at the sight of him.

Mahon, anxious to avoid recognition, hit her repeatedly on the head with a hammer wrapped in a piece of cloth, and it was said that her life was saved only by the thickness of her hair.

That was not his first crime. Five years before that he had forged cheques to the value of £123 at Liverpool, but the charge was reduced to larceny and he was bound over.

Mr. Justice Avory sentenced Mahon to death on July 21st, 1924, and there was almost immediate talk of an appeal. On August 20th, the Court of Criminal Appeal heard the grounds of the appeal.

Briefly they were that the judge was wrong in directing that women should not serve on the jury; that the judge was wrong in failing to direct the jury to consider whether Emily Kaye met her death by accident; and that Mahon's story might reasonably be true.

It was then revealed that, before he entered the Assize Court at Lewes, Mr. Justice Avory (under the Sex Disqualification (Removal) Act of 1919) directed that no women should sit on the jury.

The Lord Chief Justice (Lord Hewart) and his colleagues refused application for leave to appeal against Mahon's conviction.

"It is quite clear," said Lord Hewart, "when one looks at the whole of the evidence that this case was a most cruel, repulsive and carefully planned murder.

"Mahon has been found guilty after a perfectly fair trial and nothing except the fact, the mere circumstance, that this is a capital case prevents me from saying that this is a frivolous appeal and a waste of time of the Court."

Mahon by now had lost his debonair, handsome looks. He was haggard and drawn, and it was reported that he slept uneasily in the condemned cell at Wandsworth Goal, where he was lodged.

Mahon's only visitor was his ever-forgiving and loving wife, who still believed in his innocence of the capital crime.

But on this occasion the death sentence raised no public outcry. No member of the public made an effort to ask for a reprieve.

On September 9th, 1924, Mahon was executed. In those days, certain members of the Press were admitted to executions, and it was reported that Mahon walked firmly and unassisted his last steps from his cell door to the execution shed.

He was pinioned in his cell and he walked those fatal steps with his arms pinioned behind him. He wore one of his usual lounge-suits.

As he entered the execution shed his legs were fastened and Pierrepoint, the executioner, placed the white cap on his head. Within a few moments he had paid the penalty.

When the murder bungalow was opened to the public after the trial there were storms of protest at such a morbid display for which visitors were each charged one shilling and twopence admission fee.

Eventually, however, it became derelict, and in 1953 it was pulled down. And so ended the last link with a most repulsive murder, which started with love, inflamed into jealousy – and ended in death.

5

THE UNFORGETTABLE
WANDERER MYSTERY

Michael Grady, former chief of detectives,
Chicago police department.
As told to Robert Faherty

In twenty years in the Chicago police department I worked on countless murder cases. And, as chief of detectives, I directed the work of many men in solving murders. Of them all, the murder case I am about to relate made the deepest impression upon me. I can't forget it.

Mike Grady is hard-boiled, they said in Chicago. Murderers, thieves, blackmailers and con men who faced me told their pals I was a hard police officer. Certainly I have had to kill criminals!

But even now the memory of the fate of poor little Ruth Wanderer and her baby can very nearly bring a tear to the eye of hard-boiled Mike Grady.

Ruth was a beautiful girl, blonde and blue-eyed, scarcely more than a child it seemed to me as I saw her in death.

She deserved to live, deserved to give life to the baby she had longed for.

On that night in June, 1920, Mrs. Eugena Johnson,

elderly and motherly, was startled from her reading in the sun parlour of her apartment on the second floor of the two-flat building on N. Campbell Avenue, by the sound of shots.

As she dropped her magazine and started towards the door she heard the crash of glass. Her hands trembled as she opened the door and called:

"Who's there? What has happened?"

Out of the darkness at the foot of the stairs an excited voice answered.

"Mother, it's me, Carl. A hold up – Ruth's been shot!"

The white-haired mother hurried down the stairs. Then light flooded the scene as the door of the first-floor apartment opened and the hall bulb was switched on.

Mrs. Johnson saw her daughter, Ruth, on the floor, her eyes closed, her blonde hair awry, her arm against the jagged, broken glass of the outer door, fragments of the glass about her. Red was staining her dress above the waistline, a crimson spot, growing larger.

Near her, Carl Wanderer, husband of Ruth, was kneeling astride a man in ragged clothing, frenziedly beating the unconscious man's head against the tiled floor. Two automatic pistols lay on the ground beside him.

"Ruth, Ruth, my girl!" cried Mrs. Johnson, tenderly lifting the head of her daughter.

"Oh, Mamma," the girl said weakly, "my baby is dead! I am shot, and it has killed my baby. My hands – they're so cold. Warm them, Mamma, please, dear? I can't see."

James Williams, resident of the first-floor apartment, rushed to his telephone and called for police. Mrs. Williams brought a glass of water, and Mrs. Johnson held the glass to Ruth's lips.

Williams stepped to Wanderer's side. The young husband was still pummelling the head of the ragged man, but he looked up then. He was short, stocky, red-haired, partly bald. He was hatless, in a dark suit, and there were little stains of red on his shirt.

"Carl, did that fellow have a gun?"

Wanderer nodded at Williams' question and pointed to one of the pistols.

"That dog shot Ruth! Thank God I had my gun with me. I gave him plenty. He can't harm Ruth again now."

Again Wanderer struck out fiercely at the inert form of the ragged stranger on the floor.

Williams restrained him and the distraught husband hastened to his wife's side.

"Sweetheart, I got him," he said softly as he knelt beside her. "Ruth, he won't hurt you any more. Honey dear, does it pain?"

Tenderly he kissed her lips.

"Oh, help me, Carl," the girl gasped. "My baby, oh, our poor baby."

Patrolmen from the North Robey Street police station were at the door then. One took Wanderer by the shoulder as the young husband again struck at the still man on the floor.

"I think he's dead now, damn him!" Wanderer said. "He followed us home up to the door, tried to rob us, and he shot Ruth. See that gun!"

The policeman picked up the pistols. "That's my gun. I shot it out with him and I got him, all right. That other gun was his."

While the police continued to question Wanderer, Williams and Mrs. Johnson carried Ruth up the stairs to her bed. Police examined the body of the ragged man, meanwhile. He was bleeding from three wounds. He was nearly six feet tall, with fair hair, blue eyes and a light complexion. His age was about twenty-two years.

The torn trousers of the stranger were fastened at one knee with a safety pin. He wore a dark, ragged coat and an Army shirt. A torn felt hat was nearby.

As the ambulance took away the mortally wounded hold-up man, Wanderer went to the bedside of his wife, who moaned weakly, over and over: "Baby – baby." Police waited outside the room.

Ruth's moans ceased then and she lay quiet, scarcely

breathing. Then – a gasping, a little choking sound. Ruth Wanderer was dead.

At nearly the same moment another died, at Ravenswood Hospital. The hobo. A life had been taken for a life.

North Robey Street police took charge of the principal work in the case immediately. The homicide squad headed by Lieutenant John W. Norton also went to work on it. I was a sergeant in charge of my shift on the homicide squad.

That night we heard Wanderer's account of the shooting. "My wife and I had been at a movie," he said, "and we walked home. I saw a fellow that looked like that tramp standing near an entrance to an alley near the house. I recall now that he started walking after us.

"Ruth and I stepped into the vestibule and I gave her the key to the inside door of our apartment. She had trouble trying to turn the key. I said: 'Can't you open it, honey?' and she said: 'I'll turn on the light.'

"Then I heard someone behind me – inside the hall. It was that robber. He said: 'Don't turn on that light!' Then he shot. Ruth fell against the glass and I jerked out my automatic and let him have it. We shot it out and I got him. I was in the Army five years and I know how to use sidearms when I have to. I've kept the old gun handy, too. I was robbed of nine hundred dollars one time.

"Poor Ruth! She was going to have a baby in two months. Say, you don't have any charge to put against a fellow for killing a holdup man, do you? Anything else you want to ask me? Could I run along home – I'm feeling pretty beat?"

Assured that there would be no charge made against him for killing the stickup man, Wanderer went home.

Chicago woke up to read of the night's tragedy, to mourn with the Johnsons and the Wanderers, to pity the young husband, to applaud his killing of the hobo.

But the homicide squad and the coroner's office had work to do. An inquest was called promptly. The judgement of a jury must be written opposite the name of Ruth Wanderer and the "John Doe" designation of the vagabond.

Wanderer told his story of the shooting to the coroner's jury. The jurors quickly decided that the double slaying was a routine matter for them, and that no criminal charge should be placed against the one living principal. The jury commended Wanderer. The verdict was popular with Chicagoans. The ex-soldier's story was told again and again in the city. Wanderer was greeted by his friends as a hero.

We of the Homicide squad went on with our work. There were details that had to be cleaned up. The dead man must be identified. The file on the case must cover all the details.

I wrote down the material facts. Two Colt .45 automatic pistols had been fired. Three bullets had struck the vagabond, two Mrs. Wanderer, and five had lodged in the walls of the vestibule.

We found by examination of the discharged cartridges that seven shots had been fired from one pistol, which had the manufacturer's number C-2282, and three from the pistol marked with initials 'L.H.B.' with the inscription 'Property of the U.S Army.' The firing pins had marked the cartridges. The guns and the empty cartridges were left in custody of Robey Street Police.

I examined the effects of the dead man for a clue to his identity. A card: "E Masters, John Robinson Circus" led only to information that E. Masters was living and with the circus. He knew nothing of the stranger, nor of how his card had come into the man's possession. A button of the Chicago Chauffeurs' Union brought word that the man might have been a relief driver on a newspaper delivery truck, but none knew him. So that clue proved to be valueless.

I studied his clothing. An Army shirt – possibly he was an ex-soldier. I looked for laundry marks – there were only old, indistinguishable marks, useless. His trousers did not have the maker's name on them anywhere. I examined every button on his clothing for a clue. The buttons were old and of many kinds, giving no aid towards finding the makers of the clothing. His coat was a rag. His socks and shoes were torn. Maybe he had picked up his garb, piece by piece, in pawnshops or in missions.

Lieutenant Norton and I determined to try to identify him somehow. The squad men, aided by other police, began a city-wide search of flop-houses, missions and other havens of tramps.

And while this was going on, a puzzling little question which had come to me the day of the shooting remained in my mind. I had known flop-house tramps. I knew their habits. I had known young vagabonds, hungry hobos. I knew, too, that a good .45 automatic could be pawned for fifteen dollars in Halsted Street.

The dead man had been a youth from a camp or farm, I was sure. He was not the derelict type. He was one of the eager, wandering young ones to be seen among the old hobos along lower West Madison Street, and for that reason more difficult to trace. The old ones sleep every winter in the same police station. Young victims of wanderlust move fast and far.

What was this "John Doe' doing over in the Wilson district, not far from the bright-light centre? How had he obtained an automatic? These questions nagged me.

And why, if he had needed money, had he not pawned the gun? That question put another into my mind.

Why would a robber choose especially to lie in wait for a couple like the Wanderers, who had no jewels and who did not appear to have any money?

Would not identification of the dead man prove his vagabond's clothing a disguise? Would not another motive for the shooting be revealed?

I worked on, detail by detail, slowly, carefully, studying. I talked with the Johnsons and Wanderer. What a sad home was that at N. Campbell! The entire neighbourhood showed signs of grief for the tragedy. Many mothers in Chicago homes had tears for Ruth and for the tragic end of her dreams of holding a baby to her breast. Many thought sadly of the plight of Carl, only twenty-five years old, bereft of his young wife.

Ruth Johnson had had only one sweetheart, Carl Wanderer. She had met him when she was sixteen. He had just returned from Army Service on the Mexican border. Neighbours said he courted her ardently – she was his first sweetheart, too. The young lovers planned to marry in 1917, but America's entry into World War I caused them to defer the wedding.

Ruth promised to wait. For two years she waited. Even as in years before, she did not go to dances or parties. She helped her mother with the housework, always cheerful and willing. She went to choir practice regularly at Holy Trinity Lutheran Church.

Carl fought in France. He became a second lieutenant in the 17th Machine Gun Battalion. He came home on October 1st 1919, and he and Ruth were married that very day.

Lieutenant Wanderer put aside his khaki and went to work for his father as a butcher in a meat market on the North Side. Happily the young couple made their home with the Johnsons. Their love seemed sublime.

One day Ruth told Carl of her greatest hope, of the burning wish she had had for years – to have a baby. She had told her mother she wanted a baby more than anything else in the world.

Then had come the day of happiness when she learned she could hope for such a blessing. For seven months she planned in happy anticipation, awaiting the first day in August. In June she reserved a room at Augustana Hospital for her confinement.

Carl was always attentive. He never missed going to church services with Ruth. He saved his money, spending none on drink or tobacco. Many days and many nights Ruth whispered of her happiness to Carl.

The cedar chest in her room held little knitted boots

and tiny dresses. And now, on June 22nd, barely two months before Ruth's dream was to come true, weeping Mrs. Johnson pressed the little garments to her breast.

On June 22nd, Ruth's diary, which she had begun years before with the word "Baby," was closed forever.

"Poor boy, Carl, stay with us," urged Mrs. Johnson. And so, after Ruth was laid to rest in her grave, Carl continued to occupy the room that had been his and Ruth's.

That was the status of the Wanderer case, officially closed on the records of the coroner's office, a few days after the shooting, when I was working on cleaning up the details.

Keepers of flophouses did not know the ragged stranger. Two women came to the county morgue and looked at the white face and each said he was her son.

Neither identification proved correct. When every other means of identifying the tramp – denounced in death by the good people of Chicago – failed, our only hope lay in tracing pistol C-2282, found near his hand.

Anxiously, I awaited a reply to a letter Lieutenant Norton had sent to the Colt Company. In the meantime, I checked up on every detail of the double shooting to be written into the records with the coroner's verdict.

I learned that the vagrant had loitered near the Wanderer apartment. Otto Rehfeld, a watchman, said he had seen a man near the murder scene on the night of June 21st, pacing back and forth in the shadows with the air of a man waiting definitely for something. Other neighbours had seen him.

However, it remained hard for me to understand why a holdup man would be waiting for a young couple that had no more money than the average young couple. Waiting for a young butcher's clerk and his wife who wore no jewels except her engagement and wedding rings.

Could the ragged man have been a former sweetheart of Ruth who had killed through jealousy; who had sought to kill Carl also?

My quest of a lead along that line failed. Ruth's life

Lovesick Mildred McDonald (left) went gunning for her boy friend, but Mary DiRocco (below) was there instead

St. Helens Town Hall housed the police headquarters where James Clitheroe made his blood-chilling statement

DAY, APRIL 16, 1864,

THE FATE
Of the CONDEMNED CULPRIT,
JAMES CLITHEROE.

The following is a copy of a letter received in St. Helens from the Home Secretary on Wednesday morning, in reply to a
memorial which had been forwarded to the
Home Office.—

ST HELENS NEWSPAPER.

A portion of the following report appeared in our
Second Edition of Saturday.

EXECUTION
OF
CLITHEROE.

Wanda Stopa had been deputy assistant attorney general of the United States before a love affair led to murder.

Patrick Mahon

Miss Emily Kaye

Crowds outside the bungalow at Eastbourne as Mahon is led away. He told police he burned Emily's head, feet and legs in the sitting-room grate

MRS CARL WANDERER
CARL WANDERER
THE RAGGED STRANGER

A grim scene was enacted as Ruth Wanderer (right) and her husband climbed these steps

Ruth's killer (arrowed) told police an incredible story of cold-blooded murder

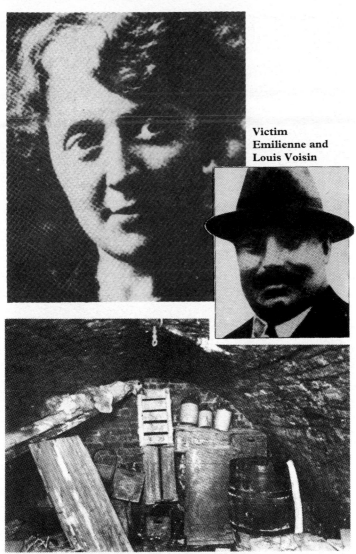

Victim Emilienne and Louis Voisin

Cellar showing the cask which contained Emilienne's head and hands

Jean Lee, left, and above after arrest

Norman Andrews

Bobby Clayton

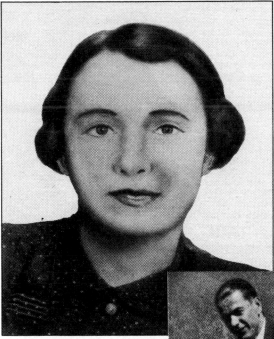

Florence Hartman and John Andrenok. His words had a deadlier effect than he intended. They led to a second murder!

ALTHORP MYSTERY.

Sir,—How true the above heading is. It is still as great a mystery to the police as it is to me and everyone else who has carefully gone through the whole of the particulars of this case. I am the wife of the condemned man, and I fully believe him to be innocent of the crime of murdering Annie Pritchard, for I believe the remains found were those of someone else. The doctor who gave his evidence at both inquests fully proved this statement to be true. As to Annie Pritchard, it is true I have known her most intimately for about seven years. She made herself a confiding bosom friend, telling me, as I thought, every feeling of her heart and action of her life during that time. How false a part, therefore, she must have played towards me all this time, as up to the last moment of her leaving Birmingham our sisterly feelings continued. I helped her to get all her clothes together and also to pack them previous to her leaving, as I fully believed, for Liverpool, to get married, and proceed to America with her husband. Our last serious conversation was my begging of her "never to trust anyone until she was married." She replied, "No, never. If I were to get in trouble I would go away and my friends should never hear from me again." The world can now judge of her deep studied deceit towards me. If I could have been called as a witness I could have said a great deal. I now firstly declare that when Annie Pritchard left Birmingham she had no green skirt, neither had she ever had one for seven years. If the Northampton witnesses are truthful the green skirt must have been bought after she left Birmingham. Therefore the Birmingham witnesses deliberately swore falsely. Again, the black trousers were sworn to by the sister and brother as being those of "their dead brother." This is absolutely false. They were my husband's, and I have mended them more than once or twice. Further, the Northampton witnesses knew full well about the clothing Annie Pritchard had, independently of those sold—that she had at least four dresses and underclothing in proportion. Where, then, are these clothes? Why with the supposed murdered woman whom I feel assured I shall live to see again, and should the law be now carried out my husband's life will have been sacrificed. The approach of death has no terror whatever for him. He declares his innocence, and I fully believe in him. I am, sir, yours truly,

HARRIET MACRAE.

Mrs. MacRae's letter to a newspaper prior to her husband's execution

Annie Pritchard   Andrew MacRae

had been open, the life of a thoroughly good girl of quiet tastes who had loved only one man, Carl Wanderer.

Blackmail? Extortion?

Couldn't the ragged man have been the agent of an extortionist, sent to collect money from Wanderer? Had he shot because payment had been refused?

But Carl's life too had been open, as far as we could see. Carl had given us every help, it seemed, in our efforts to identify the intruder. Wanderer seemed a frank, openhearted sort of fellow who would tell of an extortion attempt rather than conceal it after such a tragedy.

Then Mrs. Johnson revealed a strange fact. She had found a $1,000 bill and a $500 bill in Ruth's dresser drawer. The money had previously been on deposit in the Lake View State Bank.

I was certain that the money had a direct relation to the murder of the young woman.

It was established quickly that Ruth herself had withdrawn the money from the bank on Saturday, June 19th, two days before she was shot to death. That looked like extortion, sure.

Carl Wanderer said he did not know that his wife had withdrawn the money. The cash represented most of his and Ruth's savings. Only seventy dollars remained in the account.

Yet Ruth Wanderer's life had been that of an exceptionally fine, steadfast, good girl and wife.

The Wanderer case, I knew then, was not a routine matter for me. It was a mystery, a deep mystery, challenging all my resourcefulness.

On July 6th came the first break for us. A letter from the Colt people notified Lieutenant Norton that they had sold the .45 automatic, Number C-2282, to Von Lengerke & Antoine, sporting goods dealers with a large store in Chicago's Loop. The gun had been sold in 1913, the letter stated.

The sporting goods store found that it had sold Number C-2282 to one John Hoffman, living in N. Western Avenue, Chicago.

I was elated. At least the gun was a Chicago one. That was one bit of luck, I figured.

The night of July 6th was pleasantly warm and fresh. I was on the 4 p.m. to midnight shift of the homicide squad that night. Early in the evening I called Detective Bill Knowles and a police driver, and we left the detective bureau in a squad car to look for John Hoffman.

I rapped on the door of the house in N. Western Avenue. An elderly man answered and said he was the father of John Hoffman and that John was at home.

"You bought a forty-five automatic from Von Lengerk's in 1913, didn't you?" I asked John Hoffman.

He nodded and seemed surprised. "Yes, but I haven't got the gun now. I sold it for ten bucks a long time ago."

"Who bought it?"

"A fellow named Wanderer."

Wanderer!

I fought to keep from showing even a hint of surprise in my eyes.

I talked casually.

"Let's see – Wanderer – I've heard of the name. Oh, yes! Isn't that the name of the fellow in that shooting on Campbell Avenue?"

Hoffman nodded.

"But Fred Wanderer got the gun, not Carl. They're cousins. Fred lives down the street not far from here."

I asked Hoffman to accompany me to Fred Wanderer's home and he finally consented.

There was a light in the window of the little cottage Hoffman pointed out as Fred Wanderer's home. I ordered the squad car driver around the corner, out of sight of the front of the house. I instructed Hoffman to stay in the car with the driver. I gave Knowles directions. There must not be any slip-up now.

Mrs. Fred Wanderer admitted Knowles and me to the house and we faced Fred, cousin of Carl.

I nudged Knowles and he talked to Mrs. Wanderer.

"We're police officers," I said to Fred, "I have a little matter to talk to you about."

I walked with him to the rear door while Knowles kept the woman in the front room. We stepped into the yard and I faced him.

"You bought a forty-five automatic from John Hoffman," I said. "I just want to know what you have done with the gun."

"I gave the gun to my cousin, Carl." There was a strange look in the man's eyes as he said that.

"What did you say?" I snapped. I wanted to hear that again. "I gave the gun, the one I bought from Hoffman, to Carl Wanderer."

"That gun did not have initials cut into it? Did not have 'Property of U.S. Army' on it, did it?"

"Oh, no. I gave him my gun on the day of the shooting at his place."

I held tightly to Fred's arm. It came to me suddenly. Something was wrong with the accepted version of the double killing! There had been a mistake in identification of the guns – or someone had lied!

"Bill," I whispered to Knowles, who had joined me, "we're going to do some fast checking on the guns."

Fred Wanderer seemed puzzled as we went to the Robey Street Station as fast as that squad car could roll. I tipped off the desk sergeant – the same man who had been on duty the night of the shooting – and he laid the .45 automatics of the Wanderer case on the desk in the lieutenant's office. They looked much alike, blue steel, brown wooden grips.

"Fred," I said in a friendly tone, "I'd like to have you pick out your gun."

He glanced at both, then unhesitatingly picked up one. It was Number C-2282! It was the gun found near the hand of the slain hobo!

"You're sure?"

"Sure it's my gun, the one I lent to Carl. I never saw that other one before."

"Fred, stay with Knowles," I said. "And both of you keep out of sight when I get back. I'm going some place, quick!"

Before leaving I ordered that the guns be put away until I returned. I gave a brief order to my driver and soon the car stopped in front of the N. Campbell Avenue address. I saw a light in a window of the second-floor apartment.

I slipped my .38 from its hip holster to my side coat pocket. Just a precaution, I wanted it handy.

I opened the outside door quietly and rang the doorbell marked "Johnson-Wanderer." A man's voice answered through the speaking tube.

"I want to speak to Carl Wanderer, please," I said.

"This is Carl. What is it?"

"Police officer. I have a man over at the station we think is a pal of that tramp who shot your wife. Would you help us out by coming over to take a look at him?"

"Sure, sure. Glad to help. Come on up a minute."

I opened the door as the buzzer-lever released the lock. At the head of the stairs was the short, stocky figure of Wanderer, his red hair awry about his bald spot. He was in trousers, undershirt and slippers.

"Just going to bed," he explained. He reappeared with coat and cap and walked out with me. Carl Johnson, Wanderer's brother-in-law, hailed us and said he would come along.

"Don't hesitate to call on me for help any time, Sarge," Wanderer said, "I wonder if anybody ever will find out who that bird is."

My reply was noncommittal and I talked on – about picking up a hobo who had been seen about Wanderer's neighbourhood and had been brought in that night as a pal of the slain vagrant.

Wanderer was friendly, chatting easily. As I looked at him I was forced to doubt that he had anything to conceal, forced to consider that if anything had been covered up in the double shooting, someone else had done it.

Carl nodded to the desk sergeant as we entered the station, and talked with him for a moment.

"Where's the tramp?" Wanderer asked me. "I might have seen him before."

I touched his arm.

"Carl – I think your gun is still in the station. Isn't it, Sergeant?"

The desk sergeant nodded at my question.

"Want to look at it again?"

Wanderer agreed.

Again the two automatics were placed on the lieutenant's desk.

"Could you tell yours, Carl?" I asked.

He grinned.

"Brother, if you'd carried that rod as far as I have, you'd remember it! That's my old Betsy, there."

He picked up one of the automatics, fondling it. *Not* C-2282! He held the other one.

"I carried this baby all over France." he said.

"But those initials. L.H.B. – how'd they get on there? And it's Army property – didn't you have to turn it in?"

Wanderer smiled broadly.

"In France everybody got a little of the other guy's stuff. This gun belonged to some galoot until I nailed it. We even wore dead men's clothes over there. I took it out of the Army as a souvenir. I kept a lot of stuff."

"This other gun wasn't yours, Carl?"

"Never saw the other one before."

Carl pushed his cap back and smiled again as he held the Army gun by the grip in firing position.

"I sure could handle this rod!"

I stared at him. "Knowles!" I called, as I kept between Wanderer and the door. "Fred!"

Wanderer seemed surprised.

"You wanted me to come down here to look at the tramp," he said anxiously.

The door opened, and Knowles came in with Fred Wanderer. Carl stared at his cousin.

"Here's what I want you to look at!" I snapped. I showed the letter in my file, in which Von Lengerke & Antoine said pistol Number C-2282 had been sold to John Hoffman.

"John Hoffman sold that gun to Fred Wanderer," I said. "There it is, and you had it!"

Carl was cool.

"Somebody is mistaken. My gun is the Army gun."

Fred faced him.

"Carl, I'm telling the truth. I gave you that gun, the one with that number, the same evening Ruth was shot!"

"Sarge, I'll tell you," Wanderer said with a smile. "The gun I borrowed from Fred was the one I used. The holdup man had the Army gun."

I drew him closer to me so I could look into those pale eyes.

"Wanderer, two minutes after that shooting you said the Army gun was yours – was the one you had taken from the Army."

"Sure, sure. Of course I did. I didn't want to get Fred into trouble. I switched guns, I put Fred's near the holdup man and I took his. You know, Sarge, I liked that Army gun better, anyway, and I made a good trade before the police came."

Carl Johnson was pale as he watched the man who had married his sister. His eyes showed bewilderment.

"Did you see Carl Wanderer handle a gun in the house, an automatic, a few days before the shooting?" I asked Carl Johnson and he nodded.

"He's right," Wanderer said. " I had got a gun from my father, and I showed that one at home." Fred Wanderer shook his head, then said that Carl Wanderer's father had borrowed his gun and had given it back! Carl Wanderer trapped in another lie!

I pushed him into a chair. "Wanderer, you've got some questions to answer and you'd better be able to answer them.

"You said you saw a man following you, when you had a gun in your pocket? Why didn't you stop him? Why did you let him follow you into the house?

"You tell me that in the vestibule, as your wife lay dying, and there was a man lying shot, dying, and there was blood on the floor and powder smoke in the air and people were screaming, you thought only of your cousin, Fred Wanderer! You thought only of trying to protect him, not of your dying wife, lying there, crying for help, in death agony?

"You're a liar, Wanderer! No man, innocent or guilty, under such circumstances, would have done that."

Still Wanderer was cool. He seemed unworried as he smiled a little.

"Sarge, don't get excited. Let me explain all that."

He took off his cap and put it on the desk. He crossed his knees.

"I don't want you to get Fred mixed up in this thing. I'll tell you – I had both guns."

Carrying two automatics on an evening stroll! I awaited his words.

"I asked Fred to lend me his so I could take both apart and put the parts of one into the other. I was fooling with them when my wife asked me to go to the show. I stuck them into my hip pockets and we left in a hurry. After the show we walked home, and when I lifted one gun from my pocket to get the door key for Ruth, that robber grabbed the gun out of my hands."

I had him in more lies. I knew it. I proved it.

"Wanderer, you've been in the Army five years and you know you could not have two forty-five's in your hip pockets and sit through a show. I'll prove you couldn't."

I put two pistols into my hip pockets and sat on a chair. The heavy handles caused the guns to topple out instantly.

"And nobody will believe you would put two guns into your pockets because you were in too much of a hurry to put them down. You couldn't interchange the parts. And I don't believe any robber would come at you without a gun – you're a pretty husky fellow."

He shrugged.

"Well, now that I think about it, I had one of the guns in my front pants pocket and the other was stuck under my belt in front."

I questioned him about the $1,500 withdrawn from the bank.

"Oh, yes, Ruth took the money out to put into a bank nearer home, the Bowmanville State Bank."

I had him again.

"You previously said you did not know she had taken the money out! You're lying again, Wanderer. She left seventy dollars in that bank. By the withdrawal of the $1,500, she lost twenty-two and a half dollars' interest, due July first. She wouldn't have done that just to transfer the account. And why didn't she withdraw it by cheque instead of cash? The withdrawal was made Saturday, and there was no attempt to open a new account that day or Monday.

"And another thing, Wanderer, you were between the hobo and your wife in that hall. Not a bullet hit you!"

He blinked, but he was still cool, poised.

As I thought of the possible interpretations of his acts and his lies, I tried to read the answer in the pale eyes. Nothing there that could be read. The man was inscrutable, outwardly as calm as if we were having a friendly chat about the price of butter.

"Wanderer, you're coming with me. You're under arrest."

My words caused him to start.

"Sarge, what's the idea? I'm pretty tired. I want to go home. Any help you want on this thing I'll give you tomorrow."

Before he knew what had happened I had him handcuffed. Knowles and I put him in the car, Fred Wanderer and Carl Johnson, still mystified, rode with us. We drove to the Hudson Avenue station, where there was a good, strong lockup.

There, I had Carl Wanderer seated where I could look him squarely in the eyes. Then I voiced my hunch.

"Wanderer, you killed your wife!"

He glared at me. "I loved my wife," he snapped. "I killed the man who shot her. You can't hold me for killing him. I had a right to!"

Still the hero, he insisted. I could smile a little at that one. But I was ready to try to prove my hunch, to prove it by his own words.

I had made many another man admit crimes he had committed by allowing him to entangle himself in his own lies. It looked to me as if Carl Wanderer was well on the way to being entangled securely.

On through the night went the questioning, and I was aided by Lieutenant Michael Loftus, Lieutenant Norton and Bill Knowles. In the early morning, while lawyers were preparing to ask for Wanderer to be set free on a *habeas corpus* writ, we were still firing questions at him.

He told fifteen different versions of the shooting.

We took him to the state's attorney's office, and there Coroner Petter Hoffman, George Kenney, secretary to State's Attorney Maclay Hoyne, and Assistant State's Attorneys James C. O'Brien and John Prystalski joined in the questioning.

Wanderer insisted the stranger had snatched a gun from his hands and that he had shot it out with the vagrant. He re-enacted that version.

"You're lying Wanderer. You said the man was at the back of you – you said you had the other gun in the other pocket – you would have been shot if the hobo shot your wife – "

Hours and hours of questions, denials, lies, contradictions, word-traps. Still Wanderer showed no signs of losing his grip. Late that day of July 7th, he said unexpectedly:

"Let's end this stuff. I'll talk if you let me clean up."

He washed, shaved, had a little food and "talked". And what an amazing story the man told. What a memorable story in the annals of crime in Chicago! Carl Wanderer, who had kissed his wife as she lay dying, talked calmly while a stenographer's pencil recorded his words:

"I got tired of married life and about a week before June twenty-first I wanted to get back to the Army.

"One night when I was cutting steak in the shop I got an idea. And on the afternoon of the shooting when I went down-town with my father to buy a butcher's knife, I walked over to Madison and Halsted and looked around for a tramp. I met a young fellow and asked if he wanted a job driving a truck, to pay twenty-five dollars a week. He said yes, and I gave him a quarter to get something to eat and I told him where to meet me.

"That night I met him on Logan Boulevard and had him wait while I went to Fred's house to borrow the gun. Fred wasn't there, but I got the gun anyway. Outside I told the fellow he could make money if he would follow my instructions. I told him the truck-driving job wouldn't be open for a few days, but that I had an odd job for him. I said my wife thought I was a coward and I wanted to show her I wasn't.

"We talked it over and he agreed to pretend to hold up myself and my wife at the house. I said I would chase him away, and then my wife would regard me as a hero. He thought it sounded silly, but consented after I gave him two dollars and bought him a meal. I promised him another five dollars."

Wanderer then told how he had asked the ragged stranger not to carry a gun, "because there might be an accident." He promised the tramp that he would be unharmed and there wouldn't be any violence.

"After supper I asked my wife to go to a show," Wanderer continued. "Coming home I saw the fellow and I nodded to him and he followed. Then, when we got into the vestibule and my wife, trying to open the door, said she'd turn on the light, the tramp said, 'Don't turn on the light!' Well, I had one of my guns in my hand ready. I shot then, in both directions. I wanted to kill this man. I didn't want to kill my wife. But I had to kill that fellow. He would have squealed. And I didn't want anybody else to have my wife if I went to the Army.

"I wanted to make it appear as though he shot my wife and I shot him. No, he didn't have any gun that I know of. Yes, I saw my wife. It was dark, but I could see her face. I was not looking at her when I shot her. I shot in her direction. Who was killed first? The man. Yes, I had a gun in each hand.

"I wanted it to look like a stickup job. That's why I got the gun from Fred, although he hadn't any idea what I wanted it for, and I put it down like it was the gun of that poor boob who thought I would give him some dough.

"The money? Yeh, I got my wife to take it out of the bank. I was going to take it and blow. I wanted to go back to the Army. Maybe Ruth would have let me, though. I never asked her."

Two murders in cold blood! Calmly he talked on, about "the poor boob," and of "Ruth." He answered clearly the questions: "This is the whole truth? You have not been abused? You are not hungry? This statement is true? You will sign it?"

He signed the confession and said:

"I hated married life. I've always been adventurous. Army life is free and easy. I wanted that. And my wife was going to have a child.

"I hated her for it! The thought of being a father and nurse to a kid drove me mad!

"It's hard enough for a man to make a living for himself. I was a butcher boy when I should have been in the Army with guys saluting me. I had a wife to support and there was a child coming, maybe twins. Oh, no, none of that stuff for me!"

Chicago was astounded. The news that the "hero" had been unmasked as a cold-blooded killer was not believed by many mothers and fathers in the city.

The coroner's inquest was reopened and the confession was read, while Wanderer, bored and indifferent, listened. The verdict was:

"We find that Ruth Wanderer died at her home of shock and haemorrhage from bullet wounds. The bullets were fired from pistols held in the hands of Carl Wanderer. We recommend that he be held on a charge of murder. We commend the effective work of the police officials, of the coroner and of State's Attorney Hoyne and his staff."

A similar verdict was given in the death of the still un-identified vagrant.

But still a struggle lay ahead. Sometimes the legal battle for conviction and punishment is a harder fight for police than the solution of a crime.

To strengthen the evidence, Wanderer was made to re-enact the shooting. In the vestibule where he had slain two innocent persons, he calmly directed others in staging the crime, and even demonstrated how he knelt and kissed his dying wife.

At Hudson Avenue Station he laughed at guards assigned to prevent him from killing himself.

"Not a chance of me going out that way!" he said.

He was indicted speedily. Then it was revealed that Wanderer had gone out with a sixteen-year-old-girl three times in three weeks before the slaying of his wife, and three times afterwards.

The girl faced him in the lockup and cried.

She claimed he had planned to elope with her rather than go into the Army? He insisted that he had not.

He said he would plead guilty and take the gallows.

As the date of the trial neared, Wanderer denied he had confessed. A defence fund was raised and two successful criminal lawyers were retained for him.

In October, Wanderer was brought to trial on the charge of murdering his wife. Another indictment charging him with the murder of "John Doe" was on the court docket.

Thousands tried to witness that trial, one of the most dramatic in the city's history.

James C. O'Brien, star prosecutor, and his capable colleague, John Prystalski, asked the jury to send Wanderer to the gallows. Lieutenant Norton read Wanderer's confession. Wanderer took the stand for the defence, and denied the confession was true, saying that he had been struck on the head and that he had been forced to make the statement. Prystalki, in cross-examination, spiked that testimony by showing that Wanderer had calmly and carefully corrected typographical errors in the statement. The defence said he was insane.

O'Brien seized the two pistols and re-enacted the shooting.

The jury deliberated for twenty-six hours and brought in the verdict on October 29th. Wanderer was found guilty of murder, and the punishment was fixed at twenty-five years in prison. He had cheated the gallows!

The sentence meant it was possible he could be free in thirteen years through good behaviour.

Wanderer smirked. There was a look of triumph in his eyes. He swaggeringly shook hands with his counsel.

Judge Hugo Pam denounced the verdict and said the jurors had made a grave error in not giving the prisoner the maximum punishment. The jury had doubted the confession and did not believe there was enough evidence concerning the ownership of the two pistols, the foreman said.

Wanderer went to the Joliet prison and worked in the quarry. But the end of that strange chapter in criminal history had not yet come. An indictment for the vagrant's death remained.

In December a little woman in black came to the detective bureau. She was Mrs. Eugenia Johnson.

"Please see that Ruth's death is avenged," she pleaded. "I seem to feel that Ruth is calling me. I loved Carl once. I kissed him. He was like a son to me. Now, please, can't he be tried again – can't he get the full punishment he deserves?"

On March 1st 1921, Wanderer stood before Judge Joseph B. David in Criminal Court on the charge of the murder of "John Doe." The vagrant may have been a young man bearing a name famous in the nation's history, he may have come from a family of position and wealth, but in that courtroom he was "John Doe," the poor ragged stranger who did not have a chance to live, a mere tool in a devilish murder plot.

Four different times – twice by mothers – the ragged stranger was given a name – and four times the identifications were proved false. If the ragged stranger's real mother lived, she never appeared to claim her son.

He went to his grave unnamed, except for the name the public gave him – the Ragged Stranger.

There was no defence fund in 1921. I took the stand at the second trial. This time there was to be no doubt in those jurors' minds about ownership of the two automatics. I told how I had trapped Wanderer into admitting he had both guns. I pointed out the guns.

Mrs. Johnson testified. Pointing to Carl, she said suddenly:

"That killer! He pushed me aside and tried to take the rings from Ruth's fingers as she lay dying on their bed!"

The jurors glared in fury at the defendant.

The sixteen-year-old girl blushingly told from the stand that Carl had been out with her soon after the double slaying.

That jury was convinced of Carl Wanderer's guilt.

The verdict was "Hanging!"

Cook County, Illinois, got a rope ready for Carl Wanderer. Judge David set the hanging date for June 17th, almost one full year from the date of the murders. There were reprieves, and finally September 30th was set. Defence Counsel's final pleas failed before Governor Len Small.

On the night of the death watch, Wanderer looked up from his game of rummy with jail guards long enough to admit that his confession was true, and that he had planned from the start to kill his wife and the vagrant.

"I intended to kill that poor boob," he said.

But the "poor boob" had a decent burial, anyway. A tavern owner paid for a grave and a slab of stone marked: "The Ragged Stranger."

A cowled figure plunged through the trap that grey morning of September 30th, 1921. I saw Carl Wanderer die.

Because I had brought him to justice, a Chicago newspaper asked me to cover the hanging of Wanderer. I wrote then: "The most heartless murderer in the city's history died today at the end of a rope."

6

GIRL FROM GALWAY
Sara Lee

Dr. Johnson said, "The knowledge that he is to be hanged in the morning concentrates a man's mind wonderfully."

This was certainly true of Timothy Faherty as he sat in the death cell of New Bailey Prison, Manchester. In just under two hours, he would be swinging lifelessly from the end of a rope, and an overwhelming feeling of panic made him want to overpower the warden and run to freedom. This impulse lasted but a few seconds. He was a soldier, determined to face death with forbearance and courage, although he cried when his mother – whom he had not seen for 13 years – visited him in prison, dressed in black and weeping.

Faherty loved Mary Hanmer very much, and she was the one to blame for his becoming a murderer. If only she had behaved properly towards him, this whole sorry affair would never have happened.

His fist tightened at the memory of how she had scorned and mocked him, and for one brief moment he again felt the deadly rage which had driven him beyond the edge of control.

Twenty-seven-year-old Timothy Faherty was the son of a Galway farmer who had died when Tim was but a boy. After his mother's remarriage, Tim, unhappy with his new stepfather, left Ireland as soon as he was old enough to fend for himself and enlisted as a private in the 40th Regiment of infantry travelling to India, Australia and New Zealand. He left the Army after 12 years and went to live in Droylsden near Manchester, where he had some friends. He found work almost immediately at the mill of Messrs. Hadwen and Ashworth. In August, 1867, Faherty went to lodge with widow Mary Broaderick in a small but comfortable terraced house in Moorcroft Street.

The widow's other lodger was a mill girl named Mary Hanmer who also came from Galway. Although she was nine years Faherty's senior, her dark hair and flashing green eyes made her an undeniable beauty, and the hot-blooded Irishman was quickly smitten.

With Galway in common they had much to talk about. Mary told him that she had been sent to England as a child by her unmarried mother, who hoped that the stigma of bastardy would be less damning in a more liberal society.

Faherty easily forgave her that. He would have forgiven her anything. But Mary Hanmer was accustomed to dealing with lovesick men, and had the knack of being friendly and polite while keeping them all at arm's length. Her expectations for a serious suitor were very high indeed.

During their conversations – which Faherty lived for – Mary made no secret of what she sought in a husband. He had to be deeply pious, a devout Catholic, morally upstanding and a teetotaller. Faherty was determined to be all those things.

Mary spoke of others who had tried to court her, and Faherty listened eagerly to the stories of those who, mere mortals as they were, had quickly shown themselves to be woefully short of the qualities she found essential.

Tim Faherty was not a prude. He was fond of a drink once in a while. Life in the Army, if nothing else, had taught him that particular social grace, but if it convinced Mary he was a lifelong abstainer, then he was prepared to withdraw from the pleasures of the alehouse and swear to her he had never tasted liquor.

Before long, the bewitching Galway girl was permitting him to accompany her to church. At no time in his life before had he ever wanted to go to church so frequently. He got precious little other encouragement to be with her otherwise, so that kneeling beside her in prayer was pure joy. Would she have been shocked had she known what Tim was praying for?

The sight of Mary Hanmer made abstinence from drink very easy to bear, and Tim Faherty would gladly have sat looking at her for every minute of the day, had it been practicable.

Work, however, was one of those irksome necessities to keep body and soul together, and inevitably Faherty made friends at the mill. Furthermore, he was the only man there who did not enjoy a little outing to a public house for a beer now and again, so one or two workmates took it upon themselves to persuade him to have 'just one'.

In truth, Faherty did not need a great deal of coaxing. One drink, or even two, would not be enough to make him detectably drunk.

Unfortunately, Faherty was a great social drinker, and after one or two drinks his resolve to abstain was temporarily forgotten. Seven or eight pints later, he realised what he had done, and stumbled home in the dark on legs that seemed to be made of wayward rubber.

At the front door of his lodgings, the hapless Tim Faherty was under intense pressure to think. He had not only to get in, he had also to remember to be absolutely silent, and to move one foot in front of the other in strict rotation. Unfortunately, he was not equal to it. When the front door closed behind him, he tried to propel himself forward without moving his feet – not as a matter of bravado but simple lack of concentration. Realising his error, as he fell, he grabbed at the hallstand and took it down with him.

The thud, and the clattering as he extricated himself

from the hats, coats, umbrellas and walking sticks, woke up the entire household.

Mary and Mrs. Broaderick appeared at the top of the stairs, swathed in their dressing gowns. The light from the candles cast a halo around Mary's sweet face, making her look more like an angel than ever. But her expression was not one of sweet understanding.

Tim Faherty's blood froze for an instant. There was simply no getting out of this and he knew it. Who but a drunk would be crawling around on all fours at the bottom of the stairs, covered in coats and umbrellas?

Never again did Mary allow him to go with her to church. With her there were no second chances; she said she could not bear to see him. Tim left the lodgings in Moorcroft Road and rented a room in a house in Rochdale Road. However, he could not get Mary out of his mind, so he visited his old digs frequently.

Mary was always polite, but also very distant.

She made it quite clear that their relationship was completely at an end. Tim would not and could not accept it. By persisting, he felt certain he could win her back. Though he didn't know it, his love, perhaps spurred on by Mary's rejection of it, was quickly turning into an obsession. Day by day, as she showed no signs of warming to him, Tim in utter despair became even more angry and frustrated.

On Christmas Eve, 1867, Tim visited Moorcroft Street and found Mrs. Broaderick and Mary busy putting up Christmas decorations. He asked them if they intended going to chapel at Gorton Friary to celebrate Midnight Mass. Mrs. Broaderick said she couldn't because she didn't have any silver.

Tim looked hopefully across at Mary. "Are you coming?" he asked.

She shook her head doubtfully.

"Oh, come on, Mary, do come," he urged.

"But I shall have no-one to come home with me," she argued, pinning up a spray of holly over the fireplace.

Tim laughed. "Don't be daft, I shall walk you home," he told her.

To his shock, Mary retorted, "Oh, I'd look very well, wouldn't I, coming home with a man at two o'clock in the morning!"

Her off-hand description of him as 'a man' hurt Tim very deeply, as perhaps it was meant to. He went to the door, and Mrs. Broaderick, seeing how upset he was, followed him out.

"Oh, cheer up, lad," she told him. "After all, it is Christmas."

But Tim wouldn't be consoled. "I'm sorry I ever asked the question of a woman who promised me once and then denied me," he muttered angrily, before turning up his collar and hurrying away down the snow-covered street.

Mrs. Broaderick, sadly shaking her head, at once deduced that he had asked Mary to marry him and she had turned him down on account of his drinking. As she watched the young man go, the widow, who was very fond of her former lodger, wished with all her heart that he would forget Mary and find someone more amenable to love. After all, he was a good looking fellow. Mary, she knew, could be very wilful. Tim's wasn't the first heart she had broken.

On Christmas Day, Tim paid Mary another visit at about 3 o'clock in the afternoon. Mrs. Broaderick was not there but her daughter, Bridget Broaderick, was. She and Mary, having lived under the same roof for so many years, thought of one another as sisters.

Bridget had been at Midnight Mass and had spotted Tim in the congregation, though the two hadn't spoken. She supposed there was ill-feeling between him and Mary, so she was more than a little surprised to find him standing on the doorstep. She was even more surprised to see how smiling and cheerful he was. Then she smelt the alcohol on his breath as he went into the house.

As Tim Faherty rubbed his hands in front of the blazing fire he told Bridget and Mary he would be going to Galway in the morning to see his mother, and asked Mary if she had any messages for the folk back home. She shook her head. "No, I have no messages to send, what I had I sent to my mother the week before last. But give my respects to the green fields of Ireland and the shamrock."

As Tim chatted about his mother, Mary began to clear the table and wash up the tea things. Bridget, tired after being up so late for Midnight Mass the night before, excused herself and went upstairs for a nap.

While she was hanging her clothes up on the rack above her fire, she heard something clattering in the kitchen below, then heard Mary cry, "Oh, no, knives and forks are falling!"

Bridget knew that Mary considered this to be an evil omen. A moment later she heard Mary's voice again, shouting irritably, "Get off with you, why do you come in after me?"

Bridget assumed Tim had followed Mary into the kitchen and was trying to kiss her. She would have gone down at that point to ensure that Tim didn't annoy Mary, but being exhausted she merely got into bed. In a minute she was fast asleep.

No-one will ever know exactly what went on downstairs after Bridget dozed off. But from evidence given at the coroner's inquest, we can deduce that Tim had pleaded with Mary to marry him and she, smelling the drink on his breath, had recoiled from his embrace. Perhaps Mary's instinctive knowledge of how to wound him had made her fling some taunt at him which pushed him over the edge of reason. Mary had had many admirers, but in truth she was a remarkably naive woman who had never been able to grasp the extent of the passion she aroused in men.

Mary then accused Tim of being a Protestant, and with a laugh told him that when he died she would see to it that he would be buried in Droylsden's Protestant churchyard at St. Mary's across the street from Moorcroft

Street. His fury at this remark, coupled with months of both sexual and emotional frustration, drove Tim over the edge. Lifting the poker from beside the fireplace, he struck her over the head with it. Mary reeled backwards, screaming out, "Murder!" at the top of her voice, and then ran for her life. Tim, with the poker still in his hand, was hard on her heels.

Bridget, not surprisingly, awoke at that moment to the screaming downstairs. As she sat up and rubbed her eyes she heard Mary's voice pleading piteously, "Don't, Tim, oh please don't."

Frightened, Bridget sprang out of bed as her door opened. Mary staggered in crying, "Bridget, Bridget, I am killed."

To Bridget's horror she saw that Mary's face was covered in blood. Tim came in behind her, breathing hard. "I will kill you! I will kill you!" he screamed, as though oblivious of Bridget. Raising the poker, he struck Mary hard on the back of the head. Mary did not move again, but Tim Faherty frenziedly struck her five more blows.

Bridget could do little more than look on until the rage had abated. When the poker was raised a sixth time, it got caught up in the clothes on the rack. Snatching the few seconds it gave her to get away, Bridget ran from the bedroom. She had reached the landing when she felt Tim's hands clasp her flowing hair. Screaming at the top of her voice, Bridget broke free and leapt for the stairs.

Next door neighbour Thomas Brown had been in the street outside when he heard the screams, and pushed his way into the house without hesitation.

In the next instant, Bridget, in her blood-speckled nightgown, hurled herself from the top of the stairs, leaving Brown hardly the time to brace himself to break her fall.

Still bewildered, he held her in his arms as Bridget sobbed hysterically, "Oh, he's killed my sister, Tim's killed my sister!"

Leaving Bridget in the care of another neighbour who

had followed him in, Brown bravely ran upstairs.

He found Tim, his clothes and hands covered in blood, on his knees in Bridget's bedroom beside Mary. Blood poured from Mary's mashed head, saturating everything around her. There was even blood on the ceiling.

Brown gasped in horror as he surveyed the carnage.

"What the hell have you been doing?" he demanded angrily.

"I gave her my honour and . . . and . . . I loved her and I am now here to die for her," Tim Faherty sobbed, gently caressing Mary's bloody face.

Brown's principal concern was the injured woman, who was now making a horrible gurgling noise. Realising Tim Faherty was so shocked that he presented no further danger to anyone, he fetched a glass of water from beside Bridget's bed and tried to get Mary to drink some. Mary did not have the strength to take any. It merely dribbled down her chin and onto her chest.

At 3.45 p.m. Police Constable George Lord was making his way along Market Street when he was halted by a group of distraught women who told him there had been a murder in Moorcroft Street. Sending a boy to the police station to inform Inspector Harrop, Lord hastened to the address.

When he arrived, the policeman found Tim weeping over Mary. She was alive but unable to speak. A surgeon had already been sent for, but Lord could see from the amount of blood lost that there was little hope for the injured woman.

Later, with Inspector Harrop, Lord traced the trail of blood through the scullery and parlour, up the stairs to Bridget's bedroom.

After questioning Thomas Brown and Bridget about what had happened, Harrop promptly arrested Faherty and put handcuffs on him. As Constable Lord led him away, Faherty picked up the bloody poker from Mary's side and remarked, "Yes, this is it."

Although the poker was a heavy one, almost a yard long and an inch thick, it had completely buckled – testimony to the dreadful force of the blows.

Tim tried to pull away from the policeman, leaning back to where Mary – now breathing fitfully – had been propped and whispered frantically, "Oh, Mary, didn't I tell you . . ." Lord, however, would have no last minute nonsense. Roughly grabbing his prisoner by the collar and back of his trousers, he hauled him downstairs. He shoved the weeping Irishman through the crowd of onlookers who had clustered on the pavement outside the house, and threw him into the police van.

At the police station, Faherty was allowed to wash the blood off himself. Just before the prisoner was searched, he said, "I've nothing upon me, for I was prepared for it." As far as Constable Lord was concerned, this was a clear admission that the murder had been premeditated.

The surgeon, Robert Slater, arrived at the Moorcroft Street house at 4.15 p.m. Mary Hanmer was insensible. She had lost so much blood that there was no more he could do for her but make her as comfortable as possible until she died, which she did at 5.11 p.m.

Harrop then formally charged Tim with Mary's murder.

"Is she dead?" asked Tim in bewilderment. When Harrop assured him she was, he replied in sudden anger, "The bitch accused me of being a bloody Protestant and said she would bury me in Droylsden's Protestant churchyard."

The next day, Boxing Day, Faherty was taken by police van from Droylsden to the magistrates' court in Stamford Street, Ashton-under-Lyne. Many curious onlookers followed the van on foot through the snow, trying to catch a glimpse of the killer. As he was led into court, Faherty appeared controlled, although he must have been suffering from shock. One newspaper of the day speculated that he was now assured that if Mary Hanmer could not be his, she could not now be anyone else's either.

The magistrate, S.D. Lees Esq, heard the accounts of Thomas Brown and Bridget Broaderick. Bridget wept throughout her testimony. Inspector Harrop, Constable Lord and finally the surgeon, Robert Slater (who had completed his post-mortem on Mary Hanmer's body and concluded death was due to pressure on the brain arising from a fractured skull), gave evidence.

Lees committed Faherty for trial, and had him taken away to New Bailey Prison, Manchester.

A few days later, two mothers set out from Galway to England to say goodbye to their children for the last time.

Mary Hanmer's destitute mother went to the Roman Catholic church in Fairfield near Droylsden to attend the service. She was so poor she had only a tattered handkerchief to cover her head in church. Her daughter's friends, moved to pity for the old lady, took up a collection for her, with the result that when she went back to Ireland a few days later she was better clothed and fed than she had ever been before.

Mrs. Faherty arrived in Droylsden on the same day Mary Hanmer's mother did, but although she was neither as impoverished nor as alone (having her brother and two sisters with her) she was equally as grief-stricken to see her son in the cell.

Throwing her arms around her son, she cried, "Oh, Tim, my boy, I'm here."

From that day on she visited him every Friday, but although she gave him a lot of comfort, her visits also, inevitably, gave him a great deal of pain. He knew how much she was suffering to see him locked up for murder.

The trial opened at Manchester Assizes on Thursday March 12th, 1868, before Mr. Justice Lush. Mr. Hopwood prosecuted, with Mr. Ernest Jones defending.

Faherty pleaded not guilty. He had now spent three months in prison, during which time he had both cursed Mary and prayed on bended knees for her forgiveness. Now he cursed her again.

Inside the Assize Courts, its entrance hall decorated with illustrations of various types of punishment, Tim listened intently as his trial proceeded, but in reality he had become indifferent to his fate. Only when Mrs. Broaderick, who had always been kind to him, took the stand did Faherty display any great sorrow. Faherty's ex-landlady was very old, so the ordeal of appearing in court unnerved her to the point of collapse as she struggled to give a coherent account of what she saw on returning home on Christmas Day to find Mary had been murdered.

Giving testimony was so difficult for her that she stumbled constantly over her words, and in the end the judge completely lost patience and ordered that the old lady be led out of court for some fresh air.

If Tim no longer cared what happened to him, his counsel certainly did. Ernest Jones, in his defence speech, while agreeing that Faherty had indeed murdered Mary Hanmer, asked the all-important question of whether it was premeditated? Had Faherty been suddenly so angered by what had taken place between himself and the victim that afternoon that he snatched up the poker and battered her with it in rage?

Faherty had told Harrop that Mary had accused him of being a Protestant. Could that have triggered the assault? asked Jones. He argued that there was no real evidence to show that Faherty had harboured hostile feelings towards Mary. "Indeed," he argued, "everything showed it was an affair of the moment."

To conclude his speech, Jones appealed to the jury to take into consideration the provocation, namely Mary's continual rejection of him and calling him a Protestant.

He also asked them to consider the influence of drink on the prisoner that Christmas Day. And, Mr. Jones emphasised, they should take into account the long vigil of the Midnight Mass which Faherty had attended alone after being snubbed again by Mary. All these circumstances, Mr. Jones contended, made a strong case for the crime to be reduced from murder to manslaughter.

The judge, however, disagreed – perhaps because Faherty had admitted to Constable Lord that he had 'come prepared'. He solemnly told the jury, "If you believe the evidence, there are no circumstances in the case which could reduce the crime below that of murder. It might have been reduced to manslaughter if there was great provocation but there was nothing of that kind in this case. Words do not constitute that provocation.

"It is the clearest case of murder which could be conceived."

The jury returned a verdict of guilty, whereupon the judge passed the death sentence.

Faherty blanched but said nothing. He was led away by two warders and quietly ensconced in the condemned cell.

A priest visited him frequently to give him some crumb of comfort, but the most terrible visits were those from his mother. She was a thin woman dressed in black who looked quite out of her depth in these surroundings. As he looked at her, the embodiment of misery and bewilderment, he longed to touch her, to give her one final hug of farewell. But there could be no touching or communication between the visitors and the condemned man, for the room was divided by a passageway of iron bars along which a warder walked to make sure they could not even shake hands. Two other warders were also present to stop any signs or signals being passed between mother and son.

The effect of the inhumanity of this system of meeting brought an anguished howl from the woman's throat. Faherty's fingers convulsively clutched the bars with painful force. A warder came in and gently but firmly steered the weeping woman away, out of his sight, out into the unfamiliar streets with its bustle of uncaring strangers.

Faherty was hanged alongside the Todmorden murderer, Miles Weatherill, at 8 o'clock in the morning of Saturday, April 4th, 1868, outside the New Bailey Prison, Manchester. It was to be the last public execution to take place in Lancashire, so no one wanted to miss it. Crowds of men, women and children of the lower classes had gradually massed outside the prison during the night to see the scaffold. Many of them had dispersed by 11 p.m., but the two condemned men endured the jeering of a group of 50 youths and their girls who began marching round the prison singing loudly, "When Johnny Comes Marching Home", and an obscene version of "Glory, Hallelujah" at around 3 a.m. However, fatigue overtook even this disrespectful group and soon all those still outside the prison were sleeping peacefully at the foot of the gallows. Householders opposite the New Bailey let upstairs windows to those willing to pay for a good view, and hawkers were prepared for a brisk trade in refreshments. The crowd was also swelled by the presence of over 200 policemen who were there to control the gathering and to see that nothing untoward happened to the executioner, William Calcraft.

The crowd didn't hiss at Tim as they did at Weatherill when the two condemned men took their places on the scaffold.

"Oh, Mary, Mary," he whispered. The next moment the platform abruptly went from beneath him and he passed into eternity.

There seems to be some doubt as to whether Tim Faherty deserved the death penalty.

Despite his statement at Droylsden police station that he had 'come prepared' the murder was more likely to have been done in a fit of sudden rage. He had not taken a murder weapon with him, and Bridget had distinctly heard raised voices as if an argument was going on in the kitchen below her. Mary's cold, dismissive treatment would easily provoke a man of Faherty's nature beyond control, but curiously, the judge had disagreed that words could constitute provocation.

Perhaps, in some perverse way, Tim Faherty and Mary Hanmer both achieved their ambitions, for she died pure, as she had wished, and he laid down his life for her . . .

7

SHE LOST HER HEAD TO THE SOHO BUTCHER

Jack Carter

Early on the morning of Friday November 2nd, a roadsweeper plodded his way around Regent Square, Bloomsbury, pushing before him the debris that had accumulated during the night before.

Then, suddenly, his eyes fixed on a bulky parcel covered in what appeared to be sacking which had been tucked away just inside the railings of the gardens in the centre of the Square.

He propped his broom against the railings and stooped to examine the mysterious bundle. He pulled aside the sacking and saw what appeared to be silk. He was curious now, but anxious. This, he was quick to realise, was no ordinary parcel.

Somewhat hesitantly he removed the silk, and immediately stepped back in horror. For what he saw now was unquestionably part of a human body.

The roadsweeper ran to a side street where earlier he had seen a patrolling constable, and within a very few minutes Scotland Yard detectives were examining the torso of a woman still clad in silk lingerie.

An immediate search of the gardens and the Square were started, and very soon the officers found a second parcel wrapped in brown paper. This, it was discovered, contained the woman's legs.

But the minutest search failed to produce any trace of a head or the hands.

By now, of course, there was no shadow of doubt that this was murder, and it was equally clear that the murderer had taken steps – by hiding the head and hands – to prevent identification of his victim.

Inquiries were placed under the supervision of Chief Inspector Frederick Wensley, one of the toughest, shrewdest and most painstaking officers at the Yard, and he in turn called in Dr. (later Sir) Bernard Spilsbury, who had already won recognition for the brilliance of his pathological deductions.

Carefully and methodically the parcels were removed and unwrapped, and it was immediately established that the body was that of a woman aged about thirty.

Two other vital clues came to light. The first, and probably the most important, was that the torso had been wrapped in a sheet, on which worked in red cotton was a tell-tale laundry mark – "11H."

The second clue, also found in the wrapping of the torso, was a torn scrap of brown paper on which someone had scrawled the words "Blodie Belgium."

And so as Chief Inspector Wensley went to work on these lines of inquiry, Dr. Spilsbury probed pathologically to discover how the young woman had been killed, and to glean any information which might help in the identification of her killer.

The year was 1917, when Zeppelins were dropping their bombs on London, and while the war continued in France and hundreds were being killed daily these two great men and their aides probed this solitary murder in London.

Chief Inspector Wensley's first task was obvious. He had to identify the body, and the most important clue to this was, of course, the laundry mark.

He had this circulated to every police station in London

with instructions that every laundry in the metropolis must be visited until it was identified.

Within twenty-four hours it was established that the sheet in which the torso had been wrapped was owned by Madame Emilienne Gerard, aged thirty-two, who lived in Munster Square, Regent's Park.

Chief Inspector Wensley hurried to the flat and learned that Mme Gerard, whose husband was a French chef serving with the Army in France, had not been seen there since the night of October 31st.

This was not conclusive evidence of identification of the torso, but the Yard man felt pretty certain that she was the victim, particularly in view of the fact that Dr. Spilsbury's preliminary report said that the woman had been killed some forty-eight hours or so before the finding of her torso.

Wensley thoroughly searched her flat, and concentrated on learning as much as possible about Mme Gerard, her friends, her acquaintances, and her habits. He gave orders to the effect that he would personally interview everyone who knew her.

Among these he included a man called Louis Voisin, a Frenchman trading in London, for in Mme Gerard's flat he found not only an I.O.U. for £50 signed by Voisin, but a large photograph of the Frenchman standing in a place of honour on the mantlepiece. Meanwhile, Dr. Spilsbury had made some most interesting discoveries.

· His report to the Scotland Yard officers said that the woman had been dismembered after death by someone of abnormal strength, and someone skilled in the use of a knife.

The sharpness of the knife and the cleanness of the cuts suggested that the murderer, or at least the man who had cut up the body, was a butcher by trade. Indeed, said his report, the body had been cut in exactly the same way that a butcher would cut a carcase.

Further, there were clots of blood on the woman's heart indicating that there had been an attempt at strangulation.

Chief Inspector Wensley studied this report with peculiar interest, for he had quickly learned that Louis Voisin, the man who owed Mme Gerard £50 and whose picture stood on her mantelpiece, was a butcher trading from No. 101 Charlotte Street, Soho. He sent detectives to bring Voisin in for questioning at Bow Street police station.

When the officers called on Voisin they found him with another woman – a Mme Berthe Roche – but he made no objection to accompanying the detectives.

He was a massive, red-faced bull of a man, forty-two years of age. The only difficulty Chief Inspector Wensley had with him, however, was that he could understand very little English. However, that was overcome with the aid of a French speaking constable.

He knew nothing about a murder, of course, but he spoke at length about his work, about carving carcases and then, strangely, about taking home a calf's head.

Why, wondered Wensley, did he suddenly, out of all context, mention a calf's head? The chief inspector was most certainly interested in finding a head – the head of the torso.

Already Voisin was Wensley's No. 1 suspect, and the Yard man ordered him to empty his pockets. When this was done, keys to the man's basement flat in Soho were found. Wensley ordered that it be thoroughly searched.

Officers who went there soon discovered the missing head and hands of the murdered woman. They were hidden in tubs of sawdust in the cellar.

It now looked as if Wensley had an open and shut case against Voisin the butcher.

But did he?

The head and the hands were taken to Dr. Spilsbury, and his eventual report was of the utmost interest in view of his earlier finding that the body had been cut up by someone of great strength.

The eminent pathologist found that Mme Gerard had bled to death following a large number of wounds in her head caused by a blunt instrument.

And the startling fact was that, although there were a dozen or more wounds on the head, not one of them had been powerful enough even to fracture the skull!

That did not give the impression that it was the work of the powerful Voisin.

Dr. Spilsbury now proclaimed that Mme Gerard had been attacked by someone of *little* strength, and there were wounds on her right hand showing that she had tried to ward off the blows.

Chief Inspector Wensley was now faced with the possibility that more than one person was involved in the death of Mme Gerard, though there was no doubt that Voisin had cut up the body.

There was evidence enough that Mme Gerard had met her death in Voisin's Charlotte Street home, for in addition to the finding of the head and hands there, the kitchen walls were streaked and spattered with blood.

Wensley knew, of course, that Voisin was now having an affair with Mme Berthe Roche, whom the detectives found at his home, Wensley now wondered whether it might have been she who attacked Mme Gerard.

Immediately the head and hands of the dead woman had been found in his cellar Voisin knew he had some explaining to do, and the voluble Frenchman was now ready to give his version of what had actually happened.

On November 1st, he told Chief Inspector Wensley, he went to Mme Gerard's flat at about eleven a.m.

"When I arrived the door was closed, but not locked," he said. "The floor and carpet were full of blood. The head and hands were wrapped up in a flannel jacket which is at my place now. They were on the kitchen table. That is all I can say. The rest of the body was not there.

"I was so astounded at such an affair I did not know what to do . . . I remained five minutes stupefied . . . I thought that a trap had been laid for me.

"I then went back to my house, had lunch, and later returned to Mme Gerard's room. I then took the packet to my place. I kept thinking this was a trap. I had no intention to do any harm to Mme Gerard. Why should I kill her?"

This was, to say the least, an ingenious story. The Yard man knew that Voisin was a frequent visitor to Mme Gerard's flat, and it could account for the head and hands being found in his cellar, and the finding of the torso elsewhere.

But the wily chief inspector had one further ace up his sleeve.

He turned to the burly Voisin and said to him: "Do you mind writing the words 'Bloody Belgium'?"

Voisin readily agreed, and the big semi-literate Frenchman hunched himself over a scrap of paper and laboriously scrawled "*Blodie Belgium.*"

Wensley knew then that it was Voisin who had dumped the torso in Regent Square, Bloomsbury, for it was there that the note "Blodie Belgium" had been found.

He had to make certain, however, so he asked Voisin to write the words again. And once again Voisin wrote "Blodie Belgium." In all, the Yard man asked the Frenchman to write the words five times, and each time he made the same error and misspelt "Bloody."

Chief Inspector Wensley was now quite certain of three vital facts: That Mme Gerard was murdered in Voisin's basement; that Voisin had cut up her body, and that he had deposited the torso in Regent Square.

But he was equally convinced that Voisin had not struck the head blows with "the blunt instrument" which had felled Mme Gerard and led to her death.

Who else could have done it but Madame Berthe Roche, the butcher's latest love?

By this time, the Yard man and his assistants had dug deeply into the lives of Mme Gerard and Voisin, and had learned that at one time Mme Gerard had acted as his housekeeper.

And with her husband fighting in France this association had ripened into love. In recent weeks, however, there had been a cooling-off between the pair, evidently because Voisin had found another lover, though whether Mme Gerard was aware of this is not known.

On the night of October 31st, Wensley established, there was a Zeppelin raid over London, and Mme Gerard took shelter in a West End tube station until the "All Clear."

Evidently the raid and the barking of the defiant guns unsettled her for she decided not to return to her home, but to visit her erstwhile lover, Louis Voisin. Maybe she intended to spend the rest of the night with him.

Just exactly what happened on her arrival at Voisin's flat no-one knows. All three participants in the drama that followed are long dead, but it is quite certain that Mme Gerard's arrival was of acute embarrassment to the butcher, who at that moment was entertaining his new love, Mme Roche.

And it is equally certain that the meeting between the two women – it is believed that they were previously unaware of each other's existence – was, to put it mildly, far from cordial.

One can imagine the frigid looks, the icy greetings, and the curious, inquisitive stares. It could not have been long before Mme Gerard realised that this was the woman who had ousted her from the affections of the amorous butcher.

And it must have been with equal rapidity that Mme Roche recognised in Mme Gerard a rival who had come to regain her lover's affections.

To Voisin it must have been a moment of intense drama as the two women displayed their mutual hatred.

Detectives believe that each ordered Voisin to turn the other out, and, when he did nothing they turned upon each other and spat their animosity.

There is no knowing what names they called one another, but it was Mme Roche – the woman in possession – who proved the one with the fiery, uncontrollable temper.

Chief Inspector Wensley was quite sure that as their

tempers flared Mme Roche suddenly picked up a nearby poker, and in a fit of jealous rage, set about Mme Gerard, slashing her about the head repeatedly with blows that the unarmed woman tried in vain to ward off.

And there could be little doubt, reasoned the chief inspector, that as blow after blow descended on her head Mme Gerard screamed . . . screamed in agony, and for help from the massive butcher who watched as she was beaten to the ground.

It was equally reasonable to presume that someone became alarmed that the screams of Mme Gerard would attract the attention of neighbours or passers-by, and that someone put hands around her throat to stifle them. Hence the clots of blood on the woman's heart, indicating that there had been an attempt at strangulation.

And who else would that be but Voisin. Mme Roche still had the poker in her hands and was in an uncontrollable fury. It was not likely that she would care about her rival's screams.

So, in the kitchen of that basement flat, Mme Emilienne Gerard fell unconscious and died, and Voisin, who not so long before had been her devoted lover, watched her die.

Then came the problem of what to do with the body. And it was at this stage that Voisin, maybe with the aid of his new love, Mme Roche, thought up his diabolical scheme.

There is little doubt that he cut up the body that same night. He hacked away the head, the hands, and the legs so that it could more easily be disposed of, and he hacked away, as Dr. Spilsbury said, just as a butcher would hack at a carcase.

On the afternoon of the next day – November 1st – Voisin called at Mme Gerard's flat, of which he had the key, and collected a sheet from the linen cupboard.

He was seen by the landlord, to whom he was well known, and he explained to him that Mme Gerard had gone away for a week or two.

Then he added: "She asked me to mention to you that

she is expecting delivery of a sack of potatoes, and hopes you will be good enough to put it in her room when it arrives."

The Yard men believe that at that time, Voisin intended either to take or send the torso to the murdered woman's own flat, and no-one knows what induced him to change his mind.

That night he wrapped the torso, still clad in silk lingerie, in the sheet he had collected from the flat, added an outer covering of meat sacking, and deposited it just inside the railings of the garden in Regent Square. A little further on he left the second parcel containing the legs, and these he wrapped in brown paper.

Just what persuaded him to pencil the words "Blodie Belgium" on a piece of torn wrapping paper and place that in the torso parcel no-one knows, but it is believed that he did this as a red herring – to make Scotland Yard believe that there was some sinister political motive behind the killing.

Little did he realise that it provided, because of his ignorance, yet another vital clue to his identity and to his part in the murder.

The reason Voisin took the sheet from Mme Gerard's flat was unquestionably because – as he had indicated in his statement to Chief Inspector Wensley – his original plan was to suggest that Mme Gerard had been murdered there.

When Wensley, with the expert opinion of Dr. Spilsbury, was satisfied just how Mme Gerard had been killed, he summoned Mme Berthe Roche and questioned her closely. She swore that she had never seen Mme Gerard in her life. She knew nothing of the murder, she had never struck the woman. How could she strike a woman she had never seen?

As the Chief Inspector questioned her more and more closely her eyes flashed angrily and she showed unmistakable signs of an uncontrollable temper.

Wensley then summoned Voisin from his cell, and as

the burly butcher and his lover stood before him in Bow Street police station he told them both that they would be charged with the murder of Emilienne Gerard.

Berthe Roche immediately became livid with fury. She thought that Voisin had incriminated her, and she turned on him and spat, "You nasty man! You have deceived me!" She was still screaming with rage when officers removed her.

In due course – in January, 1918 – they appeared in the dock at the Old Bailey together, and the prosecution outlined its case with the vital evidence of the laundry mark, the misspelling of "Blodie Belgium,"and the bloodstains and discovery of the head and hands in Voisin's cellar.

The trial itself was an ordeal in more ways than one for the jury because every word, every question and answer, had to be translated into French for the benefit of the two accused. At one stage of the trial they had to examine the bloodstained door from Voisin's Charlotte Street kitchen, and later, escorted by a sheriff and the court ushers, they endured a thorough survey of the basement where the gruesome tragedy occurred.

Voisin stuck to his story that he did not commit the murder and that he found Mme Gerard's head and hands in her flat, and suspected that someone had set a trap for him. And he stoutly denied that Berthe Roche had anything to do with it.

This despite the fact that, as they sat in the dock together and a police officer translated the evidence, Berthe constantly shrieked abuse at him and insisted that he was the murderer and that she was innocent!

On the second day of the trial, Mr. Justice Darling directed that Berthe Roche could not be convicted of wilful murder, and ordered that she be remanded until the next Sessions to stand trial as an accessory after the fact.

Voisin leant over to try and pat her hand, but she turned on him like a tigress before she was led below.

Though the evidence against Berthe Roche was not

strong, that against Louis Voisin was overwhelming and the jury found him guilty of murder.

To spare him a few extra moments of torture and suspense, Mr. Justice Darling passed the death sentence in French – surely a unique happening in a British court. Voisin gripped the dock rail and in a voice which he tried to keep steady he shouted again and again that Berthe Roche had no part in the affair.

Unquestionably his gallantry had saved her life. If Mme Gerard *had* been killed as the Yard men and Dr. Spilsbury believed, Voisin was the only witness, and he never wavered from his story that she had nothing to do with it.

On the day before Voisin was executed at Pentonville Prison, Mme Roche appeared before Mr. Justice Avory charged with being an accessory after the fact. She still protested that she did not know the dead woman, but the evidence that she knew of the murder was too strong and she was sentenced to seven years penal servitude.

On the following morning, it is recorded, she was told that Voisin, her lover, had gone to the gallows, but she showed no trace of pity.

It may be that this woman with the spitfire temper was already devoid of natural emotion for, after less than a year in prison, she was certified insane. She was taken to an institution in Highgate, and died on May 22nd, 1919.

8

TILL MURDER DO US PART
John Davis

It was the first week of November, the week of the
Melbourne Cup, Australia's most important horse
race. Thousands of visitors flocked into Melbourne,
sportsmen, sheep raisers with fat bank-rolls, visitors from
near and far. Also crooks, confidence men and other
criminals on the lookout for strangers whose celebrating
made them unwary and easy prey. Detectives mingled
with the crowds, police watched airports, railway stations,
hotels, alert for malefactors.

In a quiet side street in the industrial suburb of
Carlton, Walter Symons locked the door of his furnished
room at 6 p.m. and started for the bar of the nearby
University Hotel for a couple of quick ones before dinner.
As he left the boarding house he saw through the window
of a downstairs room that his neighbour William Kent
also had begun to celebrate. Kent, though in his 70s, was
a sturdy, likable old man with an eye for pretty girls.
Symons smiled as he saw Kent holding a girl on his lap.
She was smartly dressed, a slender, curvaceous charmer,
with flame-coloured hair and brown eyes. Her head was
tipped back on Kent's shoulder and he was kissing her.
Beside them stood a table with a wine bottle and two
glasses.

Still smiling, Symons hurried on.

Like the other residents of the lodging house, Symons considered Kent something of a mystery. He let it be known that his only income was from a small pension, yet he always seemed well supplied with money. At the hotel bar he often produced a fat roll of bills and stood drinks for the crowd.

When Symons returned to the house around ten that evening a light burned in Kent's room. Through the window he thought he saw the old man lying on his bed. Must have dozed off after his festive evening, Symons concluded. But the curiously twisted position of the man's body on the bed puzzled him. Stooping, he peered into the room beneath the partly drawn shade.

He jerked back with a gasp and a shudder, ran as fast as his legs would carry him to the Carlton police station and told a constable what he had seen.

This was the evening of November 8th, 1949. Though no one suspected it then, the murder of this obscure old man in a barely furnished room was to become the most celebrated Australian murder of that era.

Among the first to arrive at the boarding house were Senior Detective Charles Currer and Dr. Keith Bowden, local government pathologist. Finding the door of the room locked, Currer and two of the constables heaved their shoulders against it. The door burst open with a splintering of wood.

The room was a shambles. Drawers were pulled open, their contents strewn upon the floor. A wardrobe closet was rifled, furniture overturned, indicating a violent struggle.

Clad only in a torn shirt and stained with blood, the body of William Kent lay on its back on the bed. His legs were bound, his arms lashed behind him with strips of a torn sheet. His thumbs were tied together with a bootlace. His face was bruised and he had been slashed across the cheeks, lips, stomach and thighs. Other mutilations, apparently inflicted while he lay bound and helpless, suggested that the old man's attacker was a sadist.

Dr. Bowden noted a bruise and gashes on the crown of the victim's head. "Looks as though he was struck over the head with a wine bottle," he said, indicating glass fragments near the bed. "But he appears to have died of strangulation. Notice the two red marks on his throat from the pressure of thumbs. He was apparently stunned by the head blow, then tied up. Before he was strangled, he was slashed and tortured, perhaps to force him to tell something. But from the look of his body, I'd say his killer was someone who hated him, tortured him for the twisted pleasure of watching him suffer."

Walter Symons told of seeing Kent with the red-haired woman on his lap, when he left the house earlier.

"Couldn't he have been killed by a woman?" Currer asked the doctor.

"Yes, if she knocked him out and tied him up first," the doctor said. "He certainly was with a woman shortly before his death. Notice the traces of lipstick." He pointed to a faint orange-red smear on Kent's mouth. "He might have been attacked by two or more persons." Dr. Bowden placed the time of Kent's death at about eleven o'clock that evening.

"By now, the killer could be anywhere," Detective Currer observed.

"Could be a decoy killing, since he had a woman here."

Fingerprint men, photographers and other experts arrived and set to work in the room. Meanwhile Currer questioned Walter Symons and the other boarders. No one had heard a disturbance, possibly because of the noisy celebration at the University Hotel. Symons explained that he had been with friends at the hotel from six o'clock until he left to come home, when he discovered the body. A check-up confirmed this and he was released from any suspicion in the case. One by one, the other boarders were also eliminated as suspects. None could offer much information about the victim. But all were unanimous in their opinions of him.

"He seemed a friendly fellow, but he never talked much about himself," Symons said. "He had lots of friends over at the hotel, but few visitors at his room."

Symons said he remembered one man he had seen there several times. Kent always closed the door when he came. "He was a much younger man than Kent, somewhere around forty, with a ruddy complexion, black hair and a little black moustache. He was a flashy dresser, always came in a sports car," Symons added.

Fingerprint experts reported that they had picked up fragments of three different sets of prints, all of them fresh.

"One set is the victim's," they disclosed. "They're all over the place, and they're on one of those two wine glasses. On the other glass there is another set of prints that look to be a woman's. There are no prints on the neck of the bottle or the door handle. Both were carefully wiped. But there are good sharp fingerprints of a third person on the door frame."

When the prints had been photographed Currer asked the expert to check them at once with the prints of known criminals on file at headquarters. Then he gave out the sketchy descriptions he had of the red-haired girl and of Kent's moustached visitor for broadcast to police cars. He also asked that detectives at railway stations, piers and airports be instructed to detain any suspicious persons attempting to leave town.

On the possibility that the murder, on the day before the Melbourne Cup, had some connection with the races, he asked officers to find out if the victim was known in horse-racing circles.

Detectives who had been searching Kent's quarters now reported that they found nothing of value. No money. The pockets of the victim's suit, which lay near the bed, had been cleaned out save for cigarettes, matches and a handkerchief.

One surprising thing was the absence of documents of any kind in the room. There was not even a personal letter or a receipted bill. No address book could be found – nothing to link the victim with any other person. Either Kent had been unusually secretive or his slayer had removed all such clues.

Another curious fact was that the lock on the door had held, while the hinges gave way. "The lock is quite new. Seems likely that Kent himself had it put on, either because he feared someone or as a precaution against burglars. It's a turnbolt type, an especially strong, heavy mechanism that must be locked from the outside," one expert said.

"The door was locked when we came," Currer observed. "So the killer either had a key to it or he took Kent's key and locked the door to delay discovery of the body."

Only one likely clue was found in the room. Around a glass ashtray which lay broken on the floor were a number of cigarette butts. All except one were of the brand found in Kent's pocket. The odd one was an oval-shaped cigarette on which part of the brand-name remained. It was an obscure brand. There were traces of orange-red lipstick on its tip.

"I know these cigarettes," a detective told Currer. "They're Egyptian and are expensive. We may get a break if that cigarette was smoked by the girl who was here tonight, because they're for sale at only a few high-class tobacconists in Melbourne. Not many are sold, and sales assistants might remember the sale."

Currer sent a detective to make the rounds of exclusive tobacconists. Then he called the police commissioner

"This is a curious case," he reported. "William Kent was presumably an obscure old man living on a pension. Still, he apparently was rich enough to put a special burglar-proof lock on his door. His room was ransacked, which would indicate robbery. But Dr. Bowden believes it was a crime also involving revenge. The killer could be any of the thousands of visitors who came especially for the big race. We've got a clue or two, but nothing very promising. And many of these people will be leaving town tomorrow night after the races."

"Every police officer in Melbourne is on overtime duty to handle the crowds," replied the commissioner. "But I'll find as many men as you need somehow. Keep me posted."

Currer had barely hung up when the telephone rang again.

"William Kent's prints are on file. He's been arrested three times on charges of off-track bookmaking. But, according to the record, the police never were able to make the charges stick and he was released," the fingerprint man reported.

"Any luck with the other prints you found?" Currer asked.

"No, we drew a blank on both sets. Neither person has a criminal record, at least not in Melbourne."

"Send the prints by plane to Canberra to be checked against the government files," Currer told him. "Also phone Canberra, ask them to check their description file for an attractive red-headed girl who has a record as a decoy."

Currer next called the police detail which dealt exclusively with racing frauds.

The detective who answered said, "We have a complete record on William Kent. Everybody knew him as 'Pop' Kent. He was one of the cleverest off-track bookies in town. His beat was the Carlton area and he worked the hotels, chiefly the University. Three times I caught him taking a bet, but he claimed the customer was a friend paying back a loan and the customer backed him up.

"When I got Kent to the station, there wasn't a betting slip on him. We searched his room but found no records of any kind. He kept everything in his head. He'd take bets and simply remember them. His clients trusted him. When they struck a winner, he'd pay off promptly. Apparently he operated entirely on his own funds, didn't have a bank account. He must have had plenty of money cached away in that room of his."

Currer asked, "Did Kent place the bets?"

"He did sometimes. But we think he also worked by telephone with a legal bookmaker named Jack McCarthy. McCarthy used to come to his room – we think to balance accounts. But we never could get anything against him either."

"Is he a flashy dresser with black hair and a small black moustache?"

"That about describes him."

"Do your best to locate him and have him taken to headquarters for questioning about Kent's death."

Currer now went to the bar of the University Hotel.

"Pop Kent? Yes, I just heard he'd been done in." The bartender shook his head.

"Did you know he ran an off-track book?" Currer asked.

"I knew. I had strict orders not to let him take bets in here. He did most of his business on the street. But I had no legal right to keep him out as a customer – and he was one of the best."

"Was Kent in here this afternoon?"

"Yes, for an hour or so. Then he went into the public lounge and had some more drinks there."

"Did you notice a pretty red-haired girl in there?"

"I certainly did. She was sitting at a table not far from Kent. She was a well-dressed, refined-looking girl. I figured she was a hotel quest."

"Did she leave with him'?

"I didn't notice either of them leave. Maybe the waiter would know." The bartender summoned him.

"That classy redhead? Sure I remember her," the waiter said. "Kent was giving her the eye and after a while he came over and sat with her and she let him buy her a drink. He pulled out a big wad of notes. Later they left together"

Currer sent for the hotel detective, who told him, "I

saw the girl you mean in the lounge yesterday."

"Was she with anyone?"

"No, she was sitting alone." He hesitated. "Is this in connection with that old man's death?"

"That's right."

"Well, then. I noticed someone else in the lounge today that you might like to hear about. Does the name Norman Andrews mean anything to you?"

Currer said it didn't.

"Well, that's natural, because he's from Sydney. He's a small-time crook who's done short stretches for burglary and robbery with violence. Once when I was working for a hotel in Sydney the police were looking for him, and issued a circular with his picture and description. I memorised them, as I always do with wanted criminals. Well, I saw Andrews in the lounge late this afternoon. I phoned the police to see if he was wanted for anything now, and the answer was no."

"Have you still got Andrews' picture?"

"Sure. I keep a file on habitual criminals. It's part of my job to keep them out of the hotel, for the protection of guests. I checked up and found that Andrews isn't registered here under his own name. Then I showed the picture around among the staff, but no one seems to remember seeing him – though they might not, even if he were staying here because the hotel is so full."

At the desk, a clerk looked through the hotel register. "Only one guest left so far tonight." he said. "Everybody is staying over for tomorrow's race. The checkout is James Robertson of Sydney. I marked him off the books at 7.21."

The house detective produced the picture from his pocket. "Is this the man who checked out?"

The clerk looked at it carefully. "Yes, I'm certain it is. I remember him, because he handed me a £50 note and I couldn't change it from the till. When I told him I'd have to go to the safe, he was annoyed."

The clerk went on to say that the guest had three suitcases. When the bell-boy attempted to carry all three to a taxi, the guest insisted on carrying the largest one. "Is that boy still on duty?" Currer asked. The clerk nodded and summoned him. But the bell-boy said he had not heard what address the man had given the cab driver.

Currer visited Andrews' hotel room. But it already had been cleaned up for another guest. He then telephoned headquarters, gave the description of Norman Andrews, alias "James Robertson," and asked for a special detail of twenty detectives to comb the city for him.

Currer then returned to his office where he mentally reviewed the case. Kent had met the red-haired girl at the hotel lounge. She had gone to his room with him after he had flashed his roll of notes. Nothing further was known of her movements. Dr. Bowden thought it possible that a woman had killed Kent.

Norman Andrews, a known criminal, had been in the lounge at the same time. He might have seen the roll, might have followed the pair out, gained admission to Kent's room after the girl left him, and committed the crime. His registration under an alias and his hasty departure from the hotel looked suspicious, though if he'd heard of the murder, a man with his record would clear out to keep from being suspected, even if he were innocent. But why would he be carrying three suitcases? Did one of them contain loot from Kent's room?

Possibly Andrews and the girl had been working a decoy game together but there was nothing yet to link the two. And what accounted for the extreme brutality of the crime?

A call came from the central identification bureau at Canberra. "About that redhead of yours," an officer said. "We've got quite a lot of them on file – both real and dyed. But there's one girl who fits the decoy role best – a slender, good-looking girl with natural flame-red hair. We've got her photograph, fingerprints and complete history. She's a Sydney girl, name's Jean Lee."

"Good. What do you know about her?" Currer asked.

"Well, she comes from a respectable middle-class

family, was given a good education. She married and had a daughter. Then the war came and her husband went to a training camp. She was lonesome. Finally she left the child with relatives and went to Brisbane to work as a waitress in army canteens. But she took to drinking, kept losing jobs, and finally became a camp follower.

"After the war she came back to Sydney, where she was convicted several times for prostitution, though she managed to keep the fact from her parents.

"In Sydney she met a criminal named Bobby Clayton – a small, thin, ferret-faced man with several convictions for housebreaking. Clayton must have been kind to her at first, because she fell violently in love with him.

"First she became his mistress and then she started working for him. She'd walk the streets at night and bring him the money. Clayton's contribution to their finances came from beating up a drunk now and then.

"Finally they were working the decoy game together. Jean would bring her pick-up home. Clayton would come in, catch them in a compromising situation and play the jealous husband. He'd give the man a savage beating, then demand money not to have him arrested.

"The law finally caught up with Clayton and Jean about a year ago. They both went to jail. We've just talked to the Sydney police and they say that while in jail Jean Lee seemed to get a grip on herself. She was only twenty-eight and she told prison authorities she was going to leave Clayton and make a fresh start in life. They say that when her term was up she went to a small town in New South Wales and got a factory job. But they don't know if she stuck to her good resolutions."

Currer said, "She may have gone through with her plan to leave Clayton – and then teamed up with Andrews. Since she's already been convicted of being a female decoy she could be the one we want. When you receive the prints we found on the wine glass, check them with hers and let me know."

Currer then telephoned the Sydney police and asked

them to contact the girl's parents and learn if they had heard from her recently.

Later a detective called him back. "I just left the Lees," he reported. "They showed me a letter from Jean, postmarked November second – a week ago. She was still at the factory, said she liked it and intended to stay there."

Reports began coming in from the detectives searching for Norman Andrews. A railway ticket clerk had sold a ticket to Adelaide to a man of Andrews' description. Andrews had reportedly been seen in a restaurant, in a club and in a waterfront lodging house. The detectives followed up all these leads. In each case the man seen had proved to be someone else.

Meanwhile, police had picked up the bookmaker Jack McCarthy at his home. He was brought to Currer's office.

"Sure I know Pop Kent," he said. "It's sure a pity what happened to him."

"When did you visit him last?" Currer asked.

"Just yesterday. Pop and I were old friends, you might say. He was lonesome in the evenings and I went to his room to cheer him up sometimes. I'd see him out at the track a lot, too. Knew a lot about horses, Pop did."

"You knew he was an off-track bookmaker."

McCarthy smiled. "Oh, Pop may have taken a few shillings from a friend now and then to bet on a horse. But I wouldn't know. That was his business."

"Come off it, McCarthy," Currer snapped. "He placed bets with you and you'd come around every week or so to settle your accounts with him. You're one of the few men he ever let into his room and probably the only one who knew how much money he actually kept there. Where were you tonight around seven?"

The bookmaker's smile faded. There was a cautious glint in his eyes as he said, "I thought you wanted me to help you figure out who done him in. Are you trying to pin the job on me?"

"Answer my question. Where were you?"

"I was out in my car. I drove to a breeding farm this afternoon to look over some horses. I must have been on the way home about seven."

"Was anyone with you?"

"No, I was alone. I stopped and had dinner on the way. I got back here around nine o'clock." He named a roadside inn where he said he had eaten.

"We'll check up on that," Currer said. "Meanwhile we want your fingerprints."

Reluctantly, McCarthy went to the laboratory with Currer. His fingerprints were taken and a technician began making comparisons between them and the prints found on the door frame of the murder room.

Currer peered through the microscope. "They look the same to me."

"They are," the expert said. "I can't tell officially until I've checked them, point for point. But there's no real doubt."

The bookmaker's jaw dropped. "I told you I was in Kent's room yesterday. I must have left my prints then."

"We won't place a charge against you yet, McCarthy," Currer conceded. "But we're holding you until we can make a thorough search of your house." Currer sent detectives to McCarthy's home.

The search for Norman Andrews yielded no result. Then at last Currer's phone rang. It was the detective he had sent to visit tobacconists.

"Currer, I've struck lucky!" he said excitedly. "I'm at the Occidental Hotel. I got here just as the cigar stand was closing for the night. A salesgirl remembers selling some packets of Egyptian cigarettes recently to a red-haired girl who came with a man. She thinks they were staying at the hotel because they used the lobby door rather than the street door."

"What did the man look like?"

"She says he was a small man, thin-faced, with hard eyes. She thinks they've both left the hotel, though, because she hasn't seen them in two or three days."

"Stay where you are," Currer told him. "I'm coming over."

He drove rapidly through streets now almost deserted.

At the Occidental Hotel he found the detective at the desk. The assistant manager was leafing through the hotel register.

"I remember that couple," the manager said, "because they nearly got us into serious trouble. Their name was Strong. Here they are, a Mr. and Mrs. Howard Strong of Sydney. They had Room 227.

Currer glanced at the signature. Suddenly his eye was caught by the name written immediately below – James Robertson of Sydney, the same name that had been signed in the register at the University Hotel.

"Do you remember this man Robertson too?" he asked.

The official looked at the signature. "I'm afraid I don't."

"See when he checked out."

The man looked in the register again. "November fifth. The same night the Strongs checked out. He left at 11.27, a few minutes after they did. They seem to have arrived here at the same time, too."

"What about the Strongs?" Currer asked. "How did they nearly get the hotel in trouble?"

"They held up one of our guests, a Mr. Murdock. But he refused to report it to the police because he feared the publicity. He's still staying with us. He must be in his room asleep at this hour."

"Call him down."

Reginald Murdock, a rotund, greying man with a prosperous appearance, was soon seated with the others in the manager's office. Beneath his eyes were purplish bruises and there was adhesive tape on his cheekbone.

"It's the old story," he said ruefully. "I'm a married man and I should have had better sense. I came to Melbourne with plenty of money to bet on the races, all set for a good time. Then, Saturday evening, I saw this red-haired girl sitting alone in the public lounge. She looked a refined type and I thought she was waiting for someone. But when nobody came, I screwed up my courage and invited her to join me in a drink. She accepted. She acted as though she liked me and kept playing up to me. When she suggested we go for a drive in her car, I thought, well, why not.

"She led the way to a touring model car parked on a dark street not far from the hotel, got in and slid under the wheel. I got in, too. But instead of starting the car, she leaned over and put her arms around me. I'm only human. I kissed her. We sat there for five or ten minutes.

"Then I felt a hand on my shoulder and a man spun me around. 'That happens to be my wife you're kissing, mister,' he said. He was a small man with a sort of rat-like face and hard eyes. He opened the car door and jerked me out. He was strong for his size, and I'd had a little too much to drink, anyway. When he hit me, I went down.

"He gave me a bad beating. There was another man there, and he hit me, too. I didn't get a good look at him. I passed out. The next thing I remember, I was lying alongside the car and my head was splitting. The man must have kicked me after I'd passed out, because my legs and abdomen were painfully bruised. I looked for my wallet. It had had nearly £100 in it. I found it lying beside me, but every penny was gone. I don't believe that car belonged to them at all. I think they just picked it out because it was in a dark place.

"I staggered back into the hotel. I was going to call the police, but then I realised the story would get into the newspapers.

"I looked up the hotel manager and told him I wanted to keep it quiet. He was worried about the hotel's reputation and wanted to keep it quiet, too. He looked in the register and found that a night clerk had just checked out a Mr. and Mrs. Howard Strong. The clerk described them. They were the couple who robbed me. I wired my bank for more money – and that's the whole story."

"I think we can keep your secret, Mr. Murdock," Currer said. "Meanwhile, you're free to go back to bed."

Though it was past three o'clock, Currer telephoned the University Hotel and asked for the house detective.

"Do you remember," he asked, "that Norman Andrews left the hotel carrying three suitcases? I thought part of it might be loot from Kent's room. Well, suppose he was carrying his own suitcase and those of two other people?"

"I don't get it. What people?"

"Two people who must have walked out another door and skipped paying their bill. See if the signature directly above Norman Andrews on the register is Mr. and Mrs. Howard Strong. I'll be there right away."

Currer found the detective waiting for him in the lobby. "That Strong couple skipped all right," he said. "Was one of them the redhead?"

Currer nodded. "I think her name is Jean Lee. The man with her probably is her boy friend, Bobby Clayton. They and Norman Andrews were working as a trio. She was the bait and it was the men's job to crash the party and do the heavy work. I believe the three of them together killed William Kent."

In their room at the University Hotel Currer found evidence in support of this theory. The washbowl showed pinkish stains. There was a bloody smear on a door frame. At the bottom of a hamper was a towel stained with blood.

"Looks as though one of them was injured during the struggle," Currer observed. "That may be why they had Andrews carry all the luggage and skipped out without paying. They were afraid the injury would attract attention."

Currer got police headquarters on the phone. "Put out a call to all cars to pick up Bobby Clayton, Jean Lee and Norman Andrews." He gave their descriptions. "One of them is probably injured. I think it's likely they robbed and murdered Kent to get money to bet on today's races and are still in town."

On the theory that the three seemed to like high living, Currer began telephoning the big hotels.

On his fourth try, he struck the jackpot. A night clerk at the New Southern Hotel stated that two men and a woman had registered in at about midnight.. The names they signed were not the ones they had used previously. But the clerk had noticed that the woman, a redhead, had a bandaged hand.

"Where are they now?" Currer demanded.

"They were all pretty drunk. The woman could hardly walk. They took their luggage to their rooms, then came down again. I thought they were taking her out to get some fresh air and sober her up."

"If they come back, don't let them suspect anything," Currer warned. "Let them go to their rooms."

He phoned headquarters again and two cars were ordered to a street corner near the New Southern. Currer met the men there and they entered the hotel by a service entrance. The trio had not returned. Currer and his men waited in an alcove near the door.

Shortly after four, the two men and the red-haired girl came in. As the detectives closed in on them they seemed amazed and put up no resistance. They were placed under arrest and taken to the Melbourne City Court. There each was taken to a separate room.

For nearly an hour all resisted the barrage of questioning. Finally they admitted that they were Bobby Clayton, Jean Lee and Norman Andrews. They denied knowing William Kent.

Then Clayton, who denied any connection with the crime, began to show signs of strain.

"You're the one who did the actual killing, aren't you, Clayton?" Currer flung at him. "You and Andrews trailed Kent and Jean waited outside. When Kent was good and drunk Jean opened the door and you went to work on him. You knocked him out with the bottle, bound him and took his money. Believing he had more money hidden in the room, you tortured him until he told you where to find it. Then to seal his lips you killed him. The strangling was your work, Clayton."

"It's a lie! " Clayton cried suddenly. "Jean and Andrews killed him. I wasn't even in the room. I was standing guard in the hall. Jean slashed him to get even with the old fool because she'd had to let him make love to her."

Clayton repeated his statement in the presence of a stenographer and signed it. Then he collapsed, sobbing.

Currer went to the room where Jean Lee was being questioned and told her of Clayton's statement.

She stared incredulously at the detective. "I want to see that statement – and him too!" she said angrily.

She was shown the statement. Then Clayton, weeping hysterically, was brought into the room.

"They call women the weaker sex!" Jean sneered. "I love Bobby Clayton and if that's the way he wants it, okay. I killed the old man. I hit him with the bottle. By the time I'd slashed him a bit, he'd lost consciousness from lack of blood and strangling him was easy. I'm the guilty one."

Jean Lee also signed a confession. Only Norman Andrews refused to make a statement. He steadfastly denied that he had had anything to do with either the robbery or the murder.

All three, however, were arraigned before a judge and formally charged with the murder.

Back in his office, Currer found a report from the detectives sent to make a check on Jack McCarthy.

"Absolutely nothing," it said. "No bloodstains in his home or his car. No bloodstained clothing. No large amounts of currency. Nothing to link him with Kent's death."

Jack McCarthy was freed, absolved of any connection with the case.

In the days that followed, Detective Currer tied up the loose ends of the case. About £73 and several blood-stained articles of clothing were found in one of the suitcases left by the trio at the hotel. The fingerprints on the wine glass were identified as Jean's. A key found in Clayton's pocket proved to be the key to Kent's room. Clayton and Jean were identified by Reginald Murdock as his assailants. Murdock said Andrews might have been the third person who beat him.

When police files were sent from Sydney, it was learned that Norman Andrews, 38, was married and had two daughters.

Nervous and depressed, he began to drink heavily and no longer was able to hold a job. He drifted into crime and early in 1949, he left his wife and family for good. Soon after that he met and teamed up with Clayton.

Bobby Clayton, 32, had been born in the slums of Sydney. His parents sent him to school and did their best to give him a good education. But by the time he was 18 he was ruthless and violent, making a living by burglary and robbery. Then he met Jean, and for a while he lived on her immoral earnings. When she attempted to go straight, he teamed up with Andrews. The murder of Kent was the first time the three had worked together.

The trio were brought to trial in the Criminal Court at Melbourne in late March, 1950, before Mr. Justice Gavan Barry. By this time, Bobby Clayton had discovered his conscience. He and Jean Lee became reconciled and sat in the dock holding hands. Under questioning by his counsel Clayton completely repudiated his previous statement.

"I turned like a yellow dog when I framed Jean that way," he said. "It was all lies and I only said what I did because I was still drunk and I was tired and my only thought was to get myself out of trouble. I killed William Kent. Jean had already left the room. But I wanted him dead so he wouldn't squeal. I and I alone did the killing. The others are innocent of that part of it."

Jean also changed her statement. She said that when she left the room, Kent was alive. "I didn't kill him and never wanted to kill him," she said. "I made that confession when I was drunk and hysterical."

Andrews still denied any connection with either the robbery or the murder.

Counsel for Jean Lee made much of the fact that her confession, upon which the Crown largely based its case, had been gained by reading to her Clayton's confession, which he since had repudiated. They also stressed the fact that Bobby Clayton had gone to the town where Jean had "gone straight".

He pleaded with her to go with him "on a holiday to the races". Her old love for him reasserted itself and she went to Melbourne with him.

As the trial continued a great deal of sympathy was built up for Jean Lee.

On March 26th, 1950, the jury retired to consider its verdict. They were out for about two hours and a half. Then they filed in and, before a hushed courtroom, the foreman announced the three verdicts separately. But all were the same. Bobby Clayton, Jean Lee and Norman Andrews were found guilty as charged. There was no recommendation for mercy.

The silence of the courtroom was broken by a scream from Jean, "I didn't do it! I didn't do it!" She fainted in the dock.

Clayton turned savagely on the jury. "You team of idiots! I hope your next meal chokes you!" he cried.

When order was restored, Judge Duffy said, "I need only say that the verdict was based on the strongest evidence and I thoroughly agree with it."

Then in a solemn voice he sentenced all three to death by hanging.

The trio's defence counsels appealed to the Court of Criminal Appeal. Their main grounds were that the confessions had not been voluntary but had been obtained under duress at a time when the suspects were intoxicated and in a semi-hysterical condition.

By a majority opinion, the court ordered a new trial for all three.

This action caused grave concern to the Victorian Crown Law Department. If these statements were not voluntary, then what constituted a voluntary statement? The Law Department expressed its opinion that if this decision were to be accepted as precedent, it would so curb the powers of the police in questioning suspects as to alter radically the course of criminal justice in Australia.

The department gave its strong backing to the Crown Prosecutor when he appealed to the High Court of Australia against the decision of the State Full Court of Criminal Appeal.

The result was that in June, 1950, the High Court, in a unanimous decision of its six judges, overruled the Appeal Court's decision and restored the death sentences of all three persons.

The morning of February 19th, 1951, dawned drizzly and grey. During the night, Jean Lee had sobbed herself into a merciful coma. She was carried to the scaffold. The noose was placed around her neck and she was hanged, still unconscious.

Two hours later, at ten o'clock, Bobby Clayton and Norman Andrews walked erectly to the gallows.

So ended Australia's most bitter trial for life. Many influential people had publicly announced their horror at the thought of a woman being hanged. Jean Lee was in fact the first woman to be so executed in over 50 years.

9

MISTRESS BOILED LIKE BACON
Stephen Bell

Saturday, August 6th, 1892, one of the hottest days on record, found young Charles Hadley at a loose end on his half-day holiday. For a lack of anything better to do he rather ghoulishly decided to investigate the stink which he had noticed about half a mile away from Althorp station. It seemed to be coming from a deep ditch which ran alongside the Northampton to Rugby road, and had plagued the locals over the Bank Holiday.

Nobody had done anything about the awful stench because they were too apathetic, he thought. Most people were quite happy simply to leave it up to the farmers themselves to discover if their dead sheep were putrefying in ditches and lanes.

Hadley followed his nose. As he got closer to the spot, the stink of the decaying mass was almost overpowering on that blazing hot day. He wrinkled his nose up in disgust, and before he got too close, he cut himself a good long stick. Breathing shallowly, but enduring a smell that might have sent anyone else reeling, Hadley leant over and poked the ragged bundle at the bottom of the six foot dyke. The grubby white mass seemed to part into two, and the rotting object was alive with more maggots than he would have dreamed possible. Furthermore, his disturbing the bundle had if anything released the foul stench even more strongly. His eyes watering, Hadley backed off, clutching his throat and hurrying to a bit of the road where the air was a little sweeter before he could breathe properly again.

Hadley's investigation had left him not much wiser, but feeling squeamish and sick. It was an adventure he wished he had not embarked on, and he took refuge in the village pub.

Somewhat soothed by the effects of a pint of beer, he started talking about his hideous experience, trying to make light of it. The village bobby's wife, however, was disinclined to laugh it off when she heard about it, and by the following morning the site was surrounded by locals. One, John Chapman, whose sense of smell was somewhat blunted, volunteered to get close enough to the bundle to find out what it was. He got near enough to report to the sea of faces peering down at him from a respectful distance that it appeared to be something wrapped in calico, tied up with string.

It was not a very good attempt at a parcel, he called up, for the whole thing seemed to have divided.

Chapman cut the string of the stinking bundle, and his face perceptibly whitened as the contents spilled out. He jumped back so none of it would splash his shoes and trousers, and got out of the ditch far more quickly than he had got into it. The people above could clearly see why, because enough was visible of two human legs and pieces of female attire for them to be able to tell that it was the corpse of a woman.

Superintendent Alexander of the Northamptonshire Constabulary showed no surprise when the local surgeon Dr. Churchouse, stated that the woman had been dead for at least a month. It was plain to see that she had been dead for a long time, as when the bundle was fully opened the female remains it contained were seen to be badly decomposed, half clothed, headless and armless. So butchered was the corpse that the clothes were the only indicators as to its sex. From the waist upwards it was just a tangle of jumbled bones, rotting flesh and maggots.

The flesh which still remained on the bones of the legs peeled away in strips when the surgeon tried to take off the stockings.

With the onlookers standing back to form a protective circle, the corpse, or at least most of it, was scraped up into fresh wrappings and conveyed on a pallet to the Red Lion at East Haddon.

It was impossible to determine the cause of death. The doctor only commented that the body was that of a female over 18 years old, and that all her internal organs were missing. Her head and arms had been removed in a savage manner, he said, possibly with a saw, because the sleeves of her dress appeared to have been hacked. The material of her dress seemed of good quality, indicating that she had come from a decent background.

The body had been wrapped originally in a sugar bag and other coarse material. The bag bore a large white label saying E.M. RAE. Northampton, L. and N.W.

Surprisingly, this vital clue was not immediately followed up. Had it been, the killer would have been caught within hours and the case cleared up. As it was, the police pocketed the label and left it until two weeks after the inquest before making inquiries as to its origin.

Police traced the label to a butcher named Edward MacRae. However, it did not take the police long to dismiss him from their enquiries. As he told them, being the proprietor of a business in Northampton, he used the bags to wrap up sides of bacon for his stall in the market. He often sold the bags separately, too, because they were very handy, and recalled having sold one during the summer to a tramp.

"I never thought to take the labels off. Why should I?" he asked. "My brother runs the warehouse in Dyechurch Lane for me, and I run stalls in Birmingham and Daventry. You can find him at the stall on Wednesdays and Saturdays. He's probably sold bags separately, too."

The police withdrew, asking him to tell his brother, should he see him, to pop into the police station opposite the warehouse at his leisure. They were certain that selling bags with that label was the only connection the MacRaes had with the case.

The MacRae family hailed from Birmingham, and it was there that Andrew George MacRae had left his wife and two sons to go to work for his brother.

The family had never done anything illegal, or crossed swords with the law, so when Andrew MacRae did not immediately present himself at Angel Lane police station, Inspector Webster pursued his enquiries elsewhere.

Many days later, MacRae did turn up at the police station, only to be told by an indifferent Superintendent Alexander that he was too busy to see him and could he call back at some other time?

The second inquest took place at the Red Lion on August 29th, with Edward MacRae present and repeating what he had already said. The victim's name and how she had met her gruesome end was still a mystery, so an open verdict was returned.

The police were baffled, but content to let the matter rest there. They made a few more enquiries for the sake of appearances, and shelved the case. Had it not been for the curiosity and stubbornness of a Northamptonshire daily reporter who published the inscription on the label, the case would never have been satisfactorily solved and brought to its ultimate conclusion.

But the day a picture of the label was published, a Mrs. Bland, who dealt in secondhand clothing, came forward and stated that Rae or MacRae was the name given by a man who towards the end of July had sold her a number of articles of women's and baby's clothing.

The police now acted swiftly. From Mrs. Bland's description, they knew that they would not be looking for Edward MacRae, so that left only the brother, Andrew George, as a suspect, and since his fruitless visit to the police station, he had made himself suspiciously scarce. However, not knowing how deeply suspected he now was, he was confident enough to show up at his brother's stall on Saturday, September 3rd, 1892. Unknown to him, however, Mrs. Bland had been asked to accompany investigators to the market to identify him as the man who had sold her the clothes. This she unhesitatingly did.

Another result of the surge of interest in the newspaper article was that two women came forward with some interesting information of their own. They too had recognised Andrew George MacRae, but they knew him as Mr. Anderson.

The police listened incredulously as the two newest witnesses told them that Mr. Anderson lived in lodgings in St. John's Street with his wife. Mrs. Anderson, so he had explained, had gone off to New Brighton with their month-old baby, on July 20th, 1892.

More witnesses who had known Anderson came forward and verified the story told by these two ladies, although some of them had heard that Mrs. Anderson had gone to Birmingham.

MacRae was arrested at once. After being shown the clothes which had given his game away, he said he had sold them for his wife. However, when the Birmingham police were contacted by telephone to confirm his story, all they could say was that the real Mrs. MacRae, ignorant of any of this trouble her husband was in, was alive and well, and had not wanted her old clothes to be sold for her.

Who then was the mysterious Mrs. Anderson? Police interest was once again centres on MacRae's home town, where they discovered more evidence to tie the case up. A near neighbour and family friend had been missing from her home since March 1892. It was vaguely thought that she had gone to marry an American artist, Guy Anderson, and settled in New York.

"There was something mythical about Guy Anderson," the Birmingham detective in charge of the case said later. He had carried out exhaustive enquiries in the area and discovered that a person of that name really had lived there previously, but had moved away to live abroad, apparently alone. Whether this person had in fact been

MacRae was never properly established, but what did surface was that Andrew MacRae had been having an illicit affair with the missing woman for nearly a year.

Annie Pritchard was a respected girl. She had won the approbation of her local community by helping her widowed father bring up her numerous brothers and sisters.

Annie was the same age as MacRae's wife and they were firm friends, often popping into one another's houses. MacRae too had been on familiar terms with the young woman, although his wife would have been surprised had she known the extent of this familiarity.

Although MacRae would admit nothing, the police were now fully confident that with the witnesses they had, and the positive identification of Annie's body and clothing by her sisters, they had solved the mystery.

Annie had left for Northampton on March 22nd 1892, pregnant, having told her family and friends that her destination was Liverpool. There she was to meet up with Anderson, marry him and sail to New York to live. So good was the description, her act so convincing, that her lover's wife had even helped her to pack, unknowingly sending her dear friend into the arms of her own husband.

To allay any suspicions, Annie had handed a letter to a commercial traveller bound for Liverpool, with instructions for him to post it when he got there.

Meanwhile, MacRae had booked lodgings in St. John's Street, Northampton, under the name of Anderson. No doubt he felt that should Annie disappear at a later date, it would be "Mrs. Anderson" who had vanished, and he would not be implicated.

The long letter, written in Annie's hand, and dated March 28th 1892, had arrived and perpetrated the charade that led ultimately to her death.

"My dear brothers and sisters," she had written, "my dearly beloved arrived safe and well. He has not altered much, but thinks that I have, a good deal. Well, I am no longer Annie Pritchard. We were married this morning by special licence and we are going back to New York till my husband has completed his engagements. Then we hope to settle in England, near you all.

"I very much regret that we cannot come home now as we sail at once. I am in very much better spirits as I know I shall have a husband and be happy. I know I shall have a good home and a good husband in my dear Guy."

Who had concocted the plan to keep the truth from both families, Annie or MacRae, was never ascertained, but other evidence came as if drawn by a magnet. The birth of the baby in St. John's Street on June 23rd; the sale of Annie's clothing – now positively identified as hers, even the hire of a cart presumably, police imagined, to transport the body to the Althorp ditch – implicated MacRae.

All that was left to find was the woman's missing head and arms, and the baby. The police felt that if MacRae had killed the woman, then he must also have disposed of the child.

Neighbours around Dyechurch Lane warehouse had noticed, they told police, thick black smoke belching from the warehouse chimney. It had not smelt like the usual smoke that came from it. The warehouse was searched in vain. Then it was searched again by Superintendent Alexander and two detectives. This time over 30 pieces of calcined human bone were found, some with saw marks. These were judged to be what remained of Annie's arms.

In the copper, too, traces of human hair, the same shade of brown as Annie's, were discovered.

Of the baby, nothing remained.

The trial opened on Thursday, November 17th, 1892, with Dr. Churchouse amending his statement regarding the length of time the body had been dead to a fortnight. This tied it in with the last confirmed sighting of Annie on July 20th, 1892.

During the adjournment for lunch one of the jurors, James Asplin, caused a serious incident when he decided that it was an ideal time to post a letter. While the other 11 jurors filed into an anteroom, Asplin slipped out of the court, returning 30 minutes later under the mortified gaze of the bailiff.

The presiding judge, Lord Justice Kennedy, had never been faced with this kind of problem before, and hastily conferred with both counsels. It was possible, because of the stupidity of this juror, that MacRae might be acquitted on a legal technicality!

Finally, the judge decided he would have to seek advice elsewhere, and Asplin and his fellow jurors were obliged to suffer the inconvenience of being locked away all night until the judge's return from London.

The court assembled the following day and Judge Kennedy promptly fined Asplin £50 for gross contempt of court, leaving him in no doubt that a substantial term of imprisonment had been considered.

The case was remanded to the next Assizes on December 20th 1892.

MacRae's defence complained bitterly about the delay, and of the protracted agony the defendant must be suffering.

The court reopened with a new jury, but this too was interrupted within 20 minutes when a juror was taken ill.

In all, 43 witnesses gave evidence, and at the conclusion, the defence counsel, Mr. Hammond Chambers, argued that there was no case to answer. He said there was no evidence of a murder having been committed, but on this Judge Kennedy interrupted and ruled otherwise. He stated that the prosecution had proved that the body was that of Annie Pritchard, that she had indeed been murdered and mutilated, and that she was unarguably dead.

The defence, however, then went on to hypothesise that Annie was still alive, and that she had left Northampton on the day she was last seen to join Guy Anderson, leaving her friend MacRae to dispose of her unwanted property.

Clutching at straws, Mr. Chambers suggested that Annie Pritchard had wished to sever all connections with Northampton and start a new life.

The judge began his summing up at 2 o'clock on Christmas Eve, saying that unless they could agree that the body was indeed that of Annie Pritchard, without going into the question of murder at all, then they should acquit.

For one and a half hours, the jury considered the evidence, and returned with a verdict of guilty. It surprised those who had heard the summing up, but a crowd of several thousand who had been waiting outside the court cheered when the news of the verdict filtered through to them.

It was in general a popular decision.

MacRae took the verdict very calmly, saying even as the judge donned the black cap, "Any sentence you pass on me has no terror. . . " The rest of his speech was drowned out by the cheers of the crowd outside, and almost stopped the proceedings.

MacRae continued to protest his innocence, calling the witnesses abominable liars, then he turned in fury to attack the jurors. "Gentlemen, you have this day, each and everyone of you, become what you have made me; a murderer. You have this day, this night, this Christmas Eve, made fatherless my loving children. As long as you live your consciences will accuse you."

The judge solemnly pronounced sentence of death.

Andrew George MacRae ate heartily on the morning of Tuesday, January 10th, 1893, and after sipping a little brandy, was hanged at Northampton Gaol. James Billington, the executioner, noted that everything had gone smoothly and that MacRae had remained calm to the end.

MacRae's body lay within the precincts of the prison until it was demolished in 1931. His body, along with others buried there, was dug up at midnight and taken on a refuse cart to be buried in a common grave in Towcester cemetery.

Annie was interred in the then newly consecrated cemetery at East Haddon. A stone purchased by the local inhabitants was erected for her. The grave lies alone along the boundary, with the inscription, "I was a stranger and you took me in."

10

SHE HELD BABY AND
EXECUTED HUSBAND

*R.C. Adamson, former Green County coroner,
as told to Aaron Green*

Elias and Rosa Marshall moved into Greene County, Pennsylvania and settled at Taylortown-Dunkard in 1907, migrating from West Virginia. With them came four children, the youngest, Florence, an infant of two. The father found steady employment on farms in the vicinity and the children, by now eight in all, attended school at Dunkard, or Taylortown.

Little Florence became the favourite of the family. She had reddish-brown hair, a flashing smile, and winning ways. At school age she was called the prettiest child in the community, and her teachers and the older children adored her. But she possessed a temper to go with her red hair, and she also had the provoking habit of flying into a tantrum when she was not the centre of attention or the winner in every game.

After leaving school, Florence met Joseph Albert Hartman. He was handsome, industrious, well-educated, and considered a "fine catch". On September 29th, 1928, they went to Waynesburg and were married in the Greene County courthouse there.

Hartman drew a good salary, considering the times and

the neighbourhood, and provided his wife with a good home. Several years passed, during which the couple appeared to be extremely happy. Then with no warning, the mines shut down, and Hartman was out of work. By this time the Hartmans had three sons to feed and clothe. They moved to Taylortown, where the ex-miner sought farm work, or any kind of job which would give him an honest living. But none was to be had. Their savings dwindled until finally his name was entered with many thousands of others on the unemployed register.

It is not clear just what happened in the Hartman home during this period. Perhaps, as so frequently occurs, when the wolf stalked to the door, love flew out of the window. At any rate they began quarrelling. At first the tiffs were not serious, but they grew in proportion until the husband and wife frequently were not on speaking terms for days at a time.

After an especially bitter quarrel which preceded the fourth of July, in 1936, Hartman announced that he was going to Cleveland to attempt to find work there. He was distressed by his inability to earn the salary to which he was accustomed, and he felt too that he and his wife would be more congenial in new surroundings. He mentioned this when he promised to return for his family as soon as he was well located.

Mrs. Hartman had sufficient funds to care for the children for a few weeks, and she was in favour of the move. Her husband departed and it was a month before she saw him again, although he wrote frequently outlining his job-hunting activities. Finally, he obtained a position on a large dairy farm at Twinsburg, Ohio, near Cleveland, and moved his family into a tenant house.

For the first couple of weeks Mrs. Hartman was busy fixing up her home, and her husband was occupied making a good impression upon his new employer, so they had no time to quarrel. But they were soon at it again. Their wills clashed over even the most trivial things, and in the harsh exchange of words that followed, there were invariably accusations – the husband accusing the wife of infidelity, and she charging him with not properly supporting her and the children.

Hartman made repeated efforts to settle the difficulties, but when in late September the tiffs became everyday occurrences, he suggested that his wife take the children back to Pennsylvania – that perhaps another separation would ease the situation. Mrs. Hartman, in high anger, immediately loaded the youngsters onto a bus bound for Taylortown. Arriving there, she placed the two older boys in the Greene County children's home, and took baby Wayne, eighteen months old, with her to her parents' home.

As her husband hoped, the separation gave Mrs. Hartman time for reflection, and she was soon back in Twinsburg, seeking a reconciliation. The husband was willing, but before they could complete arrangements another quarrel developed.

During the next few months, Mrs. Hartman made a half-dozen trips to visit her husband, each of which was climaxed by a quarrel. Finally he announced that he was going to Canada, to attempt to make a new start, and that she could do as she pleased about a divorce.

He made known his decision while visiting his wife at Taylortown, and just before he boarded a bus to return to Ohio. It was a telling blow to Mrs. Hartman. Suddenly realising that she had finally alienated her husband – that she was a loser in the game of marriage – she gave vent to her anger in a violent tantrum. She quickly regained control of her emotions, however, and appeared willing to make the best of the situation. But dark thoughts filled her mind. She no longer loved her husband, yet she vowed that if she could not have him, no one else should.

The crisis came early in January, 1937. Mrs. Hartman brooded for several days and then, taking baby Wayne with her, went to Ohio. She discovered that her husband had given up his job at Twinsburg, and had gone to Cleveland. She followed him there, and called upon

Harry Hartman, his brother. Late in the afternoon of January 18th, the brother drove her to her husband's boarding house, in East 65th Street. She found him sitting in the front seat of a car parked outside, discussing its purchase with Miss Mary King, a young friend of the family.

Mrs. Hartman greeted Miss King cordially, then got into the rear seat of the car, the two women chatting pleasantly for several minutes. Finally the wife addressed Hartman.

"Al, won't you take me back?" she pleaded.

"I took you back three times – what's the use of trying it again?" he snapped.

"What about the children, then?"

"I'll get a divorce and get custody of the children – I'll take care of them," Hartman replied.

The wife sat in silence for a few moments. Baby Wayne was teething, and he began crying. She handed him to his father in the front seat.

"Hold him while I get some things out of Harry's car," she said.

She soon returned to the back seat and her husband handed the baby back to her. He was still whimpering, so Mrs. Hartman rocked him on her knee for a few moments, then placed him in the crook of her left arm, and held him close to her side. She had not said a word since returning to the car. She slowly drew her right hand from the handbag on her lap. She was clutching a .38-calibre pistol. She carefully aimed the weapon at the back of her husband's head, and pulled the trigger.

Miss King glanced back just as the shot was fired. She leapt out of the car screaming, and ran into a near-by store. The pistol contained four shells. Mrs. Hartman fired all of them into the back of her husband's head, and calmly handed the pistol to the first policeman who arrived.

Mrs. Hartman was indicted for first-degree murder. Her trial began in Cleveland Criminal Court before Judge

Samuel H. Silbert on March 17th, 1937.

Defence attorneys claimed that "everything went black" just before she fired, entering a plea of not guilty by reason of temporary insanity, but the judge had heard this same story too many times to accept the plea. The attorneys then sought to show that their client had killed in self-defence; that her husband had not only vowed to take her babies away from her, but also had threatened her life more than once.

The jury deliberated for two hours on March 19th, and found Mrs. Hartman not guilty. The women members were in tears when Judge Silbert lectured them with sound truth about their action.

"I certainly disagree with your verdict," the judge said heatedly. "Emotion as well as facts must have entered into your deliberation."

Mrs. Hartman, who had been well pleased to be the centre of attention in the courtroom, even if it was during her trial for murder, made a triumphant exit, pausing at the door to talk to the reporters.

"I shall never marry again," she said haughtily, "and I never want to hold another pistol."

She was right on both scores. She would not marry again and would not hold a pistol.

Next time it would be a rifle!

Her first stop after leaving the court building was at a beauty shop. Its proprietor had collected a few lines of free advertising by offering her a perm, facial and manicure free of charge. Mrs. Hartman smiled coyly when it was suggested that she was being made beautiful enough to catch another husband.

Back in Taylortown, she took up her life again.

Details of the Cleveland affair had preceded her to Greene County, and she appeared not in the least displeased to discover that she had become notorious. In fact, the next several weeks may have been as happy as any in her life, for she was given plenty of the attention she loved so dearly.

Respectable people shunned her, but many of the

curious stopped on the street simply to engage her in conversation about any topic that was handy.

With only the care of her three children to keep her busy, Mrs. Hartman had plenty of time for reflection. She discussed the trial freely, and seemed to relive again and again every moment of the importance that was hers when she was the cynosure of all eyes in the courtroom. She had "put on a good act", she confided to a certain acquaintance, or else she would not have won acquittal.

How simple it had been. There was no need for any woman ever to be convicted of any crime, provided she played her role properly!

One evening late in April, a little more than a month after her trial and acquittal, Mrs. Hartman attended service in a small country church a short distance from her home. Men and women had come from miles around, and the little building was crowded. As the services progressed, the widow suddenly became aware that an attractive stranger was sitting just in front.

Mrs. Hartman paid more attention to the stranger than she did to the preacher thereafter. She knew that he did not live in Taylortown, but he undoubtedly belonged to the community.

As the service drew to an end, she saw an opportunity. The preacher was exhorting members of the congregation to come forward to pray at the altar. A couple of dozen men and women had responded, and then the young man rose, and stepped towards the centre aisle. Mrs. Hartman quickly left her pew and hastened forward. They walked to the altar side by side, and as though swayed by the fervour of the moment, the widow seized the young man's hand and clung to it. They knelt side by side at the altar, still holding hands, until the service ended, and then left the church together.

The young man drove Mrs. Hartman to her home in his car. Both were electrified by the emotional spell of the service, and it was nearly dawn when they parted. His name, he told her, was John Andrenok, and he was a miner. He was unmarried and resided with his parents in the nearby village of Moffitt-Sterling.

Although Andrenok probably did not realise it, in these first few hours he became enmeshed in a net which would hold him as firmly as though it were made from double strands of steel. The widow was 32, and he was but 21, yet this difference in their ages made no impression on him.

The young miner called at the widow's cabin again the next evening, and rarely missed a nightly visit there during the weeks that followed. He was enamoured, while for her part Mrs. Hartman was as deeply in love with Andrenok as she was capable of loving anyone. As the weeks passed into months, she began thinking of marriage, and frequently guided the conversation so that the subject came up. But Andrenok did not immediately take to the idea of taking on three children as well as a wife who was 11 years older than himself.

Several months passed and then, early in 1938, the youth's visits to the cabin became a little less frequent. He gave no indication of a change in his affections, but to a woman of Mrs. Hartman's experience, he did not need to. She sensed such a change and, by asking discreet questions in the neighbourhood, discovered that he had been seen a few times with a girl of about his own age. Mrs. Hartman did not divulge what she had learned, but one evening she made a remark that gave the youth cause for much thought, not just over her words, but over the quiet, almost ominous, tone of voice she used.

"We've meant so much to each other, Johnnie – I'd never give you up now. I'd never let another girl have you. Never!"

The words really held a more ominous implication than Andrenok realised. In fact, they signified that Mrs. Hartman had reached a decision. If, as she feared, she was losing her young admirer – losing again in the game of love – then she would act in the same way as when she had lost her husband. Why not? She had not been punished for that murder.

A few more weeks passed, in which she saw even less of Andrenok, and then on June 12th, the youth invited her to his parents' home in Moffitt-Sterling for Sunday dinner. While they were sitting together chatting, the young miner caught his mother's eye, and nodded towards Mrs. Hartman.

"How about our getting married, Mum?" he asked.

"That's up to you, John," his mother replied.

He had expected she would say this. He was silent for a few moments. He had brought the widow to his home to tell her one thing, and now that he was ready to do so, he intended to be certain his words carried the right weight. Mrs. Hartman leaned forward, listening eagerly.

"Oh, I don't think I'll get married," he finally said, striving to be casual but firm. "I'll live home here for a while yet help you and Dad for a couple more years anyway."

Mrs. Hartman, making no effort to hide her displeasure, arose and stalked from the room. Later in the afternoon, when the youth brought his car into the driveway to take her back to the cabin, her goodbyes to members of the family were scarcely civil.

Andrenok, pleading that he had been assigned extra work, told Mrs. Hartman that he would not be able to visit her again until the following Saturday evening, June 18th. She did not urge him to call earlier; in fact, she had plans that would keep her occupied during the next few days too. And, indeed, she was busy, making arrangements and outlining exactly what she would say and do the next time she saw the young man.

Days later when he arrived, she launched her scheme immediately.

The young miner had worked hard all that Saturday. She had expected that he would do so, and as soon as he appeared at the cabin, she put him to work again, chopping up firewood. He swung the axe for more than an hour, and then the widow coaxed him to accompany her on a long walk through the village while she shopped for groceries. He was extremely weary when they reached the cabin again, and she gave him warm food.

As she had planned, he became drowsy and finally stretched out on a mattress on the floor in front of the open side door, at the foot of baby Wayne's crib. Within a few minutes he had fallen asleep.

The plot was developing exactly as she had planned, and Mrs. Hartman was elated. She had rehearsed the scheme many times in her mind, and was certain it could not fail. She waited for half an hour, to be sure the youth was sleeping soundly, and then crept out of the open door and obtained the loaded rifle from its hiding place nearby. She gave no thought to Andrenok's role in the tragedy; she was intent only upon following every move as she had rehearsed it.

The widow moved back to the open door, knelt down on the lower step in front of it and leaned forward so that her elbows were resting on the step below the top. The barrel of the rifle was inside the cabin, the muzzle pointed towards Andrenok's head. Her movements were calm and deliberate. Andrenok was sleeping on his back. She carefully sighted the rifle and, exhibiting no more emotion than she would show had she been shooting at a tin-can target, slowly pulled back the trigger and fired.

Mrs. Hartman sprang to her feet and ran into the cabin. Her children had not been awakened by the gunfire. She was thankful for that. Her victim lay still and she concluded he was dead. She placed the rifle on the floor beside him, the barrel pointing to his head, glanced quickly around the room to be certain that the stage was well set, and then ran to her parents' home a few doors away. The door was unlocked and she entered and awakened her mother.

"Johnnie's killed himself!" she exclaimed.

She paused for a moment, then rushed into the room occupied by her elder brother, Theodore Marshall, and awakened him.

"Johnnie's shot himself," she said excitedly. "Run for the doctor!"

Theodore Marshall summoned Dr. Robert Gans by telephone from a neighbour's home. He arrived just before 3.00 a.m. to find Mrs. Hartman sitting on the floor beside a man, sobbing loudly.

"Johnnie dear, why did you do it?" she kept repeating.

Dr. Gans' preliminary examination told him that the young man, while still alive, was unconscious and in a critical condition. He gave him an injection and departed to summon an ambulance and to report the shooting to the sheriff's office.

Mrs. Hartman accompanied the wounded man to the hospital, where they arrived about 5.00 a.m. "There'll be a lot of gossip about me now," she told Richard Herod, the ambulance driver. "People have been saying that I carry a gun, but I haven't carried a gun since I killed my husband."

John Andrenok died without regaining consciousness that Sunday morning, June 19th, 1938. Deputy Sheriff Paul Randolph, who had been at the bedside hoping to obtain a statement, escorted Mrs. Hartman to the sheriff's office to put her account of the tragedy into writing.

Your author did not learn of the shooting until an hour or more after Andrenok died when, as coroner of Greene County, I was notified of the death by hospital authorities. I hastened to the hospital and obtained preliminary facts. Mrs. Hartman had described the affair at her home as a suicide, I was informed, and what facts were known seemed to bear her out. The dead youth's mother, who had arrived before his passing, apparently had accepted this verdict. But I was not certain that I would. I knew the facts surrounding the murder of Mrs. Hartman's husband, and if Andrenok had been shot in her cabin, I was determined to make a thorough investigation before closing the case.

I ordered the body sent to a funeral home in Waynesberg for an autopsy and then drove to Taylortown. I arrived there about 3.30 and found Greene County Sheriff Henry Flowers, Deputy Sheriff Clarence

Taylor, District Attorney Frank Throckmorton, and William E.S. Fletcher, a Waynesburg photographer, already at the scene. A number of citizens were standing nearby, watching Fletcher take photographs of the interior of the small dwelling.

Sheriff Flowers had taken charge of the death weapon, which he had found at the cabin. It was a shiny, new .22-calibre Springfield rifle, and from its appearance it had just come from a gun shop. I examined the interior of the cabin. A mattress, a couple of pillows and a blanket were on the floor in front of the side door, and the sheriff explained that the wounded man had been on the mattress when Dr. Gans arrived.

The widow explained that she was greatly distressed by the tragedy because she and the young miner had planned to be married during the summer. She could offer no reason for him wishing to take his own life, but guessed that he might have been despondent because his work had not been steady enough to permit their immediate marriage. They had been going together for about 14 months, she said. Andrenok had called at her home on Saturday evening and had gone outside some time around midnight, explaining that he intended to take a short walk before retiring.

"I was asleep and didn't hear him come back," she said. "Then I heard the shot, I saw the rifle, and ran out to get help."

At this point, tears began to trickle down the widow's cheeks. There were no apparent loopholes in her story so far, and I began to wonder if my hunch was correct. We questioned her at length, but she made no statement that might arouse suspicion. She couldn't explain where the rifle had come from, but she presumed that Andrenok had borrowed it from somewhere when he went for his midnight walk.

I had examined the youth's clothing at the hospital and found certain stains on the bottom of his trousers, and on his shoes. Finally I asked her about them.

"I don't know," she replied, looking bewildered. Then her face seemed to clear. "I'll tell you, though," she continued. "When I came back he was sitting on the floor. He fell back again, but maybe his sitting up explains it."

I let the answer pass without comment, but it was by no means satisfactory. I was certain that the stains could not have been made in that manner; that the wounded man had not been able to sit up after being shot. There was a possibility that the stains had been made while he was being removed to the hospital, but it seemed to me that the widow had given her explanation in an effort to cover up something. If so, possibly her entire statement was false. At any rate, I was more determined than ever to push my investigation to the limit.

Doctors performed the autopsy at the mortuary early on Monday and they discovered that the rifle barrel must have been approximately at right angles to the head when it was fired. Moreover – and this was vitally important – they established positively that there were no powder burns around the wound!

It was conceivable perhaps that Andrenok might have fired the rifle at arm's length, and at right angles to his head, but highly improbable that he would have assumed such an awkward position when it would have been so simple, for instance, to have held the butt of the weapon between his feet and fired while in sitting position. And anyway the matter was settled by the absence of powder burns. It would have been an utter impossibility for him to have twisted into any position to fire upon himself without leaving powder marks around the wound.

I was certain now that Andrelok was a murder victim, and that Mrs. Hartman had killed him. I enlisted the aid of Corporal H.A. Gidley, of the State Motor Police, stationed in Greene County, and when I told him the results of the autopsy he agreed wholeheartedly that the case was not suicide.

I had been given a box of .22-calibre rifle bullets, with only a couple missing, which had been taken from

Andrenok's pocket at the hospital, and also one .32-calibre pistol cartridge. The latter interested me especially, and when Corporal Gidley and I visited the Andrenok home in Moffitt-Sterling, we uncovered another important fact to support our theory. The dead youth had owned a .32-calibre pistol, in good working order, which his mother gave to us. Why, we wondered, should he have gone to the trouble of obtaining a .22-calibre rifle to fire at himself when he already had a handier weapon?

Mrs. Hartman was still being questioned at the county jail, but I realised that she would soon be released, as the sheriff was not prepared to file any kind of charge against her, I obtained a court order to hold her as a material witness at the coroner's inquest, and then got in touch with Sergeant Vincent Bunch, of the State Motor Police, then one of the best-known homicide investigators in Pennsylvania.

The box of .22-calibre cartridges which had been taken from Andrenok's pockets at the hospital were of a type sold exclusively by Montgomery Ward & Company stores, and this narrowed our search.

We soon learned that several boxes of such shells, and three of the Model 15 Springfield rifles, had been sold at the Montgomery Ward store at nearby Morgantown, West Virginia, during the several days preceding the Andrenok shooting.

John Ashburn, a clerk in the store, remembered selling the rifles, but he could not say positively that one had been purchased by a woman, as we suspected. However, we asked him to go to Waynesburg with us, to see if he could recognise Mrs. Hartman. We took him to her cell in the county jail, and our spirits fell when he shook his head, indicating that he could not identify her. But then, with no warning at all, the widow stepped to the cell door, her face beaming.

"Why, I know you," she said, addressing Ashburn. "You're the boy I bought that rifle from over in Morgantown."

Sergeant Bunch and I exchanged startled glances. This was the break we had been waiting for – but what did it mean?

"I thought you said you didn't know where the rifle came from," I snapped.

The widow turned away. "Well, I do," she said. "I haven't told everything I know yet."

She would not discuss the matter further at that time, and we were at a loss to explain her remarks. She had either made a serious error unthinkingly, we decided, or else she had concluded that Ashburn would remember her, and had thought it better to change her story accordingly. We were inclined to believe the latter was the case, and wondered what the new story would be, if and when she saw fit to tell it.

Armed with this new information, I obtained a statement from Leroy Hartman, the widow's 11-year-old-son, that he had accompanied his mother to Morgantown on a shopping trip a few days before the Andrenok shooting. He had waited for her outside the Montgomery Ward store while she made purchases inside, he said. We interviewed the boy again the following day, and showed him a cardboard box from the store. He identified it as being exactly like one his mother had carried when she had rejoined him in Morgantown. The box was one made to hold a Model 15 Springfield .22-calibre rifle!

Despite the store clerk's failure to identify the widow, we now had evidence concerning the purchase of the death weapon.

While our whole case was still largely circumstantial, we decided that we were ready for an inquest, and I set the date for July 5th, the place as the county courthouse in Waynesburg. We laid careful plans in advance, so we knew exactly how we would proceed. The doctors testified first, and then Mrs. Hartman was called to the witness stand. She had retained counsellors, and upon their advice, refused to answer any questions. This brought about the climax which we had anticipated would not come until later. Sergeant Bunch stepped forward and took hold of the widow's arm.

"Mrs. Hartman," he said, "I am placing you under arrest for the murder of John Andrenok."

The sensational trial began on September 20th, 1938, in the courthouse at Waynesburg, with County Judge Challen Waychoff presiding.

We had worked hard in preparing our case for trial, and had subpoenaed 44 witnesses to testify for the prosecution.

Early in the trial Chief Defence Attorney Thompson announced that he would attempt to prove that the rifle which had killed Andrenok had been "fired accidentally and during a struggle".

The widow appeared in the courtroom neatly dressed, and it was apparent that she was striving to "put on a good act" for the benefit of the jury of 12 men. She paled, however, and grew visibly nervous when District Attorney Throckmorton told the jury that the prosecution would demand the death penalty.

A day and a half had been spent in selecting the jury, and it was well into the morning of the third day of the trial before we began offering our strongest proof against the defendant. The medical testimony which made it apparent that Andrenok could not have shot himself scored heavily with the jury. When she left the courtroom for the noon recess Mrs. Hartman was in tears. It was the first time she had really broken since she had been taken into custody at the hospital three months earlier. I expected dramatic developments during the afternoon, but I was scarcely prepared for what actually happened.

Mrs. Hartman had suddenly realised that at long last justice had overtaken her; that she might have to pay with her life for her crimes. She begged her attorneys to make some kind of arrangement which would save her life. Soon after court opened in the afternoon, Florence Marshall Hartman pleaded guilty to murder in the second degree in the death of young Andrenok. Judge Waychoff promptly sentenced her to serve from 10 to 20 years in the State Industrial Home for Women, at Muncy, Lycoming County, Pennsylvania, and within a few hours she was locked up there.

After changing her plea, Mrs. Hartman told many of the details of her crimes, which are related here. The mysterious stains on the bottoms of the victim's trousers and on his shoes had been made, we learned, when Mrs. Hartman had endeavoured to wash Andrenok's face before the physician arrived.

Several months after she had been sent to the industrial home, Judge Waychoff was asked to sign papers committing her to a state asylum for the insane. Prison officials reported that she was suffering from hallucinations. She believed that her husband and young Andrenok frequently appeared at the prison to assure her that her sins were forgiven.

Judge Waychoff signed the order but she was transferred back to Muncy. Physicians at the asylum had pronounced her sane; their verdict was that she was faking mental symptoms.

It is not difficult to guess that she had put on a final act which she hoped might bring her freedom; probably she thought she would have more opportunity to be liberated from the mental institution than from the prison.

But she was mistaken if she thought that she would ever get out of prison before she had served her full term. A woman as deadly as she is far better off behind bars, where, it is to be hoped, she can master the truism that crime does not pay.

11

BRIGHTON WIFE
CUT TO PIECES

Bruce Sanders

On a late summer afternoon, when the punters at Brighton racecourse were discussing the prospects for one of the last races of the day, a young man was staring across the track as he made his way towards the bookmakers' stands. He certainly wasn't looking where he was going, for he bumped into a young woman who exclaimed loudly as she was spun about. The startled young man reached out a ready hand to prevent her falling. "I'm so sorry," he said, smiling. "I didn't see you."

That was not altogether surprising, for her head came barely level with his chin.

"That's because I'm so small," she said. "I'm used to walking past someone and not being seen until they bump into me. I haven't seen much of the racing today."

"We must do something about that, mustn't we?" said the young man, still smiling. "After all, it'll soon be the last race."

Thus did Celia Bashford, a young woman of 26, come to meet John William Holloway, who was six years her junior. Although he was of only modest height, his small companion for the remainder of that afternoon gave him a pleasant feeling of being tall and protective, something new in his experience. Celia was only about four feet in height. And she was certainly no raving beauty, for her head was disproportionately large for her miniature body. Though her eyes were bright, her coarse mouth could quickly assume a sulky expression, but not on that summer afternoon in 1825 when she first met Holloway.

He learned that she came from the village of Ardingly, where nowadays the South of England Show is held, had found employment in Brighton, but was not very happy in the town. He confided that he also worked in the Sussex seaside resort, having been born in Lewes.

After they succeeded in backing the winner of the last race, he asked if he might see her home.

"I would like that," said Celia, taking his arm.

As they left the course on the Downs and walked in the direction of Kemp Town, neither realised that they were beginning a courtship that was to lead first to marriage and then to a marital bitterness and enmity that ended in grim tragedy.

John Holloway was a money-squandering youth, more interested in playing Don Juan when the opportunity arose than in knuckling down to regular work. Celia Bashford, diminutive and dimwitted, had been brought up with no high ideals of romance, and felt flattered by any attention she received from men. She encouraged Holloway to see her again and to continue seeing her. Their assignations were usually made when daylight was fading, for while Holloway seemed invariably free to accompany her to some piece of woodland, he always excused himself from squiring her through the streets of Brighton in broad daylight.

A few months passed, with the unlikely lovers keeping their twilit rendezvous and later slaking their physical passions under the Sussex stars, and then Celia had to break the news that John Holloway, at 20 still not a man in the eyes of the law, was about to become a father.

"We'll have to get married," she told him.

And so the couple who had met at Brighton races duly became man and wife. Before long, Celia presented John Holloway with a baby who filled their modest home with screams and shrieks. The mother did her best to keep the child clean and to make their home a place of comfort, but it was inevitable that lack of a regular wage from a husband and father who preferred the pub to work should result in quarrels about the shortage of cash for essentials.

Now that he felt trapped by his marriage, Holloway found himself needing to leave Brighton, sometimes for weeks.

There were reunions, however, and it was on one of these that John Holloway learned for the second time that his wife was pregnant. He accepted the news glumly. It certainly didn't inspire him to make some fresh resolve to provide for four mouths, especially as he had proved, at least to his own satisfaction, that his wife could just about take care of herself. Holloway again left home, relieved to turn his back on responsibilities he was anxious to forget.

So the Holloways headed towards destitution, impelled by the husband's total lack of any sense of his marital obligations. He drifted into a shabby lifestyle, working at low-wage jobs when he had to, indulging himself in sordid liaisons with other women, whom he kept in ignorance of his wife and two children in Brighton.

For the crushed Celia, it was a dreary struggle. Her resources became slimmer as she moved from one low-paid domestic job to another, until she decided to make the effort to work for herself in a very modest way.

At the start of 1830, with some four years of unhappy marriage behind her, she moved into a single tenement room on the outskirts of Brighton. The grubby back-street neighbourhood was known locally as the Level. Having by then left her children with members of her family, she tried to follow her husband's example by setting her mob-cap at another man, but her physical attractions were indeed limited. She just could not hold on to any man she took to her bed. More frustrated and desperate than ever, this woman now turned 30 – and beginning to look 10 years older – was trying to scrape a living by selling millinery accessories, but without much success.

The Holloways, by this time, were separated by a distance covering more than half of Sussex. John Holloway had secured work in the old Cinque Port town of Winchelsea about the time his wife moved into the insalubrious Level district. He presumably felt she might appeal to the parish officers to secure payments from him, for he also covered his tracks by changing his name. He became known in Winchelsea as William Goldsmith, and before long he was also using the name in the neighbouring town of Rye, where he met a young woman who compared most favourably with the neglected wife. Such were his feelings for her that, for the first time in his life, he wished he was married.

This young woman was Ann Kennett, who remained in total ignorance that her new suitor was not the bachelor he professed to be. Nor was she aware that she was following the same dubious path taken years before by Celia Bashford.

Like Celia, Ann became pregnant by Holloway. Like the woman now living in a Brighton slum, too, she spoke of marriage. And Holloway found himself displaying more genuine enthusiasm for this idea than anything else he could ever remember. He really *wanted* this younger woman for his wife.

"We'll have a spring wedding," he told Ann, whose fears were removed by the decision.

They duly went through a wedding ceremony in the church at Rye in March, and Holloway began a new life as a bigamist who could be sent to jail for his temerity. But he felt safer when he found work farther west in the county, and moved with Ann to Pagham, on the outskirts of Bognor.

But Holloway's new feeling of security was entirely unjustified. For, as often happens in what is ironically termed real life, an outrageous coincidence occurred. On one of her emergings from the Level, Celia chanced to meet someone who had heard of Holloway's illegal marriage in Rye. The neglected woman became indignant. Not simply at her husband marrying another woman while he remained her legal spouse, but at his providing for this other woman and her child while she and her children were totally ignored. Celia decided on a confrontation.

She travelled to Pagham, inquired where Mr. and Mrs. Goldsmith lived, and presented herself at the front door to a home that was superior to any she had shared with John Holloway. At the sound of a latch being undone, she made ready to step over the threshold as the door swung open.

"Celia – you!" exclaimed Holloway, for once at a complete loss for the words that usually came so readily.

"I want to talk to you," declared the wife, determined not to remain overlooked. "About a number of things," she added pointedly.

Then Ann appeared behind Holloway, and Celia felt dwarfed by the sturdy young woman whose cheeks glowed with health and whose plump body would have made two of the short woman with the ungainly head. But she displayed no resentment to this comely woman who had supplanted her.

Celia, refusing to be intimidated, boldly entered the home as an invader and proceeded to tear the scales from a bemused Ann's bright eyes.

"I've come for what is mine by right, John," she announced. "Half your pay. I'm your wife and the mother of two children by you, and my mind's made up that you should do the right thing by us."

Somewhat to Celia's surprise, the ultimatum was accepted without quibble or argument. The bigamist, however, was in no position at that moment to further antagonise his legal wife. As for Ann Kennett, she remained almost a spectator in her own home to a meeting that was like a living nightmare. She heard with silent rage and indignation her husband agreeing to give this diminutive sullen-mouthed creature, a stranger to her, a half-share of his wages. At the sound of these words, Ann felt herself grasped in the clutch of panic.

She had heard enough to realise that the small woman's claim was true. She *was* the genuine wife. The revelation left Ann mentally tottering.

The recriminations began after Celia, clearly satisfied by the outcome of her visit, had departed from the home her presence had blighted and was on her way back to the poor comparison offered by her room in the Level. Holloway, however, was soon quietening the protestations of Ann Kennett by smoothly assuring her that he had no intention of sharing his wages with his wife.

"I had to be rid of her," he explained. "I do not consider her as my wife, whatever she says, and I am certainly not leaving you."

He obviously couldn't keep his word to both women. Ann was the one who shared his bed now and her physical presence decided any mental issue Celia's visit had given rise to in his mind.

While Celia remained scratching for pence to maintain herself in poverty, changes came about in the lives of the pair in Pagham. Holloway lost his employment and decided once more that regular work was far too demeaning for someone with his lively mind. There were better ways of coming by money. He had infringed the law once and disaster had not followed. He felt he might again thumb his nose at it, this time with profit.

He made the acquaintance of some underworld characters and joined them as a coiner, always a risky occupation, and later as a forger. One of his partners in these enterprises argued that they could do better in a town like Brighton, where so many of the nobility came from London to take the waters and enjoy a seaside sojourn. It was a move that appealed to Ann, and she supported the urgings of Holloway's partner.

A reluctant Holloway thus allowed himself to be cajoled into returning to a town he had been absent from for a considerable time. After all, he and Ann were still Mr. and Mrs. William Goldsmith to all they met, and again Celia had been lost in the past, so it was reasonable to assume that she would not learn of his return.

However, logical thinking, as has been demonstrated so frequently in criminal affairs, is no substitute for luck, and Holloway could hardly be described as a lucky man. In time, Celia heard of her husband's latest movement. And, with her birdlike pecking and persistence, she found out where the Goldsmiths were staying and again paid them a visit. This time, however, her anger was a truly frightening thing. It consumed her.

In her husband's words: "She began to be terrible."

Enough, anyway, to scare Ann Kennett into changing her mind and wishing to be well away from Brighton. Mr. and Mrs. Goldsmith fled back to Rye, where they re-entered a small circle of acquaintances who had known them before the move to Pagham. Holloway began passing spurious money there in small amounts, and his modest success as a distributor of "slush' both lined his pockets and made him apprehensive. He soon left with Ann for Hastings, where he restocked a meagre wardrobe as a first stage towards renewing adventures as a poor woman's Don Juan. For a time, at least, he had reason to feel he could enjoy life again.

The same could not be said of Ann Kennett. She was growing anxious about the future. She realised she had joined her life to that of a wastrel and ne'er-do-well, but felt that for her child's sake she had to make the best of it. And when this period of his being a coiner and forger ended with the feared visit from a constable, Ann voiced a demand for another change.

"Let's go back to Brighton," she said. "This time, though, we'll make sure Celia doesn't find us."

So the Goldsmiths arrived back in Brighton, and this time Holloway sought work rather than to invite disaster by passing more dud money. He uncharacteristically donned a painter's overalls and went to work wielding a paintbrush on the South Coast's most extravagant novelty, Brighton's Chain Pier.

If sheer persistence deserved success, then the Goldsmiths might have expected to live unchallenged by Celia. But the wife clearly possessed reserves of tenacity that the bigamist and Ann could not hope to match. For Celia not only found them and created another scene which left her having the last word, but she this time carried out her threat of taking her keenly-felt wrongs to the parish officers.

Inspection of her wedding certificate convinced these officials that John Holloway should be brought to heel. He was summoned to attend an inquiry, the outcome of which saw him being served with an order to pay his legal wife the rather modest sum, even for 1831, of two shillings a week.

True to form, Holloway was soon paring that grudgingly-paid weekly entitlement down to one shilling and sixpence. When three sixpences instead of the weekly florin were first dropped into Celia's palm, she naturally suspected Ann of deliberately short-changing her. Her fist closed over the coins, then she reached up and brought it down heavily on the other woman's hat. Ann Kennett now had fresh cause for anger.

The following week, she arrived with only a shilling – and an explanation. "When I told him you hit me, he said you should pay for it," she told the dwarfish woman.

Celia, now pregnant by an unknown lover, stared at the shilling in her hand.

"That's all you've brought me?" she shouted. "I have no food! What am I to do with a shilling?" Observing the smirk on Ann's face, she again became threatening. "I'll go to my overseer," she said angrily, "and find out who my husband is to keep! His wife – or his whore!"

She snatched up a fire-iron, but the taller woman was well able to fend off this fresh attack, sneering, "You are too small to hit." Then she became threatening in her turn, grating: "You'll suffer for this!"

Before the day was over, Holloway himself finally came to the mean lodging in the Level. He had been drinking and was thoroughly and lengthily abusive. Before leaving, he promised, "I'll do for you!"

Whether he feared that Celia might have him sent to jail, or whether he was just tired of her remaining a problem, he began to think seriously of murder as the only sure solution. He also voiced his intentions to Ann Kennett, who was either willing or coerced into complicity.

It was late on July 14th when he called again at the Level, this time in the pose of a penitent come to make amends and tell the woman he believed had trapped him into marriage that he was going to set up home with her again and leave Ann Kennett. Celia was understandably sceptical, whereupon he offered to show her the house he was going to rent for her. By then it was dusk, and she was weeping from a mixture of warring emotions. It was in this upset state that she agreed with him to go and view the house. A neighbour who saw her leave remarked later on her tears.

Holloway took her to an empty dwelling in a narrow back street called Donkey Row. He had earlier rented it for two and sixpence a week. He now produced a key and unlocked the front door.

"Come inside and see your new home," he told her. So Celia stepped into a house of shadows and growing darkness. He closed the front door behind them. "Let's go upstairs," he invited again.

Moving like someone in a dream, the small woman heavy with another man's child climbed a creaking staircase and entered an empty room. Then Holloway was upon her, attacking her with berserk fury, for this was how he planned to be divorced finally.

It didn't take him long to murder her, but it took him nearly all night to dismember her small body. Having at last reduced her to parcels of bone and flesh, he did his best to clean himself. Then he went back down the stairs and out into Donkey Row, where he paused to lock the front door, after which he hurried back to Ann Kennett. Daylight was beginning to invade the streets as he reached the house where she waited.

"Here, these are for you," he said, handing her some trinkets snatched from the corpse he had so recently butchered.

The next night, when he returned to Donkey Row pushing a wheelbarrow, Ann accompanied him. She was also with him when the laden barrow was guided to a narrow lane in the Preston Park area known as Lovers' Walk. There Holloway dug a shallow grave under some trees and interred part of his wife. He was less particular abut where he interred the other remains. They disappeared into a tenement cesspool.

A fortnight elapsed before a labourer named Mascall walked under the trees in Lovers' Walk and poked at some turned over ground with a stick, an action which produced an evil-smelling piece of red cloth. His discovery scared him, so he pushed the cloth back under the loose soil and kept his dark secret for almost another two weeks, by which time he felt the compulsion to confide in someone else. Then he told a friend and took him there, where they uncovered the shallow grave.

The pair at last went to the police, who arrived prepared to dig in Lovers' Walk on August 12th – a hot summer's day which had a promise of thunder in the air. What they removed was a woman's torso, still clothed in blood-soaked rags. It took another four days to find the other fetid remains. A jigsaw of human relics was put together and the murdered woman was finally identified as Celia Holloway. It was a remarkable feat on the part of the local constabulary, for this was barely two years after the formation of the Metropolitan Police Force in London.

It took the police even less time to find John Holloway and Ann Kennett. Both were arrested and charged with the murder, even while the good townsfolk were hot-footing it to Preston Park and paying to enter a shed, where the grim relics exhumed in Lovers' Walk had been cleansed and put up for morbid viewing. Brighton had long been noted for its peepshows and exhibitions of various kinds, but seldom have these included such a revolting spectacle. When the last groat had been collected from the crowds queueing outside the shed, the remains were finally interred in the local churchyard.

By that time Holloway, who had been lodged in the jail at Horsham, was giving trouble as the self-proclaimed leader of the worst criminals detained there. But in the idiom of a later age of crime, one of his associates there grassed about a plot to escape which included wholesale murder of the prison staff! Discovery, however, evidently moved John William Holloway into becoming a near-model prisoner until his trial, which was shared with Ann Kennett. It opened in the town hall at Lewes just 11 days before Christmas, with Mr. Justice Patteson presiding.

With a typical show of bravado, Holloway decided that he required no qualified legal guidance. But Ann Kennett, a tearful and subdued prisoner, was defended by John Sylvester Adolphus, whose competence helped to obtain an acquittal for her after Holloway himself had done his level best to relieve her of blame.

When invited by the court to offer his defence, Holloway adopted a strange mixture of cynicism and righteous indignation. What can be said for him is that he didn't try to evade the issue by lying. And once having taken his stand, he did his best for the woman he had morally terrorised into being his accomplice in the destruction of Celia Holloway.

"I know I committed murder," he said bluntly. "But it isn't plain or clear in evidence." He went on to bait his legal listeners. "The woman might have made away with herself," he said with a mocking smile, "and I might have concealed it for fear. I don't say that such *was* the case. I only say it *might* have been."

He went on: "But whether Celia was murdered or not, I don't want to live. All I want to say is that Ann Kennett is innocent. I have abused that woman shameful and she never returned an angry word," he declared. "She was always mild and submissive. She has been bruised dreadful by me. And for what reason I don't know. I suppose it was my savage nature."

So the jury had no real problem in the crucial matter of whether there was any reasonable doubt in Holloway's case. Any such doubts be concerned solely with the case against the woman, as Holloway no doubt intended.

Finding her not guilty and himself guilty must have seemed to that Lewes jury a nice way of placing the blame for the crime where it really belonged.

After hearing the judge deliver sentence of death, which was followed by a recommendation to the Almighty to have mercy on the prisoner's soul, Holloway said loudly and distinctly, "Amen."

There can be no doubt that Holloway was a person of irrational moods and manners, just as he was brutish and lazy and vicious. His irrational behaviour was clearly demonstrated by the three separate confessions he made – two of them before his trial.

He first admitted strangling his wife in the dark house in Donkey Row, then carving up the limp remains, and doing this without help from any other person. This was in accordance with his admission during the trial. But he had second thoughts during a changing mood, and revised the first confession to include the accusation that Ann Kennett had been his partner and conspirator in the crime.

But the truth was most likely that she had nothing to do with the actual murder, but had been beaten into agreeing to help him plan the crime and later to dispose of the torso and other remains.

But in the 48 hours before he met the hangman, his irrational state advanced a stage further. Then he produced his third and extremely unlikely confession. It was a claim that he had indeed had a female accomplice

in the murder. Her name was Ann Kennett, but she was
not the woman who had taken his weekly dole to Celia
and quarrelled with her. She was another woman of the
same name and unknown to the woman with whom he
was living.

It seems he must have been over-impressed by the
coincidences that had marked the passage of his 32 years
towards the gallows where, before a large Lewes crowd on
December 16th, 1831, John William Holloway's forfeited
life was finally surrendered.

12

SHE PAINTED HERSELF A MURDERESS IN HER HUSBAND'S BLOOD

R.B. McDonald

There was a strangely bird-like quality about the petite woman seated at the defence table. Her hands never moved slowly; they darted out like swooping sparrows. And her dark brown eyes had a curiously beady appearance as they focused on whatever claimed her attention.

Throughout the trial, she watched the proceedings with the interest of a participant. A stranger walking into the Johnson County courtroom at Olathe, Kansas, would never have guessed that this woman was on trial for her life, for her intensity was that of a person absorbed in the unfolding of a drama, with no personal stake in its outcome.

Attired in a black dress, she had shown no emotion as she listened to a parade of witnesses relate evidence that mounted like timbers of a gallows. Not once did she betray any sign of fear that if the jury believed these witnesses, their verdict might send her to the gallows. She never flinched, even when her lover took the stand.

Finally, all the evidence was in and on the morning of April 6th, 1955, Judge Earl O'Connor delivered his charge to the jurors.

"Three verdicts are possible in this case," he said in his 25-minute address. "You may find the defendant not guilty, guilty with a sentence of life imprisonment, or guilty with a death-penalty."

The tiny woman at the defence table fastened her eyes on the jury as they rose amid a shuffling of feet, turned and filed out of the box. She seemed oblivious to the murmur of spectators as she got to her feet and walked out of the room beside the matron.

The tragic chain of events that placed her on trial for her life began on January 1st, 1955, in the home on West 67th Street Terrace, Shawnee Village, Kansas, which John Joseph Callahan shared with his wife and three children.

Callahan, 31 years old, was known to his fellow employees at the Southern Bell Telephone Company as a friendly guy who loved a good time and was always good for a laugh. On this New Year's Day afternoon, his wife Mary would have disputed that, for there was no laughter in John Joseph Callahan that day.

There might have been the night before – although she wouldn't know about that – but now Callahan was suffering from a prodigious hangover.

Callahan's 30-year-old wife was in the kitchen, fixing supper. With her was a neighbour, Mrs. Clara Morton. Mrs. Morton complimented Mary on the heavenly aroma of her dinner, but Mary Callahan seemed in no mood for compliments.

Mrs. Morton tried to kid her out of her mood. "What's wrong – a little hangover?"

Mary echoed bitterly, "Where would I get a hangover? Jack left me alone last night on New Year's Eve. He left me alone and went out by himself."

When further attempts at conversation failed, the neighbour took her leave. The Callahans had dinner and John went out soon afterwards. Mary was sitting up when he returned after midnight, but he went straight to bed.

At 6.45 the following morning, the Callahan children were awakened by their mother's loud crying. One ran to the parents' bedroom, but stopped at the door, horror-struck.

John Callahan, covered with blood, was thrashing about on the bed. And even as the child watched, transfixed with terror, he tumbled off the bed and onto the floor, where he lay still.

Mary Callahan sobbed uncontrollably. At the sound of a knock on the front door, she said: "It's the Logans. I just telephoned them for help."

Mary Callahan bent over her prone husband, who, covered with gore and lying in a rapidly growing pool of his own blood, gave no sign of life.

The Logans were the Callahans' next-door neighbours and Mrs. Logan was a registered nurse. Mrs. Logan quickly pushed Mary aside and tried to find a pulse in John's wrist. She could not detect even the faintest tremor. His arm fell limply to the floor when she released it. Ellis Logan asked his wife if he should call a doctor, but she shook her head.

"No. He's dead. You'd better call the sheriff. I think he's been murdered."

Logan ran to the telephone. Mary Callahan was now plainly hysterical, and from the bedroom upstairs came the sound of children crying.

Mr. Logan then bent for a closer look at a gleaming object he spotted on the floor by the bed.

"What's that?" Mary cried.

"It's a .22-calibre shell," he replied.

His answer seemed to calm her. "It doesn't belong in this house," she said firmly. "I can't understand how it got here."

In a very short time, the Callahan home was bustling with activity. Johnson County Sheriff Norman Williams arrived, accompanied by Sergeants Ford and Bennett and Dr. David Long Jr., who had been summoned by the sheriff's office.

It took only seconds for Dr. Long to pronounce John Callahan dead. A slightly longer period elapsed before he rose to his feet after examining the body and told the officers that Callahan had been shot three times. One bullet had flipped through his lower lip and emerged through the right ear. The others had smashed into his chest. Death was probably caused by internal bleeding from the chest wounds. The official autopsy would later confirm this on-scene opinion.

The officers now faced the task of questioning the widow. In her highly overwrought state, this was not easy.

"I heard nothing," Mary told Sheriff Williams. "I heard no shots. I felt John moving around on the bed. That's what awakened me. Then I saw he was covered with blood. I jumped out of bed and called the Logans for help. When I got back to the bedroom, he was still thrashing around on the bed. Then he fell to the floor and lay still."

Sheriff Williams studied the bloodstained sheets, then asked: " Which side of the bed do you sleep on?"

"The right side. Why?"

Sheriff Williams chose not to answer the question, but asked her how she got on with her husband.

Mary Callahan pondered this briefly. Then her lips quivered and she burst into tears. Seconds later, she collapsed in a faint. Dr. Long tended her while Sheriff Williams conferred with his aides, who had been talking to the Logans and the Callahan children.

The Logans were sure the front door had been locked from the inside when they hurried over to the house. Investigation showed that the rear door had been similarly secure. No one heard any shots being fired, or any other undue disturbance, such as the sound of an intruder forcing an entry.

"Did you find out anything from Mrs. Callahan?" Sergeant Ford asked the sheriff.

"Only that there's no blood on the pyjamas she was wearing. She says she woke to find Callahan writhing in agony. There's blood all over the bed, but none on her. And the doors were locked on the inside. So the rifle that killed Callahan must be in the house."

The search for the murder weapon went on long after John Callahan's body had been removed for autopsy. The officers missed no possible hiding place that might conceal a weapon, either inside or outside. They found no gun, but they did find another empty shell. It was a .22 and, like the first, it was found in the bedroom.

In the end, police were faced with a set of apparent contradictions, which Sergeant Ford put into words. "It's impossible," he said. "Since the doors were locked from the inside, I don't see how Callahan could have been killed by any intruder. And since we can't find the murder weapon, I don't see how he could have been killed by his wife."

Suicide seemed the only alternative, but was ruled out because of the lack of powder burns.

"Do you suppose Mrs. Callahan could have hidden the gun some distance away from here?" the sheriff wondered aloud.

Ford shook his head. "No. Callahan was still alive – flailing around on the bed – when the child saw him. He couldn't have been shot more than minutes before – certainly not long enough for Mrs. Callahan to go out, plant the gun, return to the bedroom, change into clean pyjamas, then call the Logans."

The sheriff agreed, but said he was going to hold Mrs. Callahan on an open charge until the case could be investigated at greater length.

County Attorney James Bradley conferred with the sheriff while Mary Callahan, suffering from frequent fainting spells, was taken to the county jail at Olathe.

The search for the murder weapon continued, with more than a dozen deputies assigned to scour every nook and cranny in the neighbourhood. All residents along the street were questioned carefully, but none could shed any light on the slaying.

By January 4th, the investigation had come to a standstill and Mrs. Callahan's attorney insisted that his client should either be charged or released from custody.

Under this pressure, the prosecutor had no alternative but to take her before Magistrate Joseph Davis for a preliminary hearing. She was not required to plead at this time, and the magistrate released her on $10,000 bail.

The tide turned in the investigators' favour, however, within an hour of her release. Sheriff Williams received a call from an informant who said: "If you want to make some headway on the Callahan case, why don't you talk to Ray Tipton?"

"Who is Ray Tipton?"

"He's a truck driver. He's also the lover of Mary Callahan. He lives at the Drexel Hotel in Kansas City."

Within the hour – and with the co-operation of Kansas City police – Ray Tipton had been delivered to the office of County Attorney Bradley. "Sure," he said, "I know Mary Callahan. I've known her most of my life. She was my girl friend when I was fourteen. But I don't know anything about this killing. As a matter of fact, I've got a solid alibi."

Tipton showed no uneasiness or hesitation as he answered all the questions put to him by the prosecutor and the officers. He said he had enlisted in the Army when he was 15 by lying about his age. After his discharge, he resumed his relationship with Mary Callahan. He got married, but in 1949 he came back to Kansas City and again began to see Mary.

His alibi was that on January 1st, he had spent the entire night – from 11.30 till 8.30 next morning – drinking on Forest Avenue at the home of Mr. and Mrs. Larry Chambers.

Prosecutor Bradley had Tipton held as a material witness, pending further investigation.

Ray Tipton's alibi proved not to be quite as solid as he claimed. He had been drinking with the Chambers couple, as he said, but they insisted he arrived at their home some time after midnight and left before six in the morning. He came back, briefly, about nine.

Tipton no longer cared to answer questions. "I'm not

talking any more," he said. "I want to see a lawyer. I figure I'm in a lot of trouble and I'm not going to say any more."

From Mr. and Mrs. Chambers it was learned that Tipton had been driving a rented car on the night he visited them. Bradley ordered a check of all car rental agencies in the area. Within a few hours, Sergeant Bennett found the agency from which Tipton had rented the car, learned it had not been re-rented since Tipton returned it – and found a bag of peanuts and a .22 calibre rifle shell lying on the front seat.

Ballistics experts determined the shell had been fired from the same gun as the two shells discovered in the murder room. And on the afternoon of January 5th, the owner of a furniture repair shop reported that he had found part of a gun in a dustbin outside the shop.

Sergeants Bennett and Ford found the rifle parts to be the stock and receiver of a Mossberg .22. No fingerprints were found on them. Before a positive ballistics identification of it could be made, however, the barrel would have to be found. On a hunch, Sheriff Williams suggested that they have a look around the Chambers house.

Sergeants Bennett and Ford drove out there, although Mrs. Chambers told them she hadn't seen anything like a rifle barrel.

A search of the garden failed to uncover the weapon part, but just as they were about to leave, Bennett decided to have a look around a bench sheltered by an awning at the side of the house. An old door leaned against it, and several loose boards had been piled on it.

"He wouldn't leave it right there on the bench," Ford commented. But they decided to look anyway.

It was fortunate they did. That was where they found the rifle barrel, wrapped in four sheets of a December 19th newspaper. It bore a distinctive mark: The serial number on the barrel had been smeared with bright red lipstick, which filled the numbers stamped in the steel and made them extremely legible.

The rifle barrel fitted the stock and receiver parts found in the dustbin. A ballistics test proved it had fired the bullets that killed John Callahan. And despite the fact that someone had tampered with the firing pin, ballistics experts were sure it had also fired the shell found on the seat of the car rented by Ray Tipton.

Through the serial number, the weapon was traced to a local man, who immediately identified it as his. "I'd recognise it anywhere," he said. "I smeared that lipstick into the serial number so it would be easy to read. In case I lost it, or it was stolen, it would be simple to identify."

He said he had often lent the gun to Ray Tipton, the last time being on the afternoon of New Year's Eve.

Confronted with this evidence, Tipton admitted not only borrowing the rifle, but tampering with the firing-pin before dismantling and discarding the weapon. "But I did not kill John Callahan. You can't pin that on me and I'm not going to talk about it any more."

Events now moved rapidly. Attorney Bradley got Mary Callahan's bail revoked and she was returned to jail. She and Tipton were indicted for the murder of John Callahan. In the weeks before the trial, investigators heard from one of Mary's friends of a conversation between the woman and Mary.

She said she and Mary had been talking one day about John Callahan and divorce. The discussion somehow progressed to the subject of "perfect murder".

"Mary said she had a way to commit such a murder and get away with it," the woman said.

According to this woman, Mary seemed convinced that no murder conviction could be obtained if the prosecution failed to produce the murder weapon – and that she could hide a weapon where no one would ever find it.

Mary told this woman that Ray Tipton would help her any time she asked him to and that he would do anything in the world for her.

Mary Callahan came to trial, charged with first-degree murder, on March 29th, 1955, unaware until it got under way that the state's star witness against her was her lover, Ray Tipton. Tipton had finally decided to co-operate fully with the prosecution.

Sworn in as a witness, Tipton told in detail of the romance between himself and Mary, a romance which had existed, at intervals, over a long period of years. On one occasion, he said, he and Mary had lived together as man and wife.

Prosecutor Bradley asked Tipton to tell in his own words exactly what happened on the night of January 1st.

Testified Tipton: "Well, I got a call from Mary. She asked me to bring the rifle. She used to come to my hotel room four or five times a week and she'd seen the rifle there.

"I asked her what she wanted it for. She told me that Callahan had left her alone on New Year's Eve, that he was dumping her. She said he wasn't going to get away with it, so she wanted me to bring her the rifle."

Tipton said he rented the car and drove to her home.

He said he delivered the rifle, loaded, cocked and with the safety catch released. He deposited it on the bumper of her car, which was parked in the driveway. Then he phoned Mary and told her he'd done what she asked, adding: "All you have to do is pull the trigger."

Tipton then began drinking, ending up at the Chambers' home. At 6 a.m. he left and went back to the Callahan place. There he retrieved the rifle, which Mary had replaced on the car. Tipton said he had been convinced of Mary's "perfect crime" theory of the missing weapon.

In response to a question by Defence Attorney Jones, Tipton admitted that his feelings towards Mary Callahan had changed during recent weeks.

"And is that why," Jones asked, "you have come here to paint this woman as a murderess?"

"She has painted herself as a murderess," Tipton replied. "And in her husband's blood!"

Even then, Mary Callahan never flinched. With her eyes fixed on her lover, she merely looked disinterested, as though she was listening to him talk about something else. That was also her attitude as she listened to the judge's summing-up.

A scant two hours and 15 minutes after the jury retired to deliberate, the foreman sent word that they had reached a verdict.

Mary Callahan walked to her seat at the defence table. The judge asked the jury if they had reached a verdict. The foreman said they had. The judge then ordered the defendant to rise and face the jury.

"We find the defendant guilty and recommend life imprisonment," the foreman said firmly.

Mary Callahan reacted to these words like someone pushing a plunger on a detonator. Her iron nerve disintegrated explosively and she burst into hysterical weeping. Then, as she fainted, two court attendants caught her in mid-fall.

On April 11th, Ray Tipton came to trial for murder and pleaded guilty. He was also sentenced to life imprisonment.

Mary Callahan got a second chance. On appeal to a higher court, the verdict and sentence of her first trial were set aside and a new trial was ordered. This time the judge instructed the jury that they could find her either guilty of first-degree murder, or not guilty.

After six hours of deliberations, their verdict was guilty. On September 20th, 1956, for the second time Mary Callahan heard herself sentenced to life in the penitentiary.

13

THE LONELY HEARTS KILLERS OF HORSEPOND ROAD
Robert Reed

Early photographs of Inez Brennan depict her as an attractive girl with deep-set dark eyes. It was about that time that mechanic George Dether met her through a newspaper ad. "She was pretty – and I was lonely," he later explained. "So she became my housekeeper. We got married about two years afterwards."

The ceremony took place in 1928, at Norristown, Pennsylvania. Inez was then 25 years old and already had two children – Gertrude and Raymond – by a previous marriage to one William Pribram. Inez gave everyone to understand that Pribram had died of yellow fever while serving with the U.S. Army in Colombia. And she would usually add: "His ashes were scattered around Borneo." If she'd bothered to consult an atlas, however, she would have discovered that Borneo is halfway around the world from South America.

George Dether had been married to Inez for about 18 months when someone happened to mention to him that William Pribram was still alive and kicking. Inez, it appeared, was a bigamist. As the worried Dether sought to investigate, Inez now insisted that her first spouse, having died of pneumonia, had been buried by a

Philadelphia undertaker named Callahan. When Dether checked, however, he learned that Mr. Callahan had no record of any such burial – and neither had the Philadelphia registrar of births and deaths. The arguments with Inez became stormy indeed.

"She even tried to beat me up," Dether recalled. "But she only weighed about 140 pounds then, so I was able to hold her."

So the marriage had its problems. Yet, during the ensuing years, two sons were born of the union – George in 1930 and Robert in 1933. Then there were more violent scenes when Dether discovered that Inez was keeping company with other men. And, on one occasion, Dether was almost poisoned.

"One day," he later recalled, "she placed a bowl of vegetable soup on the table and I started on it. I noticed a peculiar taste, but I was in a hurry to get back to work, so I swallowed it. Then I left. In about ten minutes, I saw stars and I was getting dizzy. I looked into the mirror of my car and saw my eyes getting big. The white rims of my fingernails were turning black. I knew then that I had been poisoned. I stopped at a grocery store, drank a pint of sweet milk, then a glass of hot water and salt to make myself sick. I had a terrible burning pain in my stomach."

After that, there was a separation and divorce. Dether kept the children until 1947, when they decided to live with their mother. Gertrude, the eldest, was married by then, but Raymond, George and Robert went to Laurel Springs, New Jersey, where Inez had bought a pleasant little cottage.

Not long afterwards, there occurred the first of a whole series of baffling deaths and disappearances to which Inez Brennan had been linked.

Mrs. Nettie Henderson Philips, an elderly widow, lived next door to Inez. Neighbours living across the street from both insisted that Mrs. Philips had spent the night of March 16th, 1947, at the Brennan house. But Inez claimed that she called to invite the elderly woman over for coffee on the morning of the 17th and discovered that Mrs. Philips was absent from her home. Later that day, the woman's body was discovered floating face downwards in Garden Lake, half a mile away. No one could say how she got there.

Some months later, during the height of a thunderstorm, Mrs. Bessie Watkins, who lived a few doors down the street, was shot by a .22 rifle bullet. She at first thought she had been struck by lightning and tumbled to the floor with a scream.

It was this sudden shriek which so frightened Robert Brennan, then 14 years old. It was he, according to his own later admission, who had shot the woman, with the intention of robbing her house. Instead, he ran home and hid himself in bed. Mrs. Watkins later recovered, although the bullet was to remain lodged in her neck.

Shortly afterwards, Inez, who had hitherto dabbled in the writing of so-called "lonely heart" letters, began to work seriously at the task. Although she is known to have had scores of pen-pals, only one complete set of her love letters has survived. These were addressed to Fred W. Schub, a chicken farmer of Delmar, Maryland, who gave Inez $805 to buy a farm at Gettysburg.

Later, when Schub tried to get his money back and failed, he handed the letters over to Sheriff Jesse M. Pollitt. Since they so well illustrate her technique, pertinent excerpts follow. Note the gradual progress made.

July 24, 1947

Dear Sir: Mrs. E........ gave me your name but not age. Employed seamstress, taking care of home and garden, I never had time to find friends of the opposite sex. Wish you would write. Inez Brennan.

July 30, 1947

Dear Fred: Thrilled to hear from you. Glad you like children. I too raise them. My boys want to buy a farm. Last year I went to Dover looking for a small place, but my boys would get married and I would be left alone. Inez Brennan.

August 5, 1947

Dear Fred: I raised flowers last year, but they aren't doing too well this year. As you say, you need a companion and affection to go with it all. I would like a small farm and raise chickens, geese and pigs and someone to *love* me. Will close now with love, always, Inez.

August 9, 1947

My dearest Fred: That was a grand letter you sent me. It made my blood tingle. Honey, it will be wonderful to have a hubby like you. They say when a man's heart is with the soil, his soul is with God. Would you like to farm? How about near Gettysburg? Write soon, I'm so thrilled. All my love to you, honey. Inez.

August 11, 1947

To my darling Fred: Honey mine, when are we going to find our little farm? I am so happy that I have found you and we can be together for the rest of our lives. You know I am a possessive critter. What's mine will be yours, but you'll be all mine. All my love to you always. Inez.

August 14, 1947

My dearest darling: When I read your letter today, I blushed. I'm glad you like things like that. I'll be seeing you, my sweetums, Saturday. Love. Inez.

Plans to meet each other were discussed in four other letters, while the last, dated September 2nd, 1947, read:

"Writing this on van going to new farm. Wait for the kids to come for you. It will be at least a week. It's a long journey here. I.B."

Fred Schub's whereabouts are a mystery to this day. All that is known is that, on December 1st, 1947, he sold his chickens and left Delmar for parts unknown.

In early 1948, Inez moved to a farm in a lane called Horsepond Road, near Dover, Delaware. It was a gloomy place, with a stark, bare yard and gaunt outbuildings. And the strange doings of the new owner did little to improve its attractiveness.

Among her many correspondents in the various lonely hearts clubs was 67-year-old Wade N. Wooldridge. His first wife had died and he had been divorced from his second, third and fourth brides. In 1948, Wooldridge lived with a married daughter, Mrs. Bessie Ayres, on a farm in southern Virginia.

Wooldridge spent most of his spare time exchanging letters with members of the several lonely hearts clubs to which he belonged. All told, he would send and receive about 20 letters a week. While it appeared to be a harmless foible, its consequences were something to think about.

In July 1948, he announced: "I'm going to visit a widow who lives in Delaware." This occasioned no great surprise, since he often made little trips away from home to meet some of his correspondents in the flesh.

He arrived in Dover on a hot day. There is Inez Brennan's own statement of what happened at this initial meeting:

"I was very much surprised when I saw him. He was older than he said – and was almost stone deaf. He very much misrepresented himself. I even told him that.

"He gave me a line of talk, but I didn't pay much attention to it. He was dirty and sweating from riding on the train. I told him to rest up and gave him a clean shirt. Next day, one of the boys took him to the bus.

"About two weeks later, he sent me a letter. He said he'd met a lot of women and had a lot of pictures and letters, but none appealed to him like me. He said what he could do on my farm."

Although Inez's version is one-sided, there seems little

doubt that she made a strong impression on Wooldridge. When he returned home, he told his daughter that he had met a fine woman. The only drawback was that she wanted his money to pay off the mortgage on her farm.

The summer went by, Wooldridge did farm chores and carpentry and tended to his correspondence. Then one day in early October he received a letter which set him busily packing clothes and tools. He told his daughter that "the widow" had cleared her farm of debts and wanted him to come to Delaware to get married. He said that when he arrived he would send the family a card.

He packed his shirts, all of which had a little hole clipped below the last button to distinguish them from those of the other men in the household, who happened to wear the same size. He packed a shotgun, his favourite saw with its home-made handle, a pair of pig ringers, an old pair of scissors, a 100 foot steel tape, various axes, hammers and screwdrivers into two suitcases and two trunks. One of the trunks had an iron band around the top and iron cuffs at the corners.

One saw, a timber-cutter, was too big for either suitcase or trunk. On October 8th, he gave it to the express company at nearby Stone Mountain, with instructions to ship it at once to Dover, Delaware, and hold it for his call.

Before leaving, he went to his room one last time. On the bare plaster beneath the calendar which hung by his bedside, he wrote the case number of his gold watch and his future address. The inscription, a rough pencil scrawl, read:

Watch No. 516238.

WNW Dover, Del. Route 3.

He put on a dark blue pin-stripe suit. Then, at 10.15 a.m. on October 9th 1948, a son-in-law, Millard Kendrick, drove him, with his two trunks and two suitcases, to the bus station at Roanoke, Virginia.

Wooldridge's destination was the farm on Horsepond Road, Dover. Inez Brennan had undergone an appendectomy on October 2nd. Although at home, she was under the care of a nurse – a 26-year-old war widow named Dolly Thompson Dean. According to later testimony, Inez had previously told her son Robert: "Nobody will miss Wooldridge if somebody puts something through his head. He has a considerable amount of money – and we could use it."

On Sunday, October 10th, the phone at the Brennan farm rang at 8.30 a.m. Informed that Wooldridge was at the bus station, Inez said: "Bobby will go."

Robert Brennan's own words describe the events which followed:

"George and I went in the truck and got him at the bus station. He had a suitcase and two trunks. We took him out home and my mother greeted him by shaking hands. I knew she wasn't glad to see him, but she didn't let on. George and I carried his things up to the small bedroom. We had some lunch and after that we sat around and talked. George left to see his girl. My brother Ray was getting his car fixed. He got back before supper.

"Right after Ray got back, about 4.45 p.m., I decided I would get rid of Mr. Wooldridge. So I took my shotgun down to the barn and put it up in the loft. Then I went back to the house and we all had supper together, except George."

It must have been a strange meal, but apparently Wooldridge sensed nothing unusual. When it was over, he pushed back his chair and said that he wanted to look around the farm. According to Dolly Dean's account, he was "particularly interested in seeing the chickens".

As to what happened afterwards, Robert Brennan's story again gives the most precise details:

"I took him straight to the barn, a good 200 feet from the house. We went into the barn and, while he was poking around downstairs, I went on up to the loft. I only had the one shell in my gun. I picked it up and was ready for him when he started coming up the steps. He came up the steps and had his back to me. When he was halfway up, I pulled the trigger and the shot struck him in the back of the head. He rolled down the steps and lay on his back on the floor.

"I went outside the barn and I heard him hollering very loud. I knew I hadn't killed him. But I went on back to the house."

Dolly Deal recalled that, when Robert came back to the house, he was "white as a sheet". According to her, his brother Ray scolded him, saying: "Why the hell did you kill him? He sure never did nothing to you."

Inez Brennan then left the kitchen and walked out onto the back porch. Robert followed. He said later: "We could hear Mr. Wooldridge hollering real loud. My mother said, 'You can't leave him like that – go back and shoot him.' I told her I was afraid the neighbours would hear it. She said, 'It has to be done – go and do it.' "

"I went back to the barn and Mr. Wooldridge was still in the same position, hollering. I struck him on the head with the gun stock. I heard his skull crack. He was quiet after that. I knew he was dead."

Back at the house, Robert phoned a neighbour's daughter. He made some random conversation about school work, then added casually: "I been out hunting and just shot a raccoon."

Dolly Dean was crying. She had come to the house on a nurse's errand of mercy, only to find herself at the scene of a murder. She said afterwards: "If they would murder an innocent old man like that, I was afraid they would kill me next."

When George Brennan came home shortly before 9 o'clock, the first thing his mother asked was whether he would "help bury a body".

"God damn – what's happened now?" was George's retort.

Inez told him.

They were a strange crew, Inez and her brood. A short while later, company in the shape of Dolly's brother, Elmer Thompson, and a friend, Leah Loper, came to call. The group sat in the parlour. According to Robert: "We all talked, but we didn't let on what had happened."

George Brennan also recalled that occasion. "My mother and Robert were fairly calm, while Raymond and Dolly seemed to be nervous. I was also quite nervous."

So carefully did they conceal their feelings, however, that neither Elmer Thompson nor Leah Loper had any inkling of the murder. They were later unable to recall anything unusual about the visit.

The company went home and, at 9.45 that evening, everyone went to bed. Everyone, that is, except Iñez, who had difficulty in climbing the stairs. She was stretched out on the davenport in the living-room, while Dolly Dean sat in a chair, unable to sleep.

Robert said later: "Mother set the alarm for 5 a.m. We were to get up before light to bury the old man. I didn't sleep at all. I heard the alarm go off and got dressed before anyone else. Mother told me to go out and search him and bring everything back to the house. I went to the barn and went through the old man's pockets."

Robert found Wooldridge's gold watch with the initials "W.W." a wallet, a penknife and a sterling silver ring. He had a bad moment when the ring stuck. As he put it later: "I felt sick to my stomach. Mother put all the things in her apron pocket, then told me to go out and start digging a hole. I went to the pigpen and dug a hole in the right-hand corner. I told Mother I would need help to get the body from the barn. So George came out and we went to the barn and got a rope from the wall."

The rope was looped around the victim's arms and legs and the body was dragged from the barn across the yard to the pigpen, where it was buried in a shallow trench about three and a half feet deep. Then George and Ray went to work, as usual. Robert, however, stayed away from school.

According to Robert, some time during the afternoon, his mother told him she had found $134 in Wooldridge's wallet. "My mother and I started looking through his suitcase and trunks. I picked out an Army khaki shirt and about seven white shirts that were just my size. I also picked out a double-bit axe and kept it. Ray came home and when he saw what we had been doing, he said we were supposed to wait. He was mad and looked through the things. He didn't see anything he wanted, except the white shirts.

"Supper was ready and my mother told me to carry the trunks and the suitcases out and burn them, along with the clothes. I burned everything but the khaki shirt, the axe, two penknives, the silver ring, gold watch and the money."

Either by accident – or to spite his brother Ray – Robert also burned seven white shirts. However, 143 razor-blades were salvaged and put in a glass mayonnaise jar.

A few weeks later, around the beginning of November, Robert took the shotgun used in the killing to Elmer Thompson. He traded it for the latter's heavier gun, plus two dollars.

Meanwhile, back in southern Virginia, Bessie Ayres began to worry when she did not hear from her father. He had always written a "safe arrival" card on his various trips. By December 15th, she was concerned enough to bring the matter to the attention of Deputy Sheriff C.D. Ruff, who obtained Wooldridge's photograph and description and enclosed both in a letter to the police in Dover, Delaware, requesting assistance in tracing the missing man, who was supposed to have gone to a nearby farm.

Perhaps the information was too vague to have been worthwhile. At any rate, the Dover cops were unable to do much about the request. Although Mrs. Ayres had seen the name "Inez Brennan" on her father's letters, she had never noticed the address. Nor did she know that Mrs. Brennan was "the widow in Delaware".

On December 26th, Inez and Robert left Dover. Their destination was Epsom, New Hampshire, where stolid, pipe-smoking chicken farmer Hugo Schulz lived. Schulz, a sailor in the German Navy of World War I, had been writing letters to Inez for many weeks. He had often asked a friend, Charles Wende, to help him with his spelling.

Wende left for Florida before Inez arrived, but Schulz kept him informed of the progress of the correspondence.

On January 8th, 1949, Wende, still in Florida, received a letter stating that his friends Schulz was going to look at the farm in Dover – and that his wedding to Inez Brennan was planned for January 15th.

"I am very lucky to get such a woman," the letter concluded. And, that same day, in New Hampshire, Hugo Schulz obtained the marriage licence.

George Brennan left Dover by truck, arriving in Epsom on January 14th. He reached the chicken farm at nightfall and, after greeting his mother and brother, asked: "Where is Mr. Schulz?"

Robert pointed towards the yard: "Out there."

George went to the window, cupped his hands against his forehead and squinted through the pane. He saw nothing but the dim outline of a barrel against the wall of a chicken hut. "I don't see anyone."

"In the barrel," said Robert.

"What's he doing there?" asked George.

"He's dead. Mother shot him a couple of days ago."

There was a 50-gallon oil drum standing in the yard. And, as George soon discovered, the remains of Hugo Schulz were crammed inside.

The ex-sailor, it transpired, had succumbed to a shot-gun blast on January 11th, after a dosage of 22 sleeping pills and a heaped tablespoon of rat poison had failed to do any serious damage to his system, he being that strong and healthy.

Inez was busy for the next few days. She sold the farmer's chickens and geese, his generator and his sewing machine to a local auctioneer for $900. Then she had her boys load the murdered man's furniture on his own truck for the trip back to Dover.

When the furniture was loaded, the oil drum was turned upside-down over a spread of canvas. Schulz's body was rolled in the canvas and strapped to the tailgate of the truck. Then Robert and his mother started back to Delaware.

At the outskirts of town, a police officer on a motorcycle drew abreast and motioned the truck to the side of the road. It seemed that there was a sheriff's attachment for a $400 feed bill against Hugo's truck and it would not be allowed to proceed unless the debt was paid.

"Mother paid the attachment," said Robert later. "No one ever looked inside – or they would have seen the body."

It was indeed a close call. For, as the event was later reconstructed, it developed that at one time the various police officers involved were within six inches of the canvas in which Hugo Schulz had been rolled.

All told, the party was detained from 8 p.m. until 2 a.m. The rotor was taken off the distributor of the truck to make certain that it could not leave. Finally, Inez talked the authorities into accepting her personal cheque for the claim.

Hugo Schulz's egg customers were puzzled over his sudden departure, which they thought was out of keeping with his dependable character. They talked about it, but the consensus was that he had a right to live his own life, so no further inquiries were made at the time. The local bank held a mortgage on the farm, and, when the monthly payments were missed, a "For Sale" sign was put up in the front yard.

In the pigpen at Horsepond Road, Hugo Schulz was buried in a shallow grave at right angles to Wade Wooldridge. In the gloomy house, Inez continued her lonely hearts correspondence. One of the advertisements concerning her read:

"Inez Brennan, Dover, Del., age 44, weight 160lbs, height 5 feet 5, black greying hair, brown eyes, Baptist, high school education, farmerette, income not stated, widow, no dependents. Own farm and car. Prefers living in the country. Hobbies are raising chickens, flowers and gardening. Men 44 to 60 years of age write and learn more. All letters answered".

Thomas A. Stretch, a 63-year-old farmer of Canton,

New Jersey, wrote Inez a letter. After some correspondence, she urged him to make a quick settlement of a pending lawsuit, so that "you can find a respectable woman who can love you and with whom you can settle down. You know how I am, Tom. I have to know a man for a long time before I would marry because marriage is a sacred thing and should last forever."

Stretch said later that he met Inez and her sons. "They treated me fine. I thought she was a real nice woman. I looked her farm over and even stood by the pigpen. If I'd had any money, I might have ended up alongside the men who were buried there."

In March, 1949, Inez placed an ad. in the *Rural New Yorkers*, listing her farm for sale and advertising herself as a "Refined Widow, 45, with son, 16, desires position, preferably on farm."

Robert learned of his mother's plan. He said later: "I was scared, because I thought somebody might find the bodies. On March 31st, I told my mother that I was going to dig them up and burn them and she told me she thought that was best. About 6 a.m. on April 1st, I moved an oil drum in front of the pigpen and set it up on three concrete blocks. My mother got some paper and a bucket of coal."

The cremation in the drum of hot fire lasted throughout the day. And the following morning – April 2nd – the ashes were shovelled into five-gallon tar cans and then tossed onto the Dover city dump.

"There were six cans of ashes," Robert recalled. "There were some small pieces of bones, which I think were parts of the leg and arm bones. The largest would not measure over four inches long. There were some chunks of ashes stuck together, none of them any bigger than my fists."

The bodies disposed of, Inez and Robert set to work with bucket and brush to clean the bloodstains from the barn floor, walls and stairs. Robert worked half a day, but the stains proved too deep and too dark to be removed.

When Inez heard this, she gave instructions to tear down the barn wall and use it for firewood.

The work of dismantling the structure was well under way when, on April 9th, Mr. and Mrs. Charles Wende, the Epsom friends of Hugo Schulz, who were on their way north from Florida, stopped at the Dover Barracks of the Delaware State Police and talked to Captain Frederick K. Lamb.

They said that the last they'd heard from Schulz was on January 8th, when he was supposed to have visited the farm of a Mrs. Brennan, near Dover.

Lamb telegraphed authorities in New Hampshire to ask whether an inquiry into the whereabouts of Hugo Schulz was desired. Strangely enough, the answer came back: "No inquiry desired – Schulz living in Delaware, Ohio."

Where the latter report originated has never been determined. But in view of Schulz's fate, it is possible that Epsom gossip confused the state of Delaware with one of the eight communities in the United States named Delaware and, purely by chance, hit upon Delaware, Ohio.

Despite this Lamb sent officers to make inquiries about Schulz at the Brennan farm. Two troopers spoke to Inez, who said she'd never heard of the missing man. So the day ended with the Wendes going their way and the state police investigation deflected by the lack of interest expressed in the New Hampshire reply to their telegram. Yet, inconclusive though it was, this initial inquiry by the Wendes was to have one important result.

For about this same time, in Stone Mountain, Virginia, Mrs. Bessie Ayres renewed her inquiries concerning her father – Wade Wooldridge. On April 12th, she again spoke to Deputy Sheriff Ruff, who advised her that, since no reply had been received from his letter to the local authorities in Dover, she might try communicating directly with the Delaware State Police.

So on April 14th, Mrs. Ayres made a phone call to

Captain Lamb and said that her father had not been heard from for more than six months, namely since October 9th, 1948, when he left home to visit an unknown woman whom he had met through lonely hearts correspondence and who lived near Dover. She added that, before leaving home, her father had destroyed all his correspondence and had withdrawn $700 from his bank account.

Lamb promptly assigned Sergeants Joshua Bennett and Winfield Cochran to a renewed investigation of Inez Brennan and the farm on Horsepond Road. The first thing they did was to seek the whereabouts of Dolly Dean, who had been employed at the farm in October, 1948, at the time of Wooldridge's visit.

They found her at work in a local restaurant. At first, she was reluctant to talk. But on the morning of April 15th, she summoned the officers to her brother's home, where she told them what had happened to Wade Wooldridge.

Murder warrants were immediately sworn, charging Inez and Robert Brennan as principals, with Raymond and George Brennan as accessories. Dolly, who still feared for her life, went into hiding and was given police protection. And, at 2 p.m. that same day, a state police detail arrived at the Brennan farm.

Since Dolly had left the farm early in February, her last knowledge of conditions there led the officers to search for the bodies in the pigpen. A detail of workmen from the state highway department arrived and began to probe with shovels and picks. According to eyewitnesses, "the earth was loose, as though freshly turned. But when they got down to a depth of three feet, it was solid and apparently untouched." Finding nothing but bare earth, the investigators appeared to be somewhat stymied.

But not for long.

Before the digging was concluded, Sergeant Cochran had taken Robert Brennan into his car and was driving him to the state police barracks.

They were about halfway there when Robert started to cry. Then he blurted: "I'm a damn fool for killing Wooldridge!"

He then stated that it would be useless for the police to dig any further in the pigpen, since the bodies had been burned and the ashes taken to the city dump.

Cochran immediately switched on his radio, flashed a message to the farm and advised that he was returning.

Back in the farmyard, Robert pointed out the spot where the bodies had been burned, and immediate steps were taken to obtain remaining ash fragments as specimens for laboratory examination. A rubbish pile was also sifted and various pieces of metal, including a trunk band and other hardware, were recovered, plus a tie-clip with initials "W.W." a key-ring and a wallet.

A search of the barn revealed a broken set of false teeth near the spot where Wooldridge fell down the steps, together with pieces of floorboard which still bore stains and shot patterns. The soil from the pigpen grave was also gathered for analysis.

The search then shifted to the city dump. Robert pointed out the spot where the five gallon tar cans had been hidden and, at 5 p.m., a power-shovel was called into action. Every shovel load of rubbish was meticulously scrutinised until, six hours later, the makeshift burial urns of Wade Wooldridge and Hugo Schulz came to light.

Inez Brennan was already in custody.

The initial police sessions with her have been described as "like talking to a stone". But when statements given by Robert and Raymond were read to her in their presence, she finally said: "The way the boys said is just the way it happened."

Her matted grey hair was tied with a red ribbon that might have been used to tie a box of chocolates. Taken to a cell, she was examined by a physician, who said later: "I was shocked to see a very kindly, homely type of woman who spoke in a soft, modulated voice and used excellent English. On the surface, she did not seem to be different from anyone else."

George Brennan had meanwhile enlisted in the Air Force and was stationed at San Antonio, Texas. He was arrested there by Texas Rangers and brought back to Delaware. George was very bitter against his mother. He talked freely of both the Wooldridge and Schulz killings – and also revealed details of the family's earlier activities in New Jersey and Pennsylvania.

Realizing that the problem of proving the *corpus delicti* would be of major importance, the authorities strove to uncover every possible corroborative clue. Wooldridge's watch was traced to Inez's entirely respectable father, who had received it as a gift. It was identified by Mrs. Ayres from the numbers she'd found written on the wall of her late father's bedroom. She also recognised the iron trunk hoops and corners, various tools, including the saw with the home-made handle, a shotgun, scissors, steel tape and shirts recovered from the Brennan farm as having been her father's property, along with the oversize saw, which lay still unclaimed in the express office.

The murder weapon was also recovered from Dolly's brother, Elmer Thompson, who was only too willing to part with it when he learned the use to which it had been put. New Hampshire state police sent detectives to get the facts on the Hugo Schulz crime, while the New Jersey authorities were interested in the shooting of Mrs. Watkins and the drowning of Mrs. Philips. All in all, Dover, the ordinarily sleepy state capital, held the crime spotlight of America.

The murder trial began in Dover on September 12th, 1949. The stout, grey-haired widow and her pale son Robert were brought into court. Her eyes were narrow slits, her lips thinly compressed, but her jaw remained set in a firm line. Although rather smartly dressed in a well-tailored suit, with her hair trimmed in the latest feather-cut style, her stony face marked her as a person of deep-seated hostility towards her fellow-humans.

Robert, on the other hand, looked much like any other 16-year-old. He had a fresh haircut and wore a grey suit, with figured blue tie. From time to time, he chewed on his lower lip.

Chief witnesses for the prosecution were Mrs. Bessie Ayres – who identified her father's effects – and Dolly Dean, who told of the events at the farm on the night of Wooldridge's arrival. Robert Brennan's confession was also read into the record, over the objections of Defence Counsel Benjamin R. Donolow. Raymond and George Brennan, who would later receive nominal sentences, gave evidence on behalf of their mother and brother. George identified a saw, which the prosecution claimed had belonged to Wooldridge, as *his* own property.

Prosecutor Edward Duffy at one point said of Robert: "What manner of boy is this who. . . can sit across the table and eat with a visitor, knowing he is going to shoot him?" He told the jury: "These Brennans made a slaughterhouse out of their feed barn and a cemetery out of their pigpen." And he referred to Inez as having a "soft voice that cloaks a heart of steel. Mrs. Brennan's cold, clammy hands even reached out and soiled her father many miles away, when she sent him Mr. Wooldridge's watch."

The case went to the jury on September 28th, 1949. After a five-hour deliberation, Robert and his mother were found guilty of first-degree murder, with a recommendation of mercy for Robert, none for Inez.

Inez, quick to self-pity, broke into tears, while Robert seemed to sway unsteadily. A week later, mother and son were sentenced to life imprisonment.

Said the judge, in sentencing Mrs. Brennan: "It is hard to understand how a woman of average intelligence can not only lose all self-respect, but the love of her family – and entirely disregard the duty which every mother has, to nurture her children and protect them from harm. The conclusion is inescapable that, if you had not exerted such an influence over your son Robert, the crimes would not have been committed.

"If the law of this state permitted us to impose upon

you the sentence of death, we would without hesitation impose that sentence on you."

Under the law, it was not possible to sentence Inez Brennan to hang, since she was convicted as an accessory and could not receive a more severe sentence than the principal. Since the jury in Robert's case had recommended mercy, a life sentence thus became mandatory for both.

14

HORROR IN A WELSH VILLAGE

Martin Lomax

In Dolgelly, Wales, during the last century, the majority of the inhabitants were Methodists. These people lived in an atmosphere all their own, content in their comfortable obscurity, simple in their tastes and habits, and happy in an emotional religion.

Six days of the week they thrived in industry, on the seventh enjoyed hymn chanting and reverent praying.

The chapel was the sanctuary of their emotions. Nowadays the advent of materialism and commerce has replaced the simplicity of those lives, so we find it hard to understand the significance the word "chapel" held for those who lived in such districts as Dolgelly.

To them, the chapel was the supreme force in their community. First of all, it was the meeting place between man and his God; secondly, it was the appointed haven of the neighbourhood's respectability. It also provided the population with a theatre, a club-house, a social rendezvous, and in some cases a school for scandal. Cadwallader Jones was a constant attendant at the chapel, where he was known to be a devout and sincere worshipper; a reputable character, and a man of rising prosperity.

As a child, and a youth, he had been pious and

restricted, and his ethical notions orthodox and irreproachable. When he was 25 he was the model young man of the district.

Only the most skilled and malicious rumour mongers could have found a word to say against him, and that would not have been easily believed.

Cadwallader, who at a comparatively early age had attained heights of local celebrity, was a short, thick-set young man with a grave, square, heavy face and dark hair curling over his prematurely furrowed forehead.

The comparative wealth his hard work and ambition had achieved ensured that despite his mere 25 years he was looked up to and respected by everyone.

He stood upon the pinnacle of local fame, a giant amongst his fellows, and the envy of all others who aspired to be as well respected. Yet he was festering with unhappiness and discontent because at 25, he felt himself already an old man, and was conscious that he and youth had always been strangers. He had never squandered a moment in luxurious folly, never sown a single wild oat, never been drunk or caroused with other youths. He had always carried burdens of responsibility and had never known life to be different.

Cadwallader had a wife, but he had never known love, or even passion.

His wife brought him a comparative fortune, a motherly heart, a mild and tractable disposition, a pew in the chapel; but she had never set his heart on fire.

Mrs. Jones was her husband's senior by many years; she was neither beautiful nor did she have that elusive charm that bewitches without it. Her disposition was eminently sane and sober.

Cadwallader began to sicken at his own sobriety.

"I have not the manhood to sin," he said to himself. "I am not a man, I am an immaculate automaton."

He began to envy those of his own age just starting out at marriage and careers, those who envied him the head start the sacrifice of his youth had brought him.

Lonely Hearts killers Inez Brennan and son Robert

Contemporary illustration of the murder of Sarah Hughes by Cadwallader Jones

Actual woodchipper used to dispose of Helle

Richard and Helle Crafts and the woodchipper used to
dispose of her

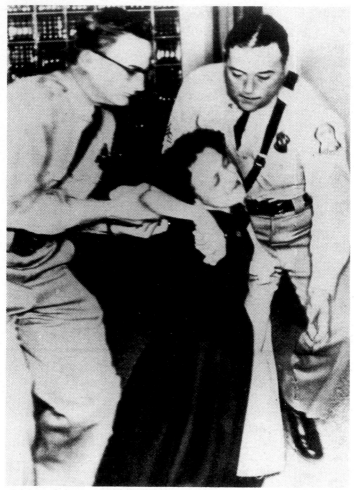

Mary Callahan after the verdict

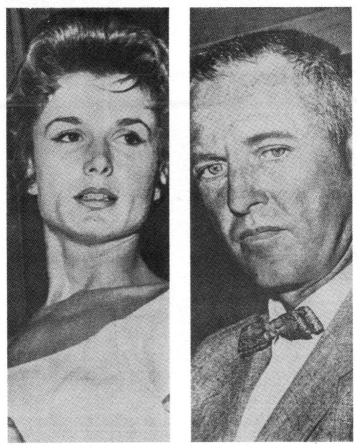

Carole Tregoff and Dr. Bernard Finch. Everything to gain somehow became everything to lose!

Effie Skinner   **Dr. Philip Cross**

Whispers turned to angry suspicions

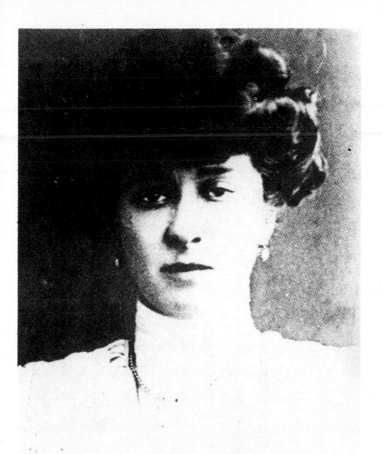

Countess Tarnowska, "Why would you want three lovers simultaneously?" asked the judge at her murder trial

Nicholas Naumoff giving evidence

Count Kamarowsky

Countess Tarnowska arriving at the court in Venice

Then one day Cadwallader had pointed out to him by a
fellow chapel-goer a strange-looking girl, who he was told,
was a model of female depravity.

For all that, she did not merit the character of common
prostitute that her sisters of the chapel bestowed upon her.
Cadwallader Jones regarded her with interest. She was tall
and slim, with a shy face, and red, eager lips. Her clothes
were garish, and covered with ribbons, but she wore no
hat.

Cadwallader left his friend and touched her on the arm.

The girl jumped at the interruption of her solitude, and
when she saw who her admirer was, she allowed her eye-
lids to droop, and blushed all over her pretty face.

"Your name is Sarah Hughes?" said Jones, speaking in
a thick voice, very seriously.

"Yes, sir."

"You live near here?"

"Yes, sir."

Each time she answered his question she curtsied
gracefully.

"Why do I never see you in chapel?"

"Me! Oh, chapel ain't for the likes of me."

"The House of God is for us all," said the good young
man sententiously. The girl shook her head, a smile crept
into her eyes, and parted her lips, revealing two rows of the
pearliest white teeth.

"Oh, no, it ain't. Now, is it?"

Cadwallader felt a sudden desire to kiss the outcast girl,
to press the warm white flesh in his strong, sinewy arms.

"Am I fit for chapel?" she asked, receiving no answer to
her previous question.

"You are fit for a place, my dear," said Cadwallader,
turning very red at his own daring in making such a
remark. His companion giggled; she began to understand
which way the wind blew. The two walked for a long time
together, and arranged a future meeting.

Cadwallader reached home in a high state of excitement. His pulses were beating in wild harmony with his

mood. He was enjoying an adventure; he was a man at last.

That night, as he lay by the side of his sober wife, he could not sleep for thought of the strange girl's beauty. He wished to devour her sweet, supple loveliness in all the fury of his passion. She delighted him in all his thoughts, distracted him from his business, and enticed him from his religion; indeed, although he had seen her only once, he was bound up body and soul to her.

When he saw the girl again she was in sore trouble. A little pin brooch that she used to fasten her dress with had scratched her throat.

"See, it has been bleeding," she said.

Without warning he took her in his arms and pressed his lips to the scar. The startled girl struggled, but he held her in a grasp of iron. He rejoiced to feel her delicate, warm limbs straining to free themselves; rejoiced at his own strength and her childish struggles. He kissed her again and again, and presently she became quiet, and putting up her lips to his, kissed him in return. He could feel the beating of her heart and could have shrieked aloud in a riot of delirious joy. This was youth, this was life, this was passion!

So Cadwallader gained the delights he had hungered for so long, he drank the cup of pleasure at such mighty draughts that he soon caught the bitter savour of the dregs. It was not long, therefore, that Sarah Hughes was telling him she was pregnant.

Such was Cadwallader's aftertaste of the nectar of folly's brewing. A child! a living witness of his shame!

This meant open publication of his infamy, his utter abasement in the eyes of his great little world. He would be denounced from the pulpit of the chapel, hunted from respectable society, hounded into the wilderness by the self-righteous voices of his present admirers; an outcast, a byword, a moral leper. Such natures as Cadwallader Jones's are subject to violent emotional reactions. Such natures also particularly desire an object when it is slipping from their grasp. He had never before prized his reputation as he did now that he seemed likely to lose it.

Besides, he was already tired of his adventure, his passion for Sarah Hughes had burned out. He had tasted sin, indeed banqueted upon it until his palate was cloyed, and he determined to return to the road of sedate travel, to his former mode of living, to the communion of saints, and to the chapel.

But this was no easy matter. The descent from righteousness had been easy enough, but to regain his former plateau of moral rectitude was an affair of harder accomplishment. He gave Sarah a large sum of money, and told her to leave the neighbourhood.

She promised to do all that he wished, and Cadwallader began to congratulate himself on an easy escape.

For a week he heard nothing of Sarah Hughes, and concluded accordingly that she had fulfilled her promise, and left the district. He spent six pleasant days in a fool's paradise. On the Saturday, however, he saw her in the company of some notorious trollops and loose young men joking in the doorway of a beerhouse. Cadwallader pretended not to see her. As he passed, the drunken company raised a concerted laugh at his expense.

"Oh, look at the man of God! Why don't you leave the girls alone?" they bawled, and jeered him until he was out of sight.

Cadwallader marched on looking neither to right nor left, but the blood mounted to his face, he felt his limbs twitch convulsively. He wanted to take to his heels and bury his dishonoured head anywhere so long as it was hidden from the wrath of society.

What a fool he had been. He might have known that she was deceiving him, bleeding him of money to squander amongst her dissolute associates, and meant to expose him publicly when funds were no longer forthcoming.

The next day a ragged little urchin called at Cadwallader's farm with a note from Sarah asking for a further sum of hush money. This was repeated again and again, sometimes with threats and menaces.

Cadwallader's life became living torture; he walked in perpetual fear of exposure and public denunciation. He could not attend to his business by day, or sleep by night. All he thought of was Sarah and the public humiliation that must surely come.

So gradually hate, fear, and dread entered into his soul, and he became a coward and a bully.

Two months before the baby was due he made one last effort to shake off the tyranny and the control that Sarah Hughes exerted over him. He refused to read her notes, sent her no money, and passed her unrecognised in the streets.

Then Sarah came to his house herself and demanded an explanation, and an immediate reckoning.

He implored her to go away before his wife discovered her, and promised to meet her the same night at the end of his garden, by the river. She accepted this compromise, but warned him of the danger of playing any tricks.

The remainder of that day dragged itself out in slow hours of burning torment for Cadwallader. Things could not continue at their present pass. Was there no escape? Other men sinned, and sinned again, and were happy in spite of it. Was he to be forever damned for one little sinful pleasure? He was a strong man, he had a strong will, he would make an escape, he would end this reign of terror once and for all to-night!

When the hour of appointment struck he put on his coat and hat and crept out of the back door. His wife was already in bed, snoring soundly.

The night was dark, and rather cold. He noticed the autumnal moon hiding behind a dense mass of black clouds. The wind blew strong, shrieked in his ears as it whirled and twirled the dead brown leaves down to the river. He crept down to the river's edge. Sarah came to meet him, her hair blown awry by the wind and her skirts swaying as she walked.

"You have come," she said, smiling triumphantly. "I knew you dare not stand me up."

"Dare! I dare anything!"

"Oh, indeed! Ain't we proud tonight!"

Cadwallader snorted in rage.

"Enough of this," he cried. "What do you want?"

"Money."

"Then you won't get it!"

"Won't get it! We'll see about that."

"Not a penny! I'll see you dead first! I've been blackmailed long enough. I mean to stop it now."

In a moment she was transformed into a blazing fury.

"You bastard! you sanctimonious blackguard! I'll go straight to the minister and tell him all. How you ruined me."

"Ruined a trull! Ha, ha!"

"Oh, I'm that, am I? It was different when you came sneaking round me with your pretty words, wasn't it?"

The girl ran from him towards his house, screaming at the top of her voice:

"Mrs. Jones! Mrs. Jones!"

He saw her intention in a moment. She was going to wake up his wife, and expose him as the father of her unborn child.

In an instant he was after her, reached her side, twisted an arm around her waist, and clapped his other hand to her mouth.

The two rolled over on the grass.

"Mrs. Jones! Murder! Help!" shrieked Sarah.

Her fine strong teeth met in the thick of his hands, and she kicked and struck him with all her might.

Cadwallader seized a large stone and brought it with a swinging blow down on her mouth with the force of a sledge-hammer.

He heard a gurgling sob in her throat, and the bones of her face crack like twigs under the weight of the terrible blow.

Her limbs twitched and her body gave a quiver of

spasmodic life, and Sarah Hughes was dead.

He laughed and cried in hysterical joy, and hit the corpse with wild, savage blows.

He tore her hair, mangled her body, trod, kicked, and danced on her, the blood lust transformed him into mad, unreasoning brutality.

He came back to consciousness in a cold sweat of fear and horror, his heart thumping like a drum, and every limb trembling. He crawled back to his house and drank a tumbler of whisky. Then he took a saw, a hatchet, a chopping block, and a bill-hook into the cowshed. He lit a lantern, and staggered back to the scene of the crime.

He carried the body to the cowshed, stripped her of her clothes, and then, with deliberate force and care, spent three hours in dismembering his victim.

He cut the body up into eleven pieces and threw them separately into the river, hoping the tide would carry them out to sea.

Then he buried his implements of slaughter in the cowshed, together with the murdered girl's clothes and his own outer garments. He took the spade and obliterated the traces of his crime from the garden, and the pale first gleams of morning lighted him to bed.

For a week Sarah Hughes's disappearance excited the local gossips. They were just tiring of that line of talk when a young man fishing in the river near to Cadwallader Jones's garden brought up a human hand.

The county was at once plunged into conjecture, suspicion, and excitement. The hand must belong to the missing girl!

The river was dragged, and eleven fragments of a female body were brought to light, all having been discovered in the neighbourhood of the prosperous young farmer's garden.

Cadwallader himself had been morose and silent, lost his colour and was generally thought to be in the grip of some debilitating illness.

So, when the police came to Cadwallader's house to

search it on suspicion, he walked out to them, and said in a clear voice, "I am the man you want. I did it. I murdered her."

He took the officers to the cowshed and showed them where he'd put the murder weapons and clothes. He told them everything, speaking like one who talks in a dream, in an unemotional and unvarying monotone.

The court was, of course, crowded with the neighbours and friends of Cadwallader. Chapel-goers turned up in full force to view the degradation of their brother, and the lamentable fall from grace of one who had been a very giant of godliness within their midst.

Cadwallader, standing behind the iron fence of the dock, studiously avoided the gaze of all with whom he had once been familiar. At times he appeared a little impatient at the length of the proceedings; indeed, he was longing for the moment when he could depart from this place of public observation.

Despite a plea of insanity set up by the defence, Cadwallader Jones was condemned to death, and there is no reason to believe that he was dissatisfied with his sentence.

His life in the condemned cell prior to his execution was spent reading his Bible, and in conversation with the chaplain. He walked to the scaffold with a firm, steady gait. His head was bowed, and he avoided the eyes of his jailers.

He stood beneath the gallows firm as a rock. Before the lever was pulled he gave one mighty shudder, then plummeted into eternity. And this was the end of the brilliant career of Cadwallader Jones, whose flirtation with the silliness of youth came too late to him, releasing instead the raging of the long-suppressed elemental savage.

15

WIFE IN A WOODCHIPPER
Bill Jones

On the night of November 18th, 1986, winter swirled prematurely into the well-to-do community of Newtown, Connecticut. It came in the shape of a swirling blizzard that piled substantial drifts on the roads and covered Newtown's densely wooded area.

Shortly before the storm broke, 39-year-old Helle Crafts, a blonde Pan American Airlines flight attendant, arrived at the Newfield Lane home she shared with her husband, Richard, and their three young children.

Helle had been dropped off there by her neighbour another Pan Am flight attendant with whom she had just flown into Kennedy Airport from Frankfurt, Germany.

The two women bade each other farewell and Helle Crafts was seen moving through the gloom of a cold November evening towards the front door of her home. She would never be seen alive again.

If the Danish-born Helle was anxious to be back with her children, she obviously had strong misgivings about a number of other aspects of her life.

Helle had been under great emotional stress during recent weeks, a fact that had become apparent to a number of her associates. These colleagues had felt a chill of dread when Helle told them, "If anything happens to me, don't think it was an accident." To some, she had already confided that she was in the process of starting divorce proceedings against her 49-year-old husband, himself a pilot with Eastern Airlines.

The reason for the ending of the Crafts' marriage was Richard's penchant for womanising.

In September, 1986, Helle had sought the services of a woman attorney who specialised in marital and family litigation. Helle's decision to act had been triggered by an out-of-state phone number frequently listed on her telephone bill.

Apprised of Helle's suspicions, the attorney recommended that Keith Mayo, a private detective, be retained to check out the phone bill.

Through his efforts, the private detective learned that the phone calls had been made to a woman in Middletown, New Jersey. He advised that a surveillance of the woman's residence be undertaken, and if possible, that Crafts be photographed in her company.

As she awaited Mayo's report, Helle checked Richard's flight schedules. She found that they added up to more than the 84 hours a month to which Eastern limited its pilots. In other words, there appeared to be times when her husband had been flying – but not aboard an Eastern aircraft.

On September 30th, 1986, after an all-night surveillance from his own car in front of the Middletown woman's home, the private detective spotted Richard Crafts leaving the premises. Crafts was accompanied by an attractive woman who appeared to be in her early 40s. The couple walked with their arms entwined and showed other signs of affection.

The pictures taken by Mayo were developed. On October 2nd they were shown to Helle and she appeared emotionally shaken by what the snapshots revealed.

In addition to Richard's sexual wanderings, there were a number of other problems in the Crafts' household. Among these was the pilot's habit of collecting weapons of all sorts. Helle felt the arsenal presented a danger to her children.

This, then, was the Crafts family's recent history when Helle Crafts disappeared inside her Newfield Lane home as the first snowflakes began to fall.

The snowstorm intensified during the night of November 18th and next morning Helle's neighbours tried to telephone the Crafts to find out how they had weathered the storm. At first, they received no answer, but finally they were able to contact Richard, who told them Helle was not at home. The pilot also said that he didn't know when his wife would be back.

The following day the neighbours called again and were told by Crafts that Helle was flying. Crafts said he was sure of that fact because her luggage was not in the house.

That afternoon Crafts called back and told the woman neighbour that he had just received a call from Helle in London.

He said Helle had told him she was on her way to Denmark to visit her mother who had been taken ill. He also told Helle's friend that he now expected his wife back on Tuesday.

In the days that followed, several of Helle's friends tried to call her mother's home in Denmark, but in each case they were told that they had dialled the wrong number.

The sense of alarm over Helle's well-being increased when the Crafts' housekeeper revealed that on November 22nd she had seen a dark stain – which she described as the size of a grapefruit – on the mat in Helle's bedroom. A few days later, according to the housekeeper, Crafts removed the mat, as well as those in his son's and daughter's bedrooms.

Then there was the matter of some telephone lists and an address book with the numbers of Helle's friends. These too had disappeared.

As the days passed and Crafts' answers to their questions continued to be evasive, a group of Helle's friends grew ever more apprehensive. The critical bomb-shell was dropped when one of them found the correct telephone number of Helle's Danish mother.

From her they learned there had been no illness, that Helle was not in Denmark, and that the mother had no idea where she might be.

Equally sinister in their view was the fact that Richard Crafts had given out his mother-in-law's number wrongly. In each case the area code and one other digit had been in error, and the same error was repeated throughout.

Consequently, on December 1st, 1986, Helle's friends filed a missing-person report with Newtown police.

From the very start, the relationship between the small-town police force (which numbered only four detectives among its personnel) and those who were seeking action in the disappearance of Helle Crafts proved a controversial one. Members of the police argued that in over 90 per cent of disappearances caused by marital difficulties, the subject has returned in a short time.

For their part, Helle's friends felt that the indifference to the situation was caused by the fact that Richard Crafts had augmented his income as a pilot by working part-time for the police as an auxiliary cop.

Meanwhile, private detective Mayo continued his own probe. He learned that Helle's car remained in the Pan Am car park and no attempt had been made to pick it up. He also discovered that Crafts had as yet failed to file his own missing-person report with the Newtown police.

Mayo received a major setback, however, when he learned that Richard Crafts had submitted to a polygraph test administered by the Connecticut state police and had passed it.

In another direction, Mayo discovered no unusual withdrawals from Helle's various banking accounts which might have been used to finance a lengthy trip.

Crafts' November comings and goings appeared more complicated. On October 29th, he'd bought a 1980 Volkswagen Rabbit in Danbury. He paid $2,500 for the vehicle, leaving $30 in cash, the balance being due when he took delivery. He collected the VW on November 17th.

On November 10th, he purchased a Ford 350 dump-truck for $15,000 in New Milford. It was to be delivered on November 13th. His reason was that he needed the truck to spread gravel on a driveway. Crafts also paid an extra $350 to have a pintle hook (used for towing heavy equipment) fitted.

On November 13th, the pilot ordered a $375 chest freezer and paid a $100 cash deposit. He also bought a pair of fireproof gloves and a flat-headed shovel.

Most crucial of all, on November 14th, Richard Crafts reserved a large woodchipper from a hire company. He made arrangements to pick the chipper up on November 18th. He claimed that he needed the equipment to clear some land.

When the Ford dump truck was not ready for delivery by November 20th, Crafts arranged to have the supplier substitute a Ford 50 U-Haul with Ohio licence plates which could be used until the Ford dump truck was ready. The truck was delivered to Newfield Lane and the pilot then drove the Ford 50 to the woodchipper hire firm and the piece of heavy machinery, weighing some three and a half tons, was attached.

These assorted purchases and rentals became vital to the probe into Crafts' operations when, on the night of November 20th, a Newtown police officer noticed a truck and woodchipper parked on Silver Bridge over the Housatonic River between Newtown and Southbury.

The officer later testified that as he passed, the woodchipper was in operation. Through the truck's door the lawman also saw two bags of woodchips as well as some bags of plastic or cloth. In addition, he remembered seeing a man dressed in a green poncho and a wide-brimmed hat who appeared to be hiding behind the truck.

Southbury Constable Richard Wildman would note that at 4.00 a.m., he came upon a chipper attached to a U-Haul. A Southbury police car was parked behind the two vehicles and he recognised Richard Crafts, who was dressed in a reversible police raincoat. Crafts was loading police equipment into the passenger side of the Ford truck.

According to Wildman, when the officer asked Crafts what he was doing with a woodchipper he was told that a number of tree limbs had snapped off in the storm and Crafts was using the chipper to clear the debris.

On December 11th, 1986, Richard Crafts was interviewed by Detective Mike DeJoseph of the Newtown police. He gave the detective the following information:

He had no idea that Helle had hired a private investigator, and he didn't know that the detective had documented his relationship with a New Jersey woman.

He couldn't imagine Helle having told friends she feared him and yes he had known Helle was leaving on the morning of November 19th.

She had taken a blue garment bag and a blue canvas bag with her. Her flight bags, passport, banking and current account statements were not in the house.

All the carpets and mats in the house were being replaced because kerosene had been spilt on the bedroom carpet.

In order to facilitate the removal of the old mats he had cut them into two-foot strips. He dumped the mat he had taken out of the master bedroom (the one with the dark stain on it) in the Newtown tip.

From all accounts by those who knew the Crafts, their personalities could not have been at greater variance. For her part, Helle was said to have been a warm, outgoing woman. Richard Crafts, on the other hand, was secretive and aloof. The marriage had been a passionate one at the outset. As time went on, however, Helle and Richard appeared to go their separate ways. Each in their own way had been devoted to their children.

As December, 1986, wore on, the local probe seemed to have stalled. Then on Boxing Day the state police entered the case and a group of detectives from the Major Crime Squad with a search warrant moved into the Crafts' home.

What they found was a residence in chaos. Items of furniture lay strewn around in rooms where they didn't belong. Christmas presents, still unopened, had been stashed in a hall closet.

Of particular interest to the detectives was the fact that not only had the blue carpet been removed from Helle's bedroom, but an underlying two-foot strip of padding had also been cut out.

The collapsible metal frame of the queen-sized bed was gone. The housekeeper told police that she had found it under the cellar steps. However, the item was now nowhere on the premises.

What amazed officers was the huge number of weapons in the house. There were at least 50. In addition, there were several grenades, one with a firing pin. Left behind were two chainsaws in the garage.

On January 6th, 1987, Richard Crafts was interviewed, this time by Connecticut state police detectives. One of the questions they asked him was, "Why does she want a divorce?"

Crafts replied, "I guess she got tired of me fooling around. Or maybe she wanted to do some fooling around herself."

Now a conference was held to determine just how strong a case the state had. Of utmost importance was what forensic specialist Dr. Lee had found, both at the Crafts' home and where the woodchipper had been spotted.

Doctor Lee's attention had been caught by the queen-sized mattress in the Crafts' home. He performed a series of tests to determine whether spots on it were bloodstains. Using orthotolidine solution (which turns blue in the presence of blood), Lee got a positive result.

Lee's best guess was that if Helle Crafts had been murdered, the slaying had taken place in the bedroom. The victim had been either standing, sitting, or kneeling on the bed with the covers pulled back. Flannels in a bucket in the bathroom and recently-washed towels tested positive for blood.

However, despite tests on the mattress that proved that

the stains were human blood and that the blood had been the same O-type as Helle's, there had not been enough evidence on which to base a murder charge.

That proof came when detectives checked out a culvert along the banks of Connecticut's Lake Zoar. There they discovered an inch-deep pile of wood chips which had been spread with a shovel or pitchfork. There were strands of bright-blue material mixed in with the chips.

Further down the culvert, they spotted an envelope bearing the return address of the "American Cancer Society". The envelope had been nicked, but, much more important was the fact that the envelope had been addressed to "Miss Helle Crafts".

Search reinforcements had been called to the scene. As they fanned out across the wooded terrain, the officers discovered a virtual trove of circumstantial evidence. Included were strands of blonde hair, a number of as yet unidentified fragments mixed in with the wood chips, and a label from a package of vitamins. (The label was of a Californian health food company which recruits part-time people to sell its products. What the police hadn't known at this time, but were to learn later, was that Helle Crafts had been augmenting her flight attendant's income by selling that company's products.)

In all, 30 bags of potential evidence were tagged for further forensic evaluation.

Among the damning items identified was the plastic crown of a human tooth, a human toe joint, a piece of bone which appeared to have been part of a human skull, and part of a human finger.

These were the items on which the state based its admittedly circumstantial case that Helle Crafts was murdered, that her body was dismembered and the body parts put through the woodchipper, and that her killer had been Richard Crafts.

On January 13th, a death certificate was issued. At 11.00 p.m. on the same night, Richard Crafts was arrested.

Now the outcome of the trial, which would not begin until March 14th, 1988, would rest almost exclusively on Dr. Lee's ability to convince a jury that the three-quarters of an ounce of human remains he was analysing proved that Helle Crafts had met a violent death at the hands of her husband.

What Dr. Lee had were 75 bone slivers, only 69 of which were certifiably human, 2,600 chopped-up strands of human hair, a fragment of human tissue, five drops of blood, a portion of a human finger and two fingernails.

Because of the publicity surrounding the case, a change of venue was ordered and the trial place and date set for New London on March 18th, 1988.

State Attorney Flanagan set the stage by calling 30 witnesses who testified about Helle's divorce demands, her fear of Richard, the rental and purchase of heavy equipment which the state contended had been used in Helle's slaying, and an assortment of Richard Crafts' girl friends who outlined the pilot's extramarital relationships.

On May 11th, a forensic odontologist took the stand to identify a capped tooth, which he said he'd X-rayed on five sides, as having been one of Helle Crafts'. The root, he said, had been sheared off by traumatic force.

Expert after expert took the stand to bolster the prosecution's forensic case. And all of this set the stage for the prosecution's star witness.

Dr. Lee took the jury step by step through his forensic findings. He also pointed out that he had tested four types of paraffin, including diesel, to determine whether the dark stains the housekeeper had found on the bedroom mat had been caused by the heater fuel. In each case, the paraffin stains had disappeared within five minutes.

After Prosecutor Flanagan rested his case, Defence Attorney Daniel Sagarin made every effort to discredit the state's view of what had happened to Helle Crafts. He also presented his own array of expert opinion, whose views were the opposite to those the jurors had already heard.

The defendant took the stand to tell the court he had

last seen his wife on November 19th, when she told him, "I'm leaving now."

Of the evening of November 18th and the following morning, he said they had discussed the divorce papers, but as for the food freezer he'd bought (which the prosecution maintained he used to preserve his wife's body until he had a chance to put it through the woodchipper) – he argued that he purchased it because a food co-op of which Helle had been treasurer had been buying foods in large quantities.

To take advantage of the savings offered, the family required larger freezing facilities. The older freezer, he maintained, had been abandoned on the Newtown landfill after the door had been removed.

There seemed to be no way that the emotional pitch which had been maintained throughout the lengthy trial could be increased as the jury listened to prosecution and defence summations and was charged as to the law by Judge Barry Schaller.

But it would be.

That came in the 17 days during which the jurors deliberated behind locked doors in an attempt to reach a verdict. At first, the 12 jurors were almost equally split between conviction and acquittal. In the give and take, however, a trend began to develop towards finding Crafts guilty.

By Friday, July 15th, the panel stood 11 to 1 for a guilty verdict. At 4.30 p.m., it reported itself hopelessly deadlocked. Judge Schaller urged the members to continue their deliberations.

But as night fell, the lone dissident bolted from the jury room and refused to re-enter. The judge had no recourse but to declare a mistrial.

Judge Schaller ordered that the defendant be held on $750,000 bail and that he be retried on the charges against him.

Time dragged on. Almost a year and a half elapsed until September, 1989, when a new jury was empanelled. This time the trial would be held in Norwalk, Connecticut.

The second time around was much the same as the first, although the media coverage was somewhat less. State Attorney Flanagan directed the prosecution, while Crafts' attorney was now Gerard Smyth.

The same arguments as had been heard in the first trial were used once more, but in one respect the second trial proved vastly different.

That was when the jury took the case. This time there were no marathon deliberations. Although the presentation of witnesses, evidence and arguments lasted over nine weeks, the jury reached its decision in only three days.

The jury this time found Richard Crafts guilty of murder. He now faced a sentence of 25 to 60 years.

Said Smyth of his client, "He wishes to appeal. And he still maintains he is innocent." The attorney also said the appeal will be based on grounds of jury selection and pre-trial publicity. Smyth pointed out that a book (*The Woodchipper Murder* by Arthur Herzog), had begun appearing in bookshops during the trial.

There was one final irony in the tragic story; one induced by a quirk of nature.

The jury decision was issued just three years and three days after Helle Crafts disappeared into a premature winter snowfall, never to be seen alive again.

On Wednesday, November 22nd, 1989, just 24 hours after the guilty verdict, the eastern seaboard was once again locked under a heavy, premature blizzard which covered Connecticut with a heavy blanket of snow.

Less than two months later, on January 8th, 1990, Richard Crafts was sentenced to 50 years imprisonment.

16

BEHIND THE SCENES OF THE FINCH MURDER FIASCO

David Bennett

From the moment it first broke into explosive headlines in the summer of 1959, the Finch case had all the ingredients to appeal to the popular imagination and then some. *L'Affaire Finch* had sex, glamour, beauty, wealth, sex, intrigue, mystery, action; sex, drama, powerful suspense – and more sex. Further touches included a "do-it-yourself murder kit," a frustrated private eye, plus a hired gunman.

Yet no self-respecting author of make-believe Whodun-its would have dared to concoct the exotic, bizarre and dramatic cast of characters and lurid events revealed in this trial. To report what actually happened would have violated every rule in the writer's craft – a bewildering chain of incredible, serio-comic climaxes and anti-climaxes that inevitably must confuse even the most orderly-minded reader.

Everyone, too, seemed to be trying to get into the act. Reporters, hard-pressed for exclusive angles, dug up "informed sources" from every place except the local cemetery. A battery of high-priced legal talent played out their roles with all the aplomb and showmanship of a Perry Mason.

It was, in short, a three-ring circus that might have been hilarious – had its pivot hinged on anything except three lives. That of the victim, Barbara Jean Finch. And those accused of her murder – Dr. R. Bernard Finch and his shapely bedmate Carole Tregoff.

At times, too, the Los Angeles courtroom's press box looked like a Hollywood set. For among the glamorous "guest reporters" were film actresses Pamela Mason and Terry Moore, scenarists Borden Chase and Irving Shulman, producer Al Zugsmith, plus many other well-known names. Terry Moore explained to her press colleagues that she was interested in watching Carole Tregoff, in preparation for her own role in the forthcoming picture *Girl on Death Row*.

Scotching the rumours of a rift, Dr. Finch and his paramour melted into each other's arms for a long kiss when they were allowed to go to a private room for a conference with their attorneys. On December 25th, 1960, Carole celebrated both Christmas and her own 23rd birthday behind county jail bars. She meekly joined other women inmates in packing Christmas stockings for orphaned children.

On December 29th, after more than 100 men and women had been examined and rejected a jury of six men and six women was finally selected as agreeable to both sides. Soon after the turn of the year, the trial proper began.

The stolid, unruffled, efficient police and medical witnesses testified to the facts their investigations had uncovered. Dr. Gerald K. Ridge, autopsy surgeon, testified that Barbara Finch's death was caused by massive haemorrhaging, produced by a downward-ranging bullet that pierced her left shoulder-blade and emerged near the breastbone.

Dr. Ridge also described two skull fractures, one over the right eye and the other on the left side of the head. He gave his opinion that these injuries could have been caused by Mrs. Finch's head striking the wall of the garage – or by her being beaten with some object, such as a pistol.

Under questioning by Deputy District Attorney Fred Whichello, Dr. Ridge stated that Mrs. Finch could not have walked or stumbled more than a few steps after being shot! Hence, she was most likely shot at the bottom of the slope, at or near the spot where she was found, rather than higher up, on the driveway near the garage.

The judge, jurors, defendants and lawyers enjoyed an outing when the court adjourned to West Covina, at the request of the prosecution attorneys, to allow the jurors to inspect the murder scene. Carole broke down and wept when they reached the Finch home, but Bernie showed little emotion. A bamboo rake was placed on the lawn to mark where Barbara's body had lain. The jury duly inspected the shattered plaster on the garage wall, where Barbara Finch's maid, who first called the police, had said Dr. Finch banged her head.

First of the key witnesses, eagerly awaited by press and public, was Marie Anne Lidholm, the pretty blonde Swedish maid. She repeated her story of the murder night – July 18th, 1959 – exactly as she had first related it to the police who came in answer to her phone call. At 11.30 p.m., she heard Mrs. Finch's car drive into the garage. A few seconds later, she heard Barbara scream for help. She ran out and found Mrs. Finch lying on the floor of the garage. As she bent over her employer, Dr. Finch suddenly appeared. He seized the young Swedish girl and banged her head against the garage wall. "His face was twisted and angry," the maid told the court.

She told of Barbara getting up, being forced into the car, then breaking away and running across the lawn. As Marie Anne ran to the house to call the police, she heard a shot. Under further questioning, Marie Anne told of previous incidents of violence.

The socialite, tennis-playing Finches, who were married in Las Vegas in 1951, had drawn apart in recent years. Principal reason was the doctor's well-known philandering. The maid, an exchange student who had been with them for 10 months, had witnessed frequent and increasingly bitter squabbles.

One Sunday morning in May, 1959, Marie Anne testified, Barbara appeared with a bandage on her head. She explained that Bernie had banged her head against the edge of the bed. "He blew up when I told him I wanted a divorce," the maid quoted Barbara as saying. "He was like a wild man. He said he'd kill me first. He tried to strangle me."

As a result of this incident, the Finches separated on May 18th. Bernie moved out – and Barbara filed for divorce on May 20th. They argued bitterly about money. Barbara wanted $1,650 monthly alimony and $250 child support. At a temporary alimony hearing in June, a Los Angeles judge issued an order restraining the battling couple from harassing each other.

On June 25th, the young maid testified, Dr. Finch broke into the house, even though his wife, in fear of him, had had the locks changed and installed new bolts. He struck Barbara, cursed her, called her vile names and threatened her life. The terrified maid called the police. By the time officers arrived, the doctor had driven off in the new white Cadillac he had recently given to Barbara.

When Defence Counsel Grant Cooper cross-examined, Marie Anne scoffed at the idea that Mrs. Finch had carried a revolver in her handbag. She believed she would have known if such were the case. But the prim little maid broke down and sobbed on the witness-stand when Cooper confronted her with a statement made to one of the original investigators, in which she had said: "It seemed like I heard shots coming from the garage while I was in the house." The maid said she did not recall having made such a statement.

Police Captain Jack Ryan was called to testify that an extensive search of the grounds around the Finch house with mine-detectors had failed to uncover the death gun, which was still conspicuously missing. Ryan also testified to finding blood smears on Mrs. Finch's car.

The prosecution then introduced a brown leather dispatch-case found at the shooting scene and identified as the property of Dr. Finch. It contained an 8-inch carving-knife, two coils of clothes-line, a leather shaving-kit bag holding a box of .38 cartridges and a flashlight, two boxes of surgical gloves, a bottle of sleeping-pills, hypodermic syringes and needles, a bottle of sedative for injection, plus miscellaneous bandages and compresses. Deputy DA Whichello called this strange collection a "do-it-yourself murder kit".

Attorney Cooper sprang something of a surprise when he contended without argument that the dispatch case and its oddly-assorted sinister contents indeed belonged to Dr. Finch. He likewise contended that the missing gun, a .38 revolver, was the property of the doctor.

Several attractive young female friends of the murdered brunette were called to the witness-stand. They testified that for some months, particularly after the Finchs' separation, Barbara had lived in constant fear of her husband. She had displayed bruises – allegedly inflicted by the doctor – and told of his threats to kill her. Barbara wanted to divorce Bernie because of his philandering, she told her friends, but the wealthy doctor was objecting, since a divorce would hit him in the wallet.

Barbara's divorce attorney, Joseph T. Forno, testified that twice within the two months before she was killed, the frightened society wife had told him how the doctor had struck her with a gun and threatened to kill her. "She said Dr. Finch had threatened to kill her in her car, then take her out to the desert or the mountains and run the car over a cliff to make it look like an accident," the lawyer said.

Heading the contingent of reporters from New York was attractive, energetic Dorothy Kilgallen. While going busily about her daily chores in the courtroom, she bade fair to top the glamour parade herself. She posed for pictures with the defendants and signed autographs for her admirers. A judge (not involved in the case at hand) sent her an orchid.

However, it was in her workaday capacity as a reporter that Dorothy Kilgallen really shone. She minced no words and pulled no punches. Her breezy, incisive observations went right to the heart of the matter.

"The best way to murder your wife," Dorothy wrote in one of her early stories, having sized up the trial and its issues, "is to have a few drinks with her, pull out your revolver and shoot her, then head for the nearest cop and hand him the gun."

Dorothy said of Carole Tregoff: "No one taking a long look at her would doubt that she was more interested in men than in sculpture, soccer or scrabble." Of the jury, she observed: "It contains in the alternate section one lady I would not care to have judging me on a jaywalking charge."

Going behind the scenes, she commented shrewdly: "The defence lawyers are fighting two formidable enemies – the prosecution and the power of sex. While they [Finch and Tregoff] are on trial, with separate counsel guiding their destinies, it is apparent that love is interfering with the lawyers. . . .

"When the worst of the prosecution's case is in, will they still be hand-in hand, or will one of them panic at the thought of the death chamber? Has any defence lawyer the power to persuade one of them to 'dump' the other? It is a small secret that Carole's attorneys would like her to unload Dr. Finch. . . ."

After interviewing the doctor, Dorothy wrote: "Dr. Finch, or Mr. Hyde? You can't tell by looking into the bright blue eyes of the accused surgeon. At close range, they glitter with sincerity."

Meanwhile, the parade of state witnesses went on. Apartment managers testified that over a period of more than a year, Dr. Finch and his redheaded paramour had rented love-nests in Monterey Park, Highland Park and Las Vegas. For 10 months, Bernie had kept Carole in a

Monterey Park hideaway apartment, not far from the Finch home in West Covina. The $175-a-month Las Vegas apartment had been rented just 10 days before Barbara was murdered.

Don Williams, Carole's childhood friend, related how Carole had sought two men who would "do a job" for her – and how he had introduced her to one of them. And when John Patrick Cody, the "hired gunman", took the stand, Dorothy Kilgallen wrote:

"A dangerous little firecracker of a man sits in the witness-box today. He is an unabashed, ungrammatical, minor crook named John Cody – Jack to his friends – and it is easy to see, by the glitter in Carole's red-brown eyes and the way she snatches up a pencil to make notes as he talks, that she knows he is hurting her and longs to strike back."

The hard-eyed, tight-mouthed Cody testified to his negotiations with Carole and the doctor. He admitted that he had sold the life of Barbara Finch for a total of $1,400 – marked down from $2,000 – and didn't deliver it.

"Dr. Finch didn't tense a muscle," Kilgallen wrote, "as Cody attributed to him a tag line worthy of a cheap paperback hard-boiled mystery – an order Dr. Finch was supposed to have uttered as he sent Cody off on his second mission to kill Mrs.. Finch. The line was:

"When you shoot her, let her know what she's getting it for. Tell her, "This is from Bernie!"

Jack Cody's dramatic testimony made a powerful impression. Defence attorneys cross-questioned him without mercy, but failed to shake the basic facts of his story. So they concentrated on attacking Cody's veracity.

"You have no compunction about telling lies, have you?" Attorney Cooper asked.

"Well, it depends on who I'm dealing with," Cody answered readily.

Carole Tregoff registered shock and indignation when one of her lawyers told her, offstage, that Jack Cody had hinted to a reporter that he had been intimate with

Carole. "There was plenty of hugging and kissing when the doctor wasn't around," Cody was quoted as saying with a leer.

"That's absolutely ridiculous!" Carole flamed. "There isn't a word of truth to it!"

Next witness was Mark Stevens, handsome film and TV actor-producer and tennis-playing friend of the Finches. Stevens testified that when Barbara told him, a week or so before her death, that she was in deadly fear of her husband, he advised her to get a gun for self-protection. "I gave her a jack handle from my car," the actor said. "And I told her that if he ever came near her, to say 'hello' to him in the face with it."

A banker and a handwriting expert then testified that two months before Barbara's death, Bernie Finch had forged a $3,000 cheque on his wife's account. It was dated the day of their separation. Barbara had wanted to prosecute her estranged husband, so her attorney had taken it up with the DA's office.

As the trial went into its eighth week, the crucial battle loomed over introduction of the fateful "Exhibition 60" – the transcript of Carole Tregoff's self-incriminating testimony at Dr. Finch's preliminary hearing in July. Deputy DA Whichello called himself as the state's 45th witness in his attempt to introduce into evidence the controversial admissions regarding both the murder night and Carole's intimacies with Finch.

The defence battled as before, contending that Carole had not been warned of her constitutional rights before testifying. And the defence scored a point when one Las Vegas detective, summoned to the witness-stand, admitted that the redhead had been under "technical arrest" when she made her original statement, which differed from her later sworn testimony.

Dorothy Kilgallen noted the possibility that if Exhibit 60 were ruled out, it was quite possible that the accused redhead might go free at once. "Carole Tregoff," Kilgallen wrote, "is a flirty redhead who started out in a bikini trying to make the cover of a girlie magazine – but today she may make legal history."

Eventually, the defence chalked up its biggest victory to date when, on February 2nd, Judge Walter R. Evans sustained objections to the admission of Exhibit 60. He ruled that Carole's two previous statements, to the Las Vegas and West Covina police, could be admitted, but that the incriminating testimony that led to her arrest could not be read to the jury. Carole didn't go free, but she was radiant at the decision. She leaned over and kissed her lawyer, Robert Neeb, who promptly pointed out that the West Covina judge had ruled that the state had no case against Carole without the disputed transcript.

With the failure of its attempt to introduce the transcript, the state glumly rested its case. As the defence of Dr. Finch got under way, the society doctor told Dorothy Kilgallen that he was eager to get to the witness-stand and tell his own story. As for Carole, Dr. Finch said: "We're pulling together – that's obvious. That's the only way it could be."

Bernie got his wish almost immediately, for Attorney Cooper called him as his first witness. The handsome physician, pictured by the prosecution as a cold-blooded, conscienceless, calculating killer, now emerged in a new incarnation – under Cooper's brilliant direction – as a loving, frustrated husband.

Volubly and glibly, to his fascinated audience, Finch bared the intimate details of his married life. He said he had been "very happy" with Barbara – until she turned frigid after the birth of their son in 1953. When his brunette wife spurned his amorous advances in their king-size double bed, the doctor testified sorrowfully, he was "driven into the arms of other women".

He related how he first met Carole Tregoff when she applied for a job as his office secretary in 1956. He told how they had fallen hard for each other, how he had rented a series of love-nest apartments. While he and

Barbara had an "armistice agreement" permitting them to date whomever they chose, the doctor blandly said, he had lied to Barbara about his affair with Carole, "in order to spare his wife's pride".

Finch explained that he and Barbara agreed to postpone divorce proceedings, in order to protect his credit rating while he was building his new clinic in association with other doctors. He presented her with the white Cadillac to seal their bargain.

Then, in the spring of 1959, Barbara started talking about filing for divorce. Irked at her breaking their truce agreement, Finch said, he hired John Patrick Cody, whom he described as "an unscrupulous gigolo," in order "to get something on Barbara – even if he had to sleep with her himself".

After paying Cody considerable money, Finch went on, he decided that the young man was swindling him and not doing his job. Finch and Carole then decided to confront Barbara and iron out their mutual difficulties.

The defendant acknowledged that he and Carole had taken the so-called murder kit along with them to West Covina. It was really only a doctor's kit that he carried for emergency calls, Finch explained disarmingly. The clothes-line was for use on his new boat, while the carving-knife was a gift for Carole's apartment.

When the pair confronted Barbara in the dark garage, Finch told the hushed, expectant courtroom, Barbara reached into her car and grabbed Bernie's gun, which he had bought for protection – and had happened to leave in his wife's car.

Carole ran away as he began struggling with his wife, the doctor told the court. Barbara fought like a fiend, according to his story. She kicked him, bit his arm, stamped on his toes. When she started to scream for help, Bernie admitted, he wrested the gun away from her and slugged her on the head. "I just couldn't get her to co-operate with me," he explained, shaking his crew-cut head.

Then, when Marie Anne came running out in her robe, Finch said, he grabbed her and shoved her against the wall, "because I thought she might have a gun". As he helped his groggy wife into the car and started to look for the keys, Barbara snatched the gun when he laid it down. She jumped from the car and started running away.

Finch got down from the witness-stand to demonstrate how he had overtaken his wife, caught her and knocked the gun out of her hand. "As she turned around, I picked up the gun to throw it away," the doctor told the attentive jurors. "I didn't want either of us to get shot. But – as I picked the gun up – it went off!"

"What happened to the gun?" Attorney Cooper pressed.

"I don't know what happened to the gun – after it went off. I went over to the edge of the hill to look for Carole. Out of the corner of my eye, I saw Barbara running down the steps. Then I saw her stumble and fall on the lawn.

"I went over and knelt down by her and asked her, 'What happened, Barb?'

"She said, 'Shot – in chest.' I was amazed. I started to get up to call an ambulance, but Barbara wanted me to wait.

"I knelt down by her head. She moved her arm. I took her hand and she sort of opened her mouth. Then she spoke – and her voice was very, very soft. She said, 'I'm sorry, Bernie, I should have listened – don't leave me – take care of the – the kids.'

"She fell back and I realised she was dead. I called her name, 'Barb! Barb!' But she couldn't answer me. . . "

At that point, he didn't know what he was doing, Finch went on, choking back his sobs. He recalled walking or running down the hill, through an orange grove and over some ploughed ground. In his distraught condition, he managed to steal two cars and drive at breakneck speed to Las Vegas.

Dr. Finch was weeping copiously when he concluded his dramatic recital. So were several spectators. Even one female juror was sniffling into her handkerchief.

Deputy DA Whichello put the amorous medico through a gruelling cross-examination that lasted more than a week. He took him back through the history of his marriage and his extra-marital affairs. Finch readily admitted affairs with other women as Whichello prepared to throw a pitiless spotlight on the doctor's secret romance with the shapely Carole.

"Dr. Finch was a guy cheating on his wife," Dorothy Kilgallen wrote, commenting realistically on this line of questioning. "A guy cheating on his wife follows a certain pattern of subterfuge. It borders on the ludicrous when Mr. Whichello registers astonishment at every lie Dr. Finch ever told in the course of his amorous pursuits, recoils at the thought of his using a false name when he rented an apartment for his liaison with Carole – and is shocked by his affectionate attentions to his wife while he was living in adultery with Carole."

Finch testified that he knew Barbara had retained a private detective to spy upon him and Carole. That was one reason why, when Barbara filed her divorce suit in May, the redhead had thought it prudent to leave the doctor's employ and go to Las Vegas.

The private eye was a North Hollywood operative, who had previously told police that the brunette socialite had been in fear of her life after filing her divorce suit. She had asked him whether she should hire a bodyguard or carry a gun. He said Barbara had hired him to tail Bernie and Carole. "But they drove like fiends, so my men could never catch up with them."

Whichello next took Dr. Finch in great detail over the exact circumstances of the fatal struggle and his wife's death. Bernie looked a mite shaken when the prosecutor introduced a tape-recording of Finch's original statement to the police in which the doctor had said he didn't know his wife was dead when he left her lying on the lawn.

"Isn't it a fact that you made up this whole touching death scene," Whichello demanded, "in order to avoid the implication that you left a dying woman on the lawn?"

"No, sir!" Finch replied hotly. "That is not true at all!"

Asked why he had fled, if he had shot his wife accidentally, Finch said, "I wasn't afraid. It was just the emotional reaction. I just – wasn't thinking of anything at all."

He admitted that when the fatal shot was fired, his first thought was of Carole's safety – not of his wife. He acknowledged that he loved Carole. And planned to marry her, "if the result of this trial permit".

The redhead, taking the witness-stand in her own defence, was asked only five brief questions by Attorney Neeb. She denied that she had entered into a conspiracy with Dr. Finch, Jack Cody, or anyone else to kill Barbara Finch. She denied that she had gone to West Covina with the doctor on July 18th with the intent to do physical violence or injury to Mrs. Finch.

Dorothy Kilgallen compared Carole, under cross-examination, to a modern Susanna facing the Elders. "The redhead is in the witness-box today, talking for her life. A tall, stern old man who could be her grandfather is trying to catch her in a lethal lie. Her lover is watching from his leather swivel chair, pretending to be calm.

"And on the jury, the elderly ladies are watching her, too, patting their carefully-waved hair rinsed in lavender – and they look so far removed from lust, or even the memory of lust, that they are not really a jury of Carole Tregoff's peers."

Assistant Prosecutor Clifford Crail bored pitilessly into Carole's story of the lethal encounter with Barbara. Thus, he was able to get into the record some of the details covered in the barred Exhibit 60.

"Mr. Crail is not dazzled by red hair or distracted by red-brown eyes," Dorothy Kilgallen wrote. "Nor is he dissuaded by youth. He is out for blood."

Carole broke down in tears at several points – and Dr. Bernie squirmed in his seat. But, on the whole, the redhead clung to her story. Nevertheless, under Crail's merciless grilling Carole had to admit that she had erred in some of her statement to the police – and that, at one point during her ordeal, she found she loved life and security more than she loved her Dr. Bernie.

In closing arguments, the redhead's attorneys told the jury: "If you think this girl is guilty, send her to the gas chamber. If not, set her free. There is nothing between." Winding up the defence, Attorney Rexford Eagan solemnly declared: "This is the age-old story of a girl in love with a man – and that is her only crime. May God grant that you take good care of her!"

In his final argument to the five men and seven women who now comprised the jury – one of the alternates having taken the place of a regular who was taken ill – Prosecutor Whichello demanded the gas chamber for both defendants. He ridiculed Finch's "soap opera" story of his wife's death. He painted Carole Tregoff as the Lady Macbeth in Dr. Finch's life, the "propelling force" of the crime.

Closing the defence of Dr. Finch, Attorney Cooper stressed Finch's own version of the shooting. Politely but insistently, he attacked the testimony of the Swedish maid. "I don't think she had any conscious bias," Cooper told the jurors. "But Miss Lidholm was confused and susceptible to suggestion by the police. She would be less than human if she didn't favour Mrs. Finch, her late employer, who had confided her innermost thoughts to her."

On March 4th, 1960, almost three months after the bitterly-fought trial began, the jurors received their instructions from Judge Evans and solemnly filed out to begin their deliberations. Speculations ran riot. The jurors sent out requests for certain exhibits. Two women jurors were taken ill and progress was delayed.

On March 6th, the jury asked that certain portions of Dr. Finch's testimony be re-read. On March 10th, Dorothy Kilgallen reported, in an exclusive headline story, that the jurors were getting ready to ask the judge to discharge one of their number, who was "not co-operating intelligently" – and substitute one of the remaining alternates.

On March 12th, on the ninth day of deliberations, the suspense was ended. The weary jurors filed back into the box, whereupon the foreman reported that they were hopelessly deadlocked. After determining that there was no chance of agreement, Judge Evans declared a mistrial and discharged the jury.

The jurors disclosed that they had been deadlocked 10-to-2 for first-degree murder conviction of Dr. Finch. As for Carole Tregoff, 16 "not guilty" votes had been cast in her favour – eight on the murder charge and eight on the conspiracy charge – but final agreement could not be reached. The vote was 8-to-4 for acquittal of both on the conspiracy charge.

Reporters quoted various jurors as to the reason for the disagreement. Several of them blamed racial resentment and tension on the part of two members of minority groups. Kilgallen's scoop, about the one obstinate hold-out who had antagonised the other jurors, was confirmed.

As the district attorney announced his determination to bring the accused pair to trial again, Kilgallen wrote: "Carole Tregoff, the little Red-headed Riding Hood of the Finch case, would like to run out of the dark forest of trial for murder, together with her basket of 16 not guilty votes cast by the deadlocked jury. But the state of California, like a big bad wolf, is holding on to her cloak with sharp fangs."

With a second trial pending. Carole's attorneys obtained her release again on $25,000 bond. There was a rumour that Dr. Finch would seek a compromise guilty plea to manslaughter, but this did not materialise.

Fred Whichello filed a claim for state compensation insurance for damage to his vocal cords, caused by "talking too loud and too long" during the protracted first trial. Deputy DA Joseph Powers replaced him as Clifford Crail's colleague. Attorney Eagan stepped out of the

Tregoff defence, blaming his ulcers.

After several delays, the second trial of the indicted lovers opened on June 27th, 1960, in the more sedate courtroom of Judge LeRoy Dawson. This time, the circus atmosphere was largely absent as a jury of eleven women and one man was empanelled to hear the defence again strive to tear down the vital and damning story of Marie Anne Lidholm. But the Swedish maid stuck to her guns.

Dr. Finch and Carole Tregoff repeated essentially the same stories. In the midst of the trial, the accused pair were sued for $1 million damages on behalf of Barbara's daughter Pattie. There were several new witnesses, with the state calling expert criminologists to dispute Finch's account of the fatal scuffle.

When the harassed redhead reported one day that she was too sick to come to court and had to be brought in forcibly by matrons, Judge Dawson revoked her bail and ordered her back to the county jail, where Deputy DA Crail had argued she belonged all along.

Through the summer and autumn months, the trial dragged on, prolonged by intensive cross-examination and bitter arguments. The bored spectators began to dwindle. So did the press coverage.

It was early in November, 1960, when the case was finally submitted to the jury, after more than four months of trial. Judge Dawson dropped a legal bombshell when, after several hours of deliberation, he called the jurors back and told them that, in his opinion, the evidence merited a verdict of guilty. Attorney Cooper objected vociferously to the judge's comments, whereupon Judge Dawson cited him for contempt.

On November 7th, after 72 hours of deliberation, the jurors filed back into the court room – to report another hopeless deadlock. The judge dismissed them, remarking that he did so "with considerable distress".

"Obviously, this case should be re-tried," the judge commented. "We cannot set a price tag on justice." The two trials had covered a total of 228 days. The first trial had cost the state an estimated $250,000. The second, the longest in California's criminal history, $350,000.

The tired jurors disclosed that, after 60 ballots, they all agreed that Dr. Finch was guilty of the murder of his wife. But while nine voted for a first-degree conviction, three held out for second-degree. As for Carole Tregoff, nine jurors voted her guilty of murder, with three believing her innocent.

So the cast of the grim murder drama gathered again on January 3rd, 1961, in the court of Judge David Coleman, for the third performance. From the outset, Judge Coleman speeded up the proceedings, cutting wordy arguments short and stopping pointless questioning. A jury of nine men and three women were seated with relative speed.

Again, the testimony was largely a repetition. Again, Marie Anne Lidholm, who had visited her home in Sweden in the interim, was a vital cog in the prosecution wheel. Bernie and Carole, both looking a little worn by this time, retold their familiar stories.

The end came abruptly and dramatically, later on the afternoon of March 27th, after the jury had deliberated for four days. This time, the verdict was sharp and clear: Dr. Raymond Bernard Finch, guilty of first-degree murder; Carole Tregoff, guilty of second-degree murder; both guilty of conspiracy to commit murder.

Carole burst into tears when the verdict was announced. Bernie was visibly shaken. His attorney appeared stunned.

Under California law, in capital cases, separate proceedings are necessary to determine the penalty. A week later, on April 4th, the same jurors solemnly heard arguments on the issue of life or death for the convicted lovers.

"These two persons planned the destruction of an unwanted wife!" Assistant Prosecutor Crail thundered. "For them, payday has arrived for the wages of their sin. Today, they are going to pay the piper. They want you to have compassion, which they never even thought of."

"It's the cry from the caves," Defence Attorney Maxwell Keith said, in arguing against the gas chamber. "Most civilised nations no longer have the death penalty. And, in this country, it is becoming a vanishing phenomenon."

"I love you," tearful Carole was heard to whisper to Bernie. Then they touched hands fleetingly as the jurors filed from the room.

After approximately two hours of deliberation on April 5th, the jury returned its fateful verdict: life imprisonment for both Dr. Finch and Carole Tregoff.

Later, the jurors told newsmen that there had been no real dissension from the first, in either of their two sessions. Several jurors said they did not believe Finch's story about the struggle for the gun. They revealed that they had re-enacted the scene in the jury room and decided that the scuffle could not have taken place as Finch described it.

"I would say that Dr. Finch and Carole were their own worst witnesses and convicted themselves," one woman juror stated.

The lethal lovers had missed the gas chamber by a hairsbreadth, it was disclosed. In their first ballot on the penalty issue, the jurors had voted 11-to-one for the death penalty for both defendants. Subsequently, they compromised on life. The jurors said they had not been swayed by Carole's tears. Most of their deliberations had been to determine whether she was guilty in the first or second degree.

Weeping Carole and stony-faced Bernie had a brief reunion before they were led away. Her head on his breast, they exchanged whispered pledges of love. But it was in half-hearted fashion.

The convicted wife-killer and his paramour were duly sentenced to life imprisonment on April 17th, 1961. Finch was paroled in 1971, Carole Tregoff having won her release two years earlier.

17

THE LETHAL MÉNAGE À TROIS

John Mead

Jeanne Favre-Bulle enjoyed in 1924 the sort of life that most women would have envied. Married to a rich industrialist, she had a luxury home with servants and every comfort in Paris, with plenty of leisure for shopping, the opera, art shows, the new films. Her husband worshipped the beauty she had retained at the age of 42. She was thoroughly spoiled – and like most of her kind she began to find life boring. But having been brought up in a convent and by tutors, she was perhaps more than usually modest – or repressed.

One day that year, she chanced to notice a young man glancing at her in the Métro. After that occasion, she became aware of his presence again and again. Indeed, whenever she travelled by Métro, he seemed to be there, looking more and more as if he wanted to speak to her. The dumb pantomime went on for nearly two and a half years!

He at last plucked up sufficient courage to talk to her. Then came the secret meetings, during which they behaved almost like schoolboy and schoolgirl, although Léon Merle was 10 years her junior. Finally, in 1927, she became his mistress. There followed two years of furtive rendezvous before Jeanne became conscience-stricken, told her husband all, and said she wanted to live with Léon.

And that was what led to Jeanne appearing before M. Bacquart, President of the Seine Assize Court, on November 25th, 1930, on a murder charge – or rather, two murder charges.

M. Bacquart started the questioning. "So you wanted to go and live with Léon Merle?"

"He was always pleading with me to get a divorce and follow him."

"Yet you knew that he had lived for years with his cousin as a mistress? She was even known as 'Mme Merle'?"

"I know. But he promised me that if I lived with him, he would give up his cousin and marry me. I'd already given him my word of honour that I would do so."

The President recalled that on September 21st, 1929, Mme Favre-Bulle left her husband, who had promised to divorce her. She went to her parents' home. But the husband visited her there several times, promising to forget what had happened if only she would return to him. She refused – and on October 15th arrived at Léon's home at Boulogne-sur-Seine, only to find the other mistress there.

The President put it to the accused, "You must have understood what a terrible situation this was? He just couldn't abandon the woman who had been with him for so long."

"He had given me his word that she would have to leave if only I would agree to live with him. He swore it. Without that promise I would never have left my husband."

"So you acted this way because you loved Merle so much? You just couldn't do without him?" the President asked.

"I'd sacrificed everything for him."

"Yes, you sacrificed your home and broke up his without thinking of the terrible situation of Mme Julliard, the cousin whose place you intended to take."

"He *had* to marry me! I was caught in an ambush."

Maître Maurice Garçon for the prosecution, then

interjected, "An ambush? But you were the killer!"

Mme Favre-Bulle looked indignant. "I'd kept *my* word. I'd left my husband. Mme Julliard hadn't kept hers.

"Horrible things happened. Léon insisted on my having intercourse with him in front of Mme Julliard. He threatened, if I refused, to have relations only with her."

"You could have refused – and left," the President suggested.

"He told me that if I went, he'd never see me again."

The court heard that on October 31st Jeanne had quarrelled violently with Léon, then went out to visit her mother. But she had her suspicions, returned quickly – and found him in bed with Mme Julliard.

She stormed out of the house, went into Paris, and bought a pistol in the Rue St. Lazare. On her arrival back at Léon's there was an angry scene between her and Mme Julliard.

Jeanne told the court, "When I suggested that she should leave, she replied, 'From the moment I help you, you should help me.' I went to complain to Léon. First of all, he said it was very natural that a man should need two mistresses. Then seeing how angry I was he suggested that I should look upon this woman as a sister."

However, the *ménage à trois* calmed down over dinner. Afterwards, Léon and Jeanne went to bed, leaving Mme Julliard to brood alone in her room. Léon never realised that Jeanne's revolver lay under her handbag on the table beside the bed.

Before they went to sleep, at about 10 o'clock, they talked about the odd situation. Léon calmly contended that Jeanne could perfectly well accommodate herself to the threesome. There was some love-making, then he fell asleep. But she was wide awake, thinking – she told the court – about her "miserable fate and hopeless situation".

The President asked, "You got up, picked up your pistol – and then?"

"Then in a moment of madness, I fired at him."

"In the darkness, you fired twice, point-blank."

As the shots rang out, Jeanne said Léon cried out, "She's shot me like a rabbit!" then Mme Julliard rushed along the corridor to Léon's room.

"What happened then?" asked the President. "I fired again, but I was crazy. I didn't even know how to handle the revolver."

"Nevertheless, you managed it and fired accurately, for all the bullets lodged in the chest," Maître Garçon put to her, then asked, "And after that?"

"I raised the revolver to my temple to commit suicide. But it didn't fire – that I could swear to. They said afterwards that the pistol was 'spiked', whatever that means."

Maître Garçon now recalled, "After mortally wounding a man and killing a woman, you calmly left the villa – without forgetting to put the dog on his chain – and went off to your former servant's lodgings to pick up the key to your old home."

"I was mad with terror. I didn't know what I was doing – I swear it."

When she arrived at the servant's address, her former maid refused to hand over the key. On that chilly night, Jeanne began to walk the streets barefoot in her night-dress, still desperately clutching the revolver in her hands. Towards 5 o'clock in the morning, she staggered on the pavement and fell in a heap in a doorway, hardly realising that she was reclining outside the local police station.

The court then heard that Léon did not die at once. Indeed, he somehow found the strength to get out of bed, chase Jeanne from the room and barricade the door, while Jeanne was wandering about the house.

A doctor told the court that Léon might have survived if he had been taken to a hospital at once. Mme Favre-Bulle, however, told Maître Garçon that she did not know where to get hold of a doctor and imagined that Mme Julliard might have looked after him. "I had gone mad," she insisted. But Maître Garçon put it to her that she was not mad at all. "You were wandering round the villa and burning various papers. In fact, you were waiting till you were sure that both were dead."

At this, Mme Favre-Bulle moaned, rose from her seat, swayed and fell into a faint. The trial was suspended until she was revived.

In her evidence, Mlle Eléonore Merle, Léon's sister, said she had regarded Mme Julliard as her sister-in-law and Mme Favre-Bulle as an intruder. She pointed to Jeanne, saying, "One day *she* told Mme Julliard – 'I'll kill you.' "

Maître Raymond-Hubert, for the defence asked, "You heard her actually say that?"

"No, but Mme Julliard told me so. The Favre-Bulle woman told my brother, in speaking of Mme Julliard, 'I tell you, I'll kill her.' My brother replied, 'You're too frightened for your own skin – you won't do it.' "

Mme Orval, who had sold Mme Favre-Bulle the automatic pistol explained that it was only on the third visit that Jeanne bought the revolver – the day of the crime. She had demanded a very detailed explanation of just how the revolver worked – even trying it out with blank cartridges.

M. Maurice Favre-Bulle said that he was completely overcome by the affair. "But I must say that this woman – my admirable wife – was always a perfect wife and totally respectable. For twenty years – and I cannot forget it – she proved to be a woman of the highest moral qualities. But what mysterious and evil force pushed her to destruction? I'm now divorced and this unhappy woman is a stranger to me – but I must say that what she did is unbelievable, even stupefying. She was the last person on earth whom I would have expected to do this."

Maître Garçon said he could find nothing in Jeanne's record to excuse or mitigate her crime. Indeed, she had tried to blacken the characters of her two victims. He said that Léon had been in a "painful situation" between two mistresses whom he cherished equally. He added, "Of these two women, one was gentle, modest, retiring –

Mme Julliard. But the other was intrusive, bossy, over-bearing. She had only one idea – that the other woman must go."

At this point, Mme Favre-Bulle fainted again and the hearing was interrupted once more. When it resumed, Maître Garçon continued: "She killed two people – Merle, because he wouldn't give in to her demand to chase the other woman away; and Mme Julliard, because she didn't want to abandon her home of 10 years standing and let herself be thrown out. She wanted to live her life, get involved in adventures, play her game of chance. She lost – now she must pay."

M. Rolland, the Advocate-General, said there could be no doubt in the case: it was premeditated double murder, justifying severe punishment.

He added, "The higher up one is in the social scale, the more one is responsible, the more vulnerable. Too much blood has been spilt. I ask the jury to make an example of this woman."

Maître Raymond-Hubert asked the court to picture the state of mind of Mme Favre-Bulle when she found herself first deceived on arriving at her lover's house, then disgusted with the promiscuous *ménage à trois*. Her love for Léon was desperate, the more so because she was revolted by this state of affairs.

"This unfortunate woman, for all her forty-eight years, knew little of life," he told the court. "When her former husband has pardoned her, could not the jury show mercy and generosity in their verdict?"

The jury found her guilty, but with extenuating circumstances. She was sentenced to 20 years hard labour – and was carried away from the dock, having fallen into yet another faint.

18

AS PEACEFUL AS A SUMMER EVE

Patrick Carroll

Effie Skinner's got to leave this house," Laura Cross angrily told her husband, Dr. Philip Cross. Laura, the mother of five children, had been happily married to her husband, a former Army surgeon, at their home at Shandy Hall, Coachford, County Cork – until the couple engaged pretty Miss Effie Skinner as governess to the children in the autumn of 1886. Within a few weeks, husband and governess were having an affair which was the talk of the neighbourhood.

Laura was therefore mildly surprised when her husband raised no objection to Effie getting her marching orders.

"Perhaps it would be a good thing," he said smoothly, "if that's how you feel about it. I'll give Miss Skinner a cheque in lieu of notice and say that she must leave at once. I'll tell her we're making fresh plans for the children's education."

"Tell her what you please," said Laura tartly.

Effie actually heard a different version. She was told by Philip Cross that his wife was sick of them both. He told her not to worry, but to leave for Dublin: he would join her the next day. He did – and they posed as "Mr. and Mrs. Osborne" at a hotel there. Then Effie went to her home in London and Philip Cross returned to Shandy Hall.

There he found a Miss Margaret Jefferson, a friend of his wife's, looking after her, for Laura had been taken ill the very day Effie had left. He told Miss Jefferson not to worry – and that he would prescribe for her himself.

But Laura became worse. Despite the medicine she was taking, she was prone to violent spasms. However, when neighbours called they were told that she had a touch of fever and couldn't see anyone, but was otherwise doing well.

Miss Jefferson saw Laura alive for the last time on June 1st, 1887. Early the next morning, hearing groans, followed by an eerie silence, she hurried into Laura's room. Dr. Cross was bending over the bed. "My poor Laura has passed away – it's a happy release," he said.

He insisted that the funeral arrangements should be made at once because of the risk of infection. Miss Jefferson left Shandy Hall. As soon as she had gone, Dr. Cross registered his wife's death – with his own signed certificate – as being due to typhoid fever. He gave instructions that the funeral should take place at 6 a.m. two days later, with only the clergyman and himself being present.

Of course, tongues soon wagged – it was noticed that he told some people that his wife had died of typhoid, others that she had had a heart attack. Still more startling was the fact that only ten days after the funeral he married Effie Skinner in London.

The whispers turned into angry suspicions. Police made inquiries and it was decided to exhume the body and hold an inquest.

Professor Pearson, a Dublin medical expert who carried out the autopsy, said at the inquest that Laura Cross had not died of fever, but of irritant poisoning caused by arsenic and strychnine, of which there were traces in her stomach.

As a result of this evidence, Dr. Cross was arrested and charged with wilful murder. The case came into the local police court the next day. The magistrate asked Inspector

Tyacke of the Royal Irish Constabulary, "Did Dr. Cross say anything when you arrested him?"

"He said, 'My God, to think that a man at my time of life should be accused of committing murder. There is a God above me who will see the villainy of such a charge.' I warned him that it would be better not to say any more just then."

The inspector told the court that in searching the house he had removed two medicine bottles from the wardrobe – one of them labelled "dog poison". He found Dr. Cross's diary, one extract from it read: "June 2nd. Mary Laura Cross departed this life. May she go to Heaven is my prayer. Expenses of funeral &c. five guineas."

The inspector also discovered letters written by Dr. Cross to Humphrey Marriott, Laura's brother. One said: "The last rites were carried out this morning. I had her buried quietly, with a carriage and pair to take her to what, I feel sure, is her heavenly home. . . In time I will lie side by side with her I loved."

Philip Cross's trial opened at Munster Assizes on December 13th, 1887, before Mr. Justice Murphy.

Prosecuting, the Attorney-General, John Gibson QC said, "The Crown charges the prisoner, who is 64 years of age, with murdering his wife under particularly horrible circumstances. There is positive evidence that this lady did not die, as he alleges, from either fever or heart disease. You will hear what the real cause was. The case I am presenting is a combination of horrors until now happily unknown to us.

"It is that of a husband murdering his wife, 20 years younger than himself, in his own house, in order to fly back to his paramour, and to elevate her to the position of the wife he had poisoned."

A chemist said in evidence that some months before the arrest Dr. Cross had bought a quantity of arsenic from him.

"Did he tell you why he wanted it?" asked the prisoner's counsel.

"Yes," was the answer. "He told me he wanted it for sheep-dipping."

"Is not arsenic used for that purpose?"

"Sometimes it is," replied the chemist guardedly.

The strong evidence for the prosecution lay in the bottles collected by the medical expert, Professor Pearson, which were shown to the jury. They contained the quantities of arsenic and strychnine taken from Laura Cross's stomach.

Dr. Cross's counsel begged the jury to "rid their minds of the crop of rumours that discredited the prisoner." He stressed that no guilt had been established – and that the evidence offered by the prosecution was purely circumstantial.

A great deal had been made of Dr. Cross's action in letting time elapse before telling anyone that his wife was dead. But a guilty man, said counsel, would have "immediately summoned the household and wept tears of sorrow". Dr. Cross had felt it better to wait a little.

Moreover, he did not attempt to conceal or destroy – though he had every opportunity to do so – the poison which Inspector Tyacke later found in the house. No evidence was offered as to who put it there – though anyone might have done this. Ladies did use preparations of arsenic to improve their complexions. It was just possible that Laura Cross *did* consider it a "beauty treatment".

Defence counsel also made the point that, as a medical man, Philip Cross had access to drugs that left no traces in the body. So if he meant to poison his wife he would not have had recourse to one detected as readily as arsenic.

He agreed that Dr. Cross's second marriage could not be defended on strictly moral grounds. But he insisted that that had nothing to do with the case; the principal thing was the evidence of Professor Pearson.

"If this be disregarded," he concluded, "the whole case must collapse. I most solemnly beg of you not to attach undue importance to what Professor Pearson has said."

In his summing up, Mr. Justice Murphy warned the jury that the charge was not one of "immorality or a callous indifference to the proper decencies of domestic conduct, but a much more serious one." All they had to determine was if the death of Mrs. Cross was due to the deliberate action of her husband.

He thought it very significant that no second doctor was called to prescribe for the invalid when her illness developed. Then, in one of his letters to his brother-in-law, Dr. Cross had said that his wife's heart failed from exhaustion: the jury must consider what caused that exhaustion.

The judge then drew attention to what happened on June 2nd. "At an early hour," he said, "the prisoner calls the servants together and – without any sign of natural feelings on his part, no wailing or expression of grief, and no bustle or confusion – calmly tells them that their mistress is dead. Under his directions, the corpse is hurriedly washed, clad in a flannel nightdress, and then coffined."

There was no doubt, he said, that there was an adulterous relationship between Philip Cross and Effie Skinner and that Cross "hurried with callous and wicked speed to replace the faithful wife not yet cold in her grave."

The jury unanimously found Dr. Cross guilty. Philip Cross made a long rambling speech in which he declared he was innocent.

"The only wrong I did anyone was to Miss Skinner," he said. "Well, I am sorry about that. But I married her because I thought that, under the circumstances, it was required of me. . . When a man is abused like me, all sorts of things are said against him. . . The prosecution even say that I poisoned my wife. Well, I once poisoned a dog, and that gave me horror of poisoning ever since. Then, as to this charge of killing my wife, is it likely that as a medical man – and knowing its properties and the certainty of detection – I would have used arsenic for such a purpose? The suggestion is ridiculous. That is all I have to say."

He was sentenced to death. Two petitions seeking a reprieve were sent to the Lord Lieutenant of Ireland, but were turned down.

James Berry, the public executioner of England, crossed to Cork Jail for the hanging in January, 1888.

"Quite a good job," Berry told a journalist. "I give you my word – Dr. Cross passed away as peaceful as a summer eve."

And Effie Skinner, the "other woman"? She left Ireland when Philip Cross was arrested and vanished from view.

19

THE BRIDE USED ANTI-FREEZE

Robert Woods

On November 1st, 1982, Lloyd Allen died. His death did not appear to involve any foul play. Yet soon after he died, the St. Charles County sheriff's office in Missouri began receiving phone calls from people who hinted that Allen did not die from natural causes, but was poisoned.

Sheriff Edward Uebinger did not usually pay much heed to these calls. He had received more than his fair share of crank calls over the years. Nevertheless, he knew it was his duty to investigate any death in which there might be the suggestion of foul play. So Uebinger had a talk with the district attorney's office, with the result that an autopsy was ordered to determine the cause of Lloyd Allen's death.

The autopsy report, however, was specific. It revealed that Lloyd Allen's deterioration and death had been because of repeated doses of ethylene glycol. In short, he had ingested anti-freeze. Sheriff's Detectives Kenneth Brockel and Bob Boerding now felt that they had a homicide, but they kept open minds.

The detectives, in their questioning, found out plenty about Lloyd Allen – and all of it was good. He was considered by both neighbours and friends to have been an excellent man. No one had known him to lose his temper, or make enemies of anyone.

Investigators were shown his wedding picture, taken in September, 1981. In it Lloyd, a rotund fellow, was smiling next to his striking blonde wife. It was a picture that simply shouted the happiness of the just-marrieds.

But detectives working on the case soon learned that Lloyd's new wife did not have as sunny a reputation as her husband. There were many questions in her rather chequered past which investigators decided to look into.

To begin with, Uebinger's investigators learned that the woman had four marriages on record, two divorces (from the same man), plus one widowhood behind her. While this game of musical chairs was not considered bad, it was found that there had also been two, perhaps three, also-rans, maritally speaking.

Brockel and Boerding reported that flawed happiness was par for the course in the marital history of Shirley Allen, and it was while detectives were putting together a dossier on Shirley's life that something curious occurred. One of Shirley's ex-husbands insisted that she had tried to poison him. "I couldn't prove it, though," he told interested investigators.

"Once," he explained, "I drank coffee. It tasted sweet, like Listerine. My head suddenly felt like somebody was using an axe to split it in half and I couldn't see for hours."

One member of the family told detectives that she had seen Shirley give this husband rat poison. Rat poison is an anti-coagulant – and it can cause internal bleeding and blindness. And anti-freeze, the cops mused, would come very close to Listerine in sweetness. Anti-freeze had killed Lloyd Allen. So why, probers wondered, hadn't this been spotted immediately?

The doctor provided detectives with the answer. According to the physician, substances so esoteric as this ". . . couldn't have been discovered, unless specifically looked for."

As detectives delved into the couple's marital relationship, they learned that insurance had been taken out on Lloyd in the first weeks of the new union. The insurance was for a tidy sum, $25,000. The beneficiary was Shirley Allen. Then, five months after the wedding, Lloyd had made out a new will. His blonde wife was now his sole heir.

Less than a month later, Lloyd started feeling poorly. Probers learned from the hospital records that he continued to worsen until his death in November, when according to a witness, he died reaching for a phone – a phone pulled just out of reach by his loving bride.

Shirley had given various stories about Lloyd's illness to different people. She had told one curious neighbour that Lloyd had a brain tumour. To another, she explained that her husband suffered from hypoglycaemia. A third neighbour was ticked off by an angry Shirley when she suggested that Lloyd should get another medical opinion.

This neighbour confided to detectives that she had been called to the Allen house, where she saw Lloyd surrounded by medicine bottles. "I'd begged Shirley Allen to call an ambulance, but she said he was drunk and would come out of it," she told lawmen. Later, after Allen's death, the neighbour herself had called the sheriff's office.

"You suspected foul play?" Brockel inquired.

"Yes," she replied, "from the moment she wouldn't call for the ambulance."

After hearing this statement, Sheriff Uebinger felt there was a strong possibility that not only was Lloyd Allen fatally poisoned, but that Shirley's previous husband – who had allegedly died of a heart attack – was also a victim of poisoning. If it could be proved that this husband had been poisoned, detectives would have an excellent case against Shirley Allen. An exhumation order was issued, but it would still take some days for an autopsy to be performed.

In the meantime, detectives learned a good deal of chilling information. They learned that Shirley had phoned the life insurance company before Lloyd's demise and asked if the house mortgage would be paid off in the event of her husband's death, while she had earlier asked about the amount she could expect when the policy she had taken out on his life paid out.

Probers were also told that Shirley had become violent and once hit Lloyd in the back with a baseball bat when he tried to go to the bathroom. This had caused him to fall back on the bed and pass out.

Other witnesses claimed that Shirley had doctored Lloyd's beer and wine, putting anti-freeze in it over a period of eight months. When Lloyd sank into a stupor, Shirley would take a nose-dropper and pour anti-freeze down his mouth.

A search warrant was taken out and detectives conducted an extensive search of the premises. A container of anti-freeze was found, together with a nose-dropper, insurance papers, plus papers on the house mortgage. The detectives' reports were taken by Sheriff Uebinger to the district attorney's office, which immediately issued a warrant for the arrest of Shirley Allen for the first-degree murder of her husband.

On November 8th, 1982, a week after the death of her husband, Shirley Allen was arrested and charged with poisoning him.

When her trial got under way, it drew a large crowd. The state's two prime witnesses were the pathologist and one of Shirley Allen's children.

The pathologist testified that Lloyd Allen's body was saturated with ethylene glycol, the major ingredient of anti-freeze, a substance so lethal that a mere three fluid ounces taken internally could cause death.

One of Shirley's daughters testified that she had seen Shirley give Lloyd anti-freeze and a petrol additive at least eight times in the two months before his death. In the early morning hours of the day he died, she related, Shirley had physically prevented him from calling a doctor. When Lloyd reached for a phone, the daughter continued, "she moved it away from him."

Shirley Allen dabbed at her eyes as her daughter

related the damning evidence to the court. But she fixed her eyes over her mother's head and continued her evidence. She related that, in the second week of October, she had seen her mother put a mixture of anti-freeze and liquor in a glass that contained cold medicine. She then handed the glass to another of her children, telling her to give the solution to the bedridden Lloyd.

There was a deathly hush as the witness told the court that on Lloyd Allen's last day of life, Shirley had sent her children to buy more anti-freeze, and had made the statement: "That's what I'll use to finish him off."

Shirley's daughter when cross-examined said she had seen her mother give Lloyd a solution of petrol additive, warm water, sugar and orange food colouring on at least four occasions. According to her, Shirley had told Lloyd that the mixture was an "iron supplement".

On the morning Lloyd died, the daughter testified, she and her sister had been sent by Shirley to St. Louis to obtain money to pay the water bill. When they returned at 8.30 a.m., they heard Shirley say over the phone: "There has been a death in the family."

"I went into the bedroom and he was already gone," Shirley's daughter recalled. "His lips were blue and his eyes were rolled back." She also recalled that Shirley had waited hours before calling an ambulance. When the ambulance got there, Shirley told the medics that Lloyd had only been dead for 15 minutes.

After all the testimony was concluded, on April 27th, 1984, Shirley Allen was found guilty of capital murder in the death of her husband, Lloyd Allen. In July, 1984, she was sentenced to life imprisonment without the possibility of parole for 50 years.

20

COUNTESS TARNOWSKA: RUSSIA'S LOVE VAMPIRE

Jonathan Reed

The sensational story of a sex-crazed Russian countess who brought men to their doom in a drama of sex, drugs, passion and intrigue began when 17- year-old Maria Nicolaevna, brought up in a noble household near the Russian city of Kiev, told her parents that she would not marry their choice of husband, Prince Troubetzkoi.

She preferred Vassili Tarnowsky, an aristocratic rake who kept a string of mistresses in St. Petersburg and Moscow. They eloped and married; she became Countess Tarnowska. A year later after setting up home in Italy, the first of their two children was born.

It was a little after this happy event that Maria learned that Vassili's brother Peter, only 16 years old, had hanged himself for love of her. She had cared little for him but did return to Kiev with her husband, saw the boy's body lying in state – and sought consolation with Alexis Bozevsky, a handsome officer of the Imperial Guard.

Bozevsky met the Tarnowskys at a ball, where the handsome guardee whirled Marie away in a wild *czardas*. She suddenly fainted, recovering to find a family friend, Dr. Vladimir Stahl, giving her an injection. Her husband

Vassili tried to pull her away, Bozevsky intervened, and other guests had to drag them apart to prevent a fight.

The rivals met again at a farewell party given before the Tarnowskys returned to Italy. Bozevsky drunkenly toasted Maria with a verse which ended:

"*I bless the hour that brings me death*
For the hour that thou wert mine!"

The party broke up with Vassili storming out angrily. Maria was about to step into the sleigh, when Bozevsky strode rapidly to her, saying, "So it's all over!" A shot rang out, followed by a crazy cackle of laughter from Vassili. Still clutching Maria's hand, Bozevsky wrenched himself upright, shivered convulsively, and fell in a faint, covering Maria with blood.

He hung between life and death, with strength only to whisper to Maria, "Stay with me." Vassili gave himself up to the police but was later acquitted by a jury, on the grounds of justifiable attempted homicide.

Needing more expert care than Dr. Stahl could give, Bozevsky went from town to town for medical help, with Maria following faithfully. At Yalta, in the Crimea, his condition worsened and Maria telegraphed to Stahl to come at once. Dr. Stahl was thinner, with dishevelled hair and dull, sunken eyes. He had become a drug addict, secretly crazed with love for Maria.

At Bozevsky's bedside, she heard him mutter, "I can wait a little longer – yes, I can wait a little longer."

With Bozevsky in delirium, Stahl said suddenly to Maria, "Come here – why should I let you suffer." He whipped out a morphia syringe, seized her wrist and pricked her arm with the needle. Bozevsky, his face grey with approaching death, looked imploringly at Maria. But her quivering nerves were already relaxing – she began to sink into a doped sleep. A few minutes later, Bozevsky was dead – the second of Maria's victims.

Distraught with grief, but heavily drugged herself, Maria scarcely noticed that Dr. Stahl had deserted his wife and his practice to stay at her side.

Then, one night, she learned that Stahl had poisoned himself. There came a note from him, written in a shaky hand on a torn scrap of paper: "Maria! I have only half an hour to live! Come to me, I implore you!"

She tossed the paper aside, reached for the syringe and gave herself another shot of morphia. A few minutes later her third victim died. Stahl's body was returned to Kiev for burial: it was to play an unforeseen part in the tragedy.

Deserted by her husband, Maria was sinking into poverty in Moscow in May, 1903, when she decided to telegraph despairingly to her mother. She was about to write the message in a post office, when she felt a hand touch her shoulder. She turned to see Donat Prilukoff, one of Moscow's most successful young lawyers. She had met him some months earlier, at a party, and it wasn't long before she began pouring out her troubles to him. He told her not to worry – he would look after her. Soon she had become his mistress.

One day, Maria was told by a fortune-teller, "Two men have yet to enter your life. One will bring salvation, the other ruin. Choose the One, and you will obtain happiness. Choose the Other, and you will perish . . . you will choose the Other – for it's your destiny."

The gipsy's warning still rang in Maria's ears on the day she encountered a handsome, middle-aged man dressed in deep mourning. He was Count Paul Kamarowsky, the husband of one of her closest friends, whom she had not seen for two years. Maria inquired after his wife's health. "Poor Emilia!" he cried – then his voice broke. Maria felt suddenly tender towards the widower, and they spent many passionate hours together.

But she also carried on her spendthrift, careless way. She once asked lawyer Prilukoff for 5,000 roubles.

"I haven't got them," he said, "at least, not unless I steal them."

He suggested that she should obtain them from Kamarowsky – but without asking directly. She was to telephone Kamarowsky to ask him to dinner. Prilukoff ordered Maria, "Do nothing and say nothing – and mind you don't open any letter in his presence."

Immediately after the tête-à-tête dinner, Prilukoff entered, holding a big sealed envelope. He pretended to be disconcerted at finding Kamarowsky there.

"What is it?" Maria asked.

Glancing uneasily at Kamarowsky, the lawyer said stiffly, "This morning, Countess, you did me the honour of confiding to me the fact that you needed ten thousand roubles. I shall be most grateful and honoured if you will accept that sum from me."

He gave her the envelope, bowed deeply to the pair of them, and left.

Kamarowsky looked stunned when she explained that Prilukoff was a friend.

"You must have very confidential relations with him if he permits himself to give you ten thousand roubles," he said.

"Oh – no – no," she stammered. "He – he's only lending them to me, I'll pay them back, of course."

Kamarowsky took her hands, pressing them to his breast.

"How can you accept assistance from a stranger when I am here – I, who am so devoted to you?"

She burst into tears. In a moment, his arms were round her – and he was begging her to accept the money from him.

"Let me be your friend – now and for ever," he said.

Maria nodded. He wrote out a cheque for 10,000 roubles and gave it to her.

"I wanted five thousand roubles and now I've got twenty thousand," thought Maria. She fingered Prilukoff's envelope. "Why should I return it?" she said to herself.

Idly, she broke the seals. Inside the envelope were a random selection of old newspaper cuttings!

Maria continued to take money from Prilukoff and Kamarowsky, but when she found out that she could get a divorce from the vanished Vassili Tarnowsky, she became engaged to the more polished and wealthy Kamarowsky. Before they went on a French Riviera holiday, Maria wrote to Prilukoff begging for his forgiveness, thanking him for his help and suggesting that it was time he returned to his family and career.

They had spent only a few days at Hyères, by the Mediterranean, when Prilukoff arrived, gaining admission to her suite by a ruse.

"Are you cross with me?" Maria asked.

"Cross!" he shrieked at her. "You ruin a man and then you inquire whether he is cross! You take an honourable man in your little talons, you turn and twist him round your fingers, you mould him and transform him and turn him into a coward, a rogue and a thief – then you throw him aside like a dirty rag – and you ask him if he's cross!"

Maria burst into tears, but he stormed on, "I had a wife, and I betrayed her for you . . . I had two children and I forsook them for you . . . I had a career and I lost it for you . . . I was a man of honour and I have turned thief for you!"

He drew a wad of banknotes from his pocket and flung them in her face.

"I stole all this – because you needed money, you vampire!" he hissed. He began to weep hysterically and declared, "If I go to penal servitude, so shall you. I swear it. I am a thief – but if I go to prison, you go, too!"

She fell on her knees at his feet, asking for his forgiveness. "Go back and become an honest man again," she said.

"There's no going back," he sobbed. "By this time, all Moscow knows that I've absconded with my clients' money. I'm a thief – and I'm done for."

A strange situation developed. For days, Prilukoff haunted Maria's suite. Elise Perrier, Maria's Swiss maid, kept Kamarowsky away as much as possible with stories of her mistress's "headaches". Sometimes Prilukoff even forebade her to go out with Kamarowsky! On other occasions he followed them through the streets. Though

Maria hinted that she was being spied on, Kamarowsky suspected nothing.

But he agreed that she might enjoy herself more in Vienna: she left without saying goodbye. Elise went with her, carrying a small satchel stuffed with the money Prilukoff had stolen. Three days later, Kamarowsky joined them. Then the three moved on to the Russian city of Orel.

The evening they arrived, Kamarowsky saw the satchel on Maria's dressing table. Maria claimed that it belonged to Elise and that it contained only Elise's old love letters. When he teased Elise about the letters, she blurted out that the bag contained money that didn't belong to her.

Kamarowsky grew angry when neither woman would give him the key. He told Elise to go, then he cut the satchel with his penknife and found 35,000 roubles.

"You told me you were penniless," he screamed.

Maria claimed the money was not hers, but Kamarowsky stormed downstairs to the hotel bar.

Maria, trembling violently, put the notes back in the satchel. She had given Prilukoff the slip: now she wished that he was with her. She collapsed weeping on the sofa.

She did not hear the door open. When she finally raised her head she saw a slender, fair-haired youth on the threshold.

"I was looking for Count Kamarowsky," he told her. "He has invited me to dine with him – my name is Nicholas Naumoff."

"And mine is Maria Tarnowska," she said, pressing his hand warmly.

At dinner, Kamarowsky spoke only to the 20-year-old Naumoff, son of the Governor of Orel. Naumoff looked with longing at Maria. To ease the constraint, Naumoff said, "I hear that Delphinus, the famous crystal-gazer, has arrived in Orel. You should get him to tell your fortune."

"Is that so?" she smiled. Suddenly, memory stabbed her. Delphinus was the Moscow crystal-gazer who had told her of her two men of destiny. Was the sullen, dark-bearded Kamarowsky the "One" and the boyish, fresh-faced Naumoff the "Other?" She touched Naumoff's hand under the table: he tensed with hidden passion.

After dinner, the morose Kamarowsky changed his mood. "I love you and I trust you utterly," he told Maria.

"Leave me – let me go away," she cried, "I do not wish to speak to you any more. I do not wish to marry you now. I want to go away and never see you again."

"You've promised to be mine – and I'll make you keep your word," Kamarowsky cried as he left her.

As the days passed, Naumoff became madly jealous of Kamarowsky.

One night Naumoff came to her and pleaded with her not to marry Kamarowsky. He was embracing Maria when Prilukoff came through the open French window of her bedroom. He levelled a revolver at Naumoff but did not fire. Maria, in the darkness, manoeuvred Naumoff to the window and pushed him out, then shut it.

Alone with Prilukoff, Maria begged, "I implore you – do not betray me. Do not let them hear you . . . Forgive me. I am yours – yours only!"

Prilukoff raised the revolver to his temple. There was a rattle at the door as Naumoff tried the handle.

"Swear to me that you loathe that man – and the other!" hissed Prilukoff. "Swear that if I murdered them both you would still be mine. . . Swear that they shall both die, that you will help me to rid the world of them. . . Unless you swear it, I shall shoot myself here – this instant!"

"I swear that they shall die," she murmured.

Prilukoff left and Naumoff entered – just in time to turn the key in the lock against Kamarowsky, who called out from the hallway, "Goodnight, my darling." Maria staggered and sank to the floor, only to feel Naumoff's hands passing over her face in the dark. "Go!" she said weakly. Naumoff, always obedient, stumbled away.

Early in August, 1907, Maria fled to Vienna, followed first by Prilukoff, then by Kamarowsky, then by Naumoff.

When Prilukoff showed Maria the syringe and ampoules of poison he proposed using to eliminate Kamarowsky and Naumoff, she was horrified – and a wild plan began to form in her mind.

Maria first went to Naumoff telling him she wanted Kamarowsky killed to avenge her honour. The lovesick Naumoff agreed to go to Venice where Kamarowsky was staying and shoot him. She then contacted Prilukoff and explained how Naumoff could be deliberately sacrificed so that there would be no awkward questions.

It was arranged that two private detectives, hired by Prilukoff, should watch Kamarowsky's villa when Naumoff went in to kill him. When the assassin came out they would arrest him.

At seven o'clock on the morning of September 3rd, Naumoff went to the villa, confronted Kamarowsky and fired five pistol shots into his body.

Naumoff emerged safely into the street – where the murder plot collapsed. The detectives weren't there to arrest Naumoff. They had expected him at dawn; tired of waiting, they had gone to breakfast.

Kamarowsky died three days later in hospital, but named Naumoff to the police. They trailed him to Verona – and he talked freely of Maria, who was then in Kiev. The police knew that Prilukoff, who had arrived in Venice a few days before, was repeatedly telegraphing her. He had done so within an hour of Kamarowsky's death, but had left Venice: he was arrested in Trieste.

When she learned of Kamarowsky's death, Maria made for Venice. She was arrested when the train arrived at Vienna. Escorted to Venice, Maria confronted Prilukoff at police headquarters there, claiming that he had masterminded the murder, with Naumoff as his cat's-paw.

"My only guilt is that I have been connected with men of bad character," she said. "That is regrettable, perhaps, but it is not criminal."

Prilukoff spat out, "This woman has always been my evil genius: she has ruined me, body and soul!"

The police had plenty of evidence, including compromising telegrams she had sent Prilukoff from Kiev. "I love you more than anybody in the world – you are doing just what I want," said one.

For two and a half years, Maria paced her prison cell while the case was prepared. The trial of Maria, Naumoff and Prilukoff, which opened in Venice on March 4th, 1910, was a great public spectacle, reported by the world's Press. Journalists dubbed her "The Vampire," the "Sphinx in Crepe" and the "Little Wax Madonna."

Naumoff, almost a nervous wreck, told the court that he had shot Kamarowsky under Maria's evil spell. "I was her slave," he wept.

During ten hours of examination and cross-examination, Prilukoff told much the same story. "She was too strong for me," he said. "There was nothing I would not have done at her command."

When it came to her turn, Maria freely admitted her liaisons, but insisted that all arose from her husband's misconduct, years before.

When the prosecutor taxed her with Dr. Stahl's suicide, she coolly replied, "Surely I'm not responsible if men do foolish things?"

"Why should you want three lovers simultaneously?" Judge Fusinato asked her.

"It was because I was endeavouring to find someone who would really love me," she replied. "Instead, I was always deluded. Nobody corresponded with my ideal."

"Yet you allowed each of these three men to think you would marry him?"

"Ah – but the engagement was not official, she replied."

The jury found all three defendants guilty, though Naumoff's responsibility for the murder was lessened by his partial mental collapse at the time.

Naumoff was sent to prison for three years and four months, Maria to eight years and four months – and Prilukoff was sentenced to ten years' solitary confinement.

Maria died of natural causes in 1923.